Fantasy has been an important and much-loved part of children's literature for hundreds of years, yet relatively little has been written about it. *Children's Fantasy Literature* traces the development of the tradition of the children's fantastic – fictions specifically written for children and fictions appropriated by them – from the sixteenth to the twenty-first century, examining the work of Lewis Carroll, L. Frank Baum, C. S. Lewis, Roald Dahl, J. K. Rowling and others from across the English-speaking world. The volume considers changing views both on the nature of the child and on the appropriateness of fantasy for the child reader, the role of children's fantasy literature in helping to develop the imagination, and its complex interactions with issues of class, politics and gender. The text analyses hundreds of works of fiction, placing each in its appropriate context within the tradition of fantasy literature.

MICHAEL LEVY is Professor of English at the University of Wisconsin-Stout. He is the author of *Natalie Babbitt* (1991), *Portrayal of Southeast Asian Refugees in Recent American Children's Books* (2000), editor of *The Moon Pool* by A. Merritt (2004) and co-editor of the peer-reviewed journal *Extrapolation*. Levy was awarded the Clareson Award for Distinguished Service to the fields of Science Fiction and Fantasy (2007).

FARAH MENDLESOHN is Head of the Department of English, Communications, Film, and Media at Anglia Ruskin University. She is the author of *Rhetorics of Fantasy* (2008), *The Inter-Galactic Playground: A Critical Study of Children's and Teens' Science Fiction* (2009), co-author of *A Short History of Fantasy* (2009) and co-editor of the Hugo Award winning *The Cambridge Companion to Science Fiction* (Cambridge, 2003) and *The Cambridge Companion to Fantasy* (Cambridge, 2012).

# CHILDREN'S FANTASY LITERATURE

## LITERATURE

*An Introduction*

MICHAEL LEVY AND FARAH MENDLESOHN

CAMBRIDGE
UNIVERSITY PRESS

# CAMBRIDGE
## UNIVERSITY PRESS

University Printing House, Cambridge CB2 8BS, United Kingdom

Cambridge University Press is part of the University of Cambridge.

It furthers the University's mission by disseminating knowledge in the pursuit of
education, learning and research at the highest international levels of excellence.

www.cambridge.org
Information on this title: www.cambridge.org/9781107018143

First published 2016

Printed in the United Kingdom by Clays, St Ives plc

*A catalogue record for this publication is available from the British Library*

*Library of Congress Cataloguing in Publication data*
Levy, Michael, 1950 April 15-
Children's fantasy literature : an introduction / Michael Levy, Farah Mendlesohn.
pages cm
Includes bibliographical references and index.
ISBN 978-1-107-01814-3 (hardback)—ISBN 978-1-107-61029-3 (paperback)
1. Children's literature—History and criticism.  2. Fantastic, The, in literature.
3. Fantasy fiction—History and criticism.  I. Mendlesohn, Farah.  II. Title.
PN1009.5.F37L48  2016
809'.89282—dc23
2015029104

ISBN    978-1-107-01814-3 Hardback
ISBN    978-1-107-61029-3 Paperback

# Contents

# Contents

# *Acknowledgements*

This book is the result of long-term collaboration and discussion between the two authors – some by email, some in person during intercontinental visits – discussions and sometimes disagreements (occasionally in print) over the nature of fantasy literature. Each of us, as editor of the other's work, has occasionally felt the need to play the heavy and request edits that led to still further interesting conversations. In general, however, compromise has been the nature of the game and each of us has convinced the other of things we didn't originally agree with. In truth, like all such books, this one is the result of multiple collaborations with many other scholars, librarians, readers and friends.

We would like to thank the scholars, editors and students with whom we have held many discussions over the years, who have shaped our thinking. Particularly important to us has been the work of Brian Attebery, Holly Virginia Blackford, Cathy Butler, Mike Cadden, Maria Nikolajeva, Charles W. Sullivan III and Virginia L. Wolf.

For actual assistance with the book we would like to thank Charles Bayliss for his database; Ann Dowker, Eileen Gunn, J. P. Satyamurthy, Aishwarya Subramanian and also friends on Child_Lit for assistance with fact-checking; Josh Steans of the University of Wisconsin-Stout's Robert S. Swanson Library Learning Center Interlibrary Loan Department; Susan Thurin, owner of Bookends on Main; Diane Roback and John Sellers, children's book editors at *Publishers Weekly*, for supplying books; Sue Foxwell of the University of Wisconsin-Stout's Research Services and Angela Soutar for help on New Zealand's fiction; Judith Ridge and Stefan Ekman for Australian fiction; Cathy Butler, Hallie O'Donovan and Gillian Polack for reading the manuscript; Hazel Sheeky for taking on the arduous task of checking a bibliography that contained so many different primary texts; and Maureen Kincaid Speller for making sure that two Englishes appeared as one and spotting titles we had omitted from the bibliography.

Both of us are grateful for the material and professional support we have received from our own and other institutions. Michael Levy would like to thank the UW-Stout sabbatical, professional development and named professorship committees for release time, travel funds and the Reinhold and Borghild Eng Dahlgren Endowed Professorship. Farah Mendlesohn is deeply appreciative of the kindness of Eileen Wallace and Sue Fisher of the Eileen Wallace Collection at the University of New Brunswick.

More general thanks go to Michael Levy's colleagues and friends: Jerry Kapus, Laura McCullough, Kelly McCullough, Mandy Little, Matt Kuchta, Quan Zhou, Joan Menefee and Andy Cochran for ideas, support and good fellowship; and to Farah Mendlesohn's colleagues at Middlesex University, particularly Ben Little, Maggie Butt, David Rain, James Charlton and Lorna Gibb, and to her new colleagues at Anglia Ruskin University, which includes her whole department and many of the faculty but in particular Nina Lübbren and Andy Salmon, who helped to carve out time for the last stages of the book. Her PhD students Tiffani Angus, Agnieszka Jedrzejczyk-Drenda and Audrey Taylor have been unfailingly supportive and patient.

Finally, we would like to thank our partners, Sandra Lindow and Edward James. Both are respected science fiction and fantasy scholars in their own right, and their critical input has been invaluable. Edward James provided essential practical support and assistance in the final stages of this project.

# Introduction

The aim of this book is to bring together two traditions of criticism, that of the literature of the fantastic, and that of children's literature. In addition, this book aims to situate children's fantasy in the context of changing ideas of childhood across three centuries; and perhaps most crucially, to consider the effect which the extension of childhood has had upon the writing and publishing of children's fiction. It is a story of separate but overlapping traditions, that of the British Empire and later the Commonwealth, and that of the United States and eventually North America, and of European traditions that have influenced both.

The study of the literature of the fantastic is relatively recent, and in some ways still underdeveloped: the crucial critical texts in the field still number less than ten, and until recently focused primarily on defending and defining fantasy. That fantasy has needed defending stems from the division between high and low in our literary culture, in which belief in mimesis, the idea that a writer or artist can accurately describe reality, took centre stage. Kathryn Hume, in her landmark 1984 study *Fantasy and Mimesis: Responses to Reality in Western Literature*, wrote, 'It is an astonishing tribute to the eloquence and rigour of Plato and Aristotle as originators of western critical theory that most subsequent critics have assumed mimetic representations to be the essential relationship between text and the real world', but it is in some ways not astonishing at all. Christianity is a hybrid of Greek and Judaic ideas of the world: the first saw literature as primarily moral, the second as primarily historical. The Greek gods and their fantastical adventures were *not* moral, and to Christians were positively immoral; it was easiest to dismiss the unreality that they represented. Kathryn Hume constructs a critical thread through Tasso, Hobbes and David Hume, who, she reminds us, actually 'disparages literary fantasy as a threat to sanity'.[1] John Bunyan, author of one of the great taproot texts of the quest fantasy, explicitly denied that *The Pilgrim's Progress* was fantasy. During the Renaissance, perpetrators of such 'lies', from Boccaccio to Sir Philip Sidney, complained about those who criticized their work on these grounds.

If fantasy was a species of lie, then it should not be fed to children. Before the eighteenth century, fantastical tales – folk tales such as Robin Hood, Tom Thumb or Mother Hubbard (already a familiar figure when she appeared in Edmund Spenser's 'Mother Hubberd's Tale', 1578–9, a satire, not a children's story) – were tales not for children, but for the peasantry. Children were taught (if they were taught) from hornbooks, the Bible and, as this story opens, from primers grounded in mimesis. Mother Goose was first mentioned by a French writer, Jean Loret, in *La muse historique* in 1650, and was made more popular by Charles Perrault's *Contes de ma mère l'Oye* in 1695. These stories were intended for the amusements of adults. The transition will be discussed in greater detail in Chapter 1, but it is worth noting that the raising of tales originally intended for the peasantry into fare for the court and for adults may well be a reaction to the civil wars that raged across Europe in the seventeenth century.

The wars had led to unprecedented social mixing, which may have spread the tales, but in addition may well have created a climate in which realist literatures were risky: better to take refuge in folk tales, and per-haps tone them down a little to remove their more subversive elements. At the end of the eighteenth century a change in the way (middle- and upper-class) children were understood enabled the fantastical to enter the sphere of children's reading. The perception of the child who is born sinful, who must be tamed and led away from the fantastical to a realist understanding of his or her Christian responsibilities, is gradu-ally exchanged for a notion that the child is born innocent, and can be tempted through the fantastic to the marvellous in Christianity. When fantasy emerges as part of the creative upsurge and response to industri-alization in the nineteenth century, many Christians are at the heart of it. The legacy of John Bunyan had been to legitimize fantasy as an accept-able mode of allegory and moral instruction for the Christian, and the immense popularity of *The Pilgrim's Progress* with families demonstrates its utility in moral instruction. This is perhaps epitomized in the work of George MacDonald: both *At the Back of the North Wind* (1871) and *The Princess and Curdie* (1883) are explicitly concerned with the shaping of the Christian child.

It would be nice to say that fantasy no longer needs defending, but hostility to it as a literary form reappears periodically. *The Wizard of Oz* is one of the most frequently banned books in the United States;

J. K. Rowling's *Harry Potter* sequence arouses the ire of fundamentalists; modern Islam is often uncomfortable with fantasy – while, at the same time, Christians (e.g. G. P. Taylor) as well as Muslims (e.g. Najiyah Diana Helwani) continue to write allegorical fantasy. Jews, interestingly, seem to have had little tension with the form: the best-known Jewish children's fantasy writer is perhaps Jane Yolen but there are many more. On the secular stage, the division remains closer to that of the eighteenth century: the fantastic is to be regarded primarily as children's literature, and children's literature is to be regarded as innately inferior and less complex.

If the defence of fantasy is ultimately a rather pointless task, the act of defining it was crucial to its early critical history. Rosemary Jackson, Tzvetan Todorov, W. R. Irwin, Brian Attebery and a group of other hardworking scholars have explored the concept in great depth in an attempt to delineate the fantastic, to greater (Jackson, Irwin, Hume) or lesser (Todorov) utility; but apart from the general understanding that the fantastic is the realization of the *impossible* (distinguishing it from science fiction which attempts to realize a possible), a paradigmatic approach grounded in reader response, which assumes that the existence of the fantastic is a constant negotiation between author, publisher and reader, rather than a delineation, has become the dominant narrative.

Brian Attebery's use of the fuzzy set (a mathematical term for sets whose elements have degrees of membership and in which case means a set whose core we can identify but whose edges are ambiguous) to identify a core of texts to which we can point and say 'This is fantasy, and as we move from the core it becomes less fantastical' has worked well, even as it is now being challenged by Farah Mendlesohn and Helen Young, not for its lack of utility but because the original material on which it was based was biased by the selections of respondents and texts, and perhaps most significantly – given the rapid shifts in the field traced in Mendlesohn and James's *A Short History of Fantasy* (2009) – because it reflected a very specific moment in time.[2]

In her introduction to *Rhetorics of Fantasy*, Farah Mendlesohn has suggested that it is no longer worth engaging in a debate over the exact definition of fantasy: 'A consensus has emerged, accepting as a viable "fuzzy set" a range of critical definitions',[3] in which the mode of fantasy rather than the nature of fantasy is crucial to an understanding of the form. The four modes Mendlesohn outlines are the *portal-quest fantasy*, a fantastic world entered through a portal and told as tourist narrative in which the protagonists have little access to the underpinning of the world; the *intrusion* fantasy in which the fantastic intrudes upon the normative world, disrupting it until defeated; the *immersive* fantasy, in which the fantastic world becomes the primary world for all the participants and is constructed as such, with little explanation; and the *liminal* fantasy, in which reader and protagonist may have very different ideas about what is fantastical and Todorovian doubt underpins the rhetoric.

The concept of a fuzzy set enables two highly opinionated scholars to come to terms with their own differences over whether a given work is fantasy, horror, science fiction or something else entirely. This is possible even when one scholar (Levy) has Coleridge's 'willing suspension of disbelief' firmly lodged in the back of his mind, while the other (Mendlesohn) prefers to argue for the intensification of belief.

The study of children's literature is far more established than that of fantasy, with the first studies of children's literature appearing in the 1920s, along with *The Horn Book Magazine*, now the most prestigious review journal of children's literature. By the 1960s Margaret Meek and Humphrey Carpenter, among others, had begun the work of establishing respectability for the field, and academic journals, such as *Children's Literature*, *Children's Literature Association Quarterly* and *The Lion and the Unicorn*, appeared in the 1970s. However, while the infrastructure of children's fantasy criticism is strong in these journals, and in the general introductory texts such as John Rowe Townsend's *Written for Children* and Peter Hunt's *An Introduction to Children's Literature*, the specialist material is more problematic. Ann Swinfen's *In Defence of Fantasy* (1984) does not position itself as a book about children's literature although it cites only children's texts, and it lacks a historical paradigm (the books are dated according to the edition read); Sheila Egoff's *Worlds Within: Children's Fantasy from the Middle Ages to Today* (1988) is an excellent introduction but now old, and concludes prior to the development of Canada and Australia as significant voices in the English-speaking book market. (A good replacement is K. V. Johansen's *Quests and Kingdoms: A Grown-Up's Guide to Children's Fantasy Literature*, 2005.) The rapid development of Canadian and Antipodean fantasy is why Colin Manlove's otherwise excellent *From Alice to Harry Potter: Children's Fantasy in England* (2003) is problematic: it is simply too narrow and ignores the partial merger of the British Commonwealth and American traditions in the 1990s. Pamela Gates, Susan Steffel and Francis Molson's *Fantasy Literature for Children and Young Adults* is probably the closest to what we have set out to achieve, but its categorization of fantasy into fairy tales, mixed fantasy and heroic-ethical traditions is unilluminating and lacks a contextual or historical overview.[4]

All of the above titles are highly selective in terms of the texts they study, leaning towards the best of children's fantasy, or simply that which has been loved enough to survive. We have been less so: we began our bibliographies from scratch, creating lists from each period and including lesser-known texts or those which have completely vanished, as we strove to create a narrative history of the field. The working definition of fantasy in this book is broad and to a degree ad hoc. We have excluded obvious science fiction (time travel with equipment or vehicle), alternative history (including steampunk, which is grounded in the early expansion of the rational and mechanical) and tales of horror that lack a fantastical element. We have included time-slips where the facilitating device is magical, and alternative worlds that embrace magic. Animal tales are included where animals behave as humans and there is no attempt to create a mimesis of animal life (so *Redwall*, but not *Watership Down*). We cover all historical genres: myths and legends, fairy tales, romances, ghost fantasies, quests, nonsense tales and paranormal romance.

We have, however, placed genre and media limitations on this book: it is predominantly about what the American publishing industry labels chapter books; we have excluded picture books, poetry, television and film. We have included non-English-language fantasy where it has been foundational (Hans Christian Andersen) or absorbed into the traditions we describe (Tove Jansson). In the early chapters we have attempted to be comprehensive. By Chapter 5 we have moved to tracing strands in the weave. It is a given that whoever you are, wherever you are from, you will discover that a number of your favourite children's fantasies are not discussed or done justice to in this volume, as there is simply too much to cover.

We have used a range of ways to describe and classify fantasy: high fantasy for medievalist and court fantasy, but indigenous fantasy (Attebery) rather than low fantasy for the fantasy of the everyday; urban and pastoral fantasy; and on occasion Mendlesohn's quartet of immersive, portal-quest, intrusion and liminal fantasy when we have wished to describe the narratology of the text. But ours is a book that argues there are more ways than one to consider literature: the filters and questions applied each produce very different and fruitful understandings.

We have also taken decisions around the definition of children's literature that reflect our goal of a flexible and reader-oriented understanding. The first is that children's literature is fiction read to or by children, whether or not it was originally published for children and whether or not adults have approved of children reading it. This particularly affects the early chapters of this volume, which concern a time before children's fiction was a category, but it also applies to the work of John Bunyan, Charles Kingsley, Stephen King, Anne Rice, Terry Brooks and Trudi Canavan, whose books have been appropriated by younger readers.

The second decision is almost more important because it explains the changing scope of the book as it proceeds to narrate three centuries of fiction for children: this book might best be understood as a history of fantasy for school-age children. It is very noticeable that the age at which fiction specifically for children is pitched has been gradually extended. In our earliest chapters the protagonist is rarely over eight years old; by the 1930s twelve seems to be the cut-off point; by the 1950s and into the 1980s fourteen-year-olds are regularly appearing in children's fantasy. From the 1980s onwards a new category begins to develop – first through appropriating the work of adult writers, later as new teen lists, until it emerges as Young Adult – which features protagonists in their late teens. By the time this book concludes, there is a swathe of fiction labelled Young Adult (or more recently New Adult) which features protagonists in their early twenties and is clearly aimed at late teens and early twenties readers, readers who are in this modern world still quite likely to be in school or college.

Our aim is to create an overview of the development of fantasy literature within the English-speaking world. This is a tale of distinct but converging book markets: as late as the 1980s and well into the 1990s, there were two children's book markets, one in the USA which eventually extended to collaborate with Canada, and one focused on Britain, which encompassed the British Empire, later the Commonwealth (Ireland declined to join the Commonwealth but it remains part of this nexus). Although some influential books crossed lines, the markets were sufficiently distinct that readers from Singapore, Delhi, Sydney and London were more likely to share their childhood reading with one another than with a reader from New York. These book markets had different flavours. The great outdoors is a feature of American, Canadian and Australian fantasy a full century before it becomes the norm for the British market, where over seventy years we will trace a very distinct trajectory out of the home, into the garden and finally into the streets. This is also a tale of absorption and sometimes appropriation, in which we will trace different source materials, the stuff of fantasy – folk tales, fairy, Greek myth and legend, science, Arthuriana, paganism, medievalism, orientalism – new cultural voices, and different ideologies, particularly feminism, as they shape the emergence of the field.

We begin with 'How fantasy became children's literature' and in Chapter 1 consider tales such as *Aesop's Fables* (1484), *The History of Reynard the Fox* (1481) and *The History of the Seven Champions of Christendom* (1596), and the ways in which they entered the popular imagination and did or did not receive approval from the cultural elites of their day. We then move on to a discussion of fairy tales, as peasant or Mother Goose stories, as bourgeois *Märchen* and as courtly tales retold and refined, and discuss their influence on the Romantics and on nineteenth-century English writers. This takes us to Chapter 2, in which we explore the British fascination with 'Fairies, ghouls and goblins: the realms of Victorian and Edwardian fancy' and the movement of writers such as Charles Dickens and Charles Kingsley, Lewis Carroll and Edward Lear against the dominant narrative mode of realism, until the point at the end of the century when the majority of that Victorian and Edwardian British children's literature which has survived is firmly in the fantastical vein.

Immigrants to America brought their own folklore with them, but as Chapter 3, 'The American search for an American childhood', argues, it did not easily survive the hostile environment in which it found itself – fascinatingly, this itself would become a theme in the American urban fantasy of the 1990s. When Washington Irving wrote his folk tales, he often stripped them of their fantastic elements, or offered rationalist explanations of his apparently fantastical tales. Yet a strong Gothic tradition developed for adults in the works of Charles Brockden Brown, Herman Melville and Edgar Allan Poe, and this was quickly appropriated by young readers. Hawthorne published two collections specifically for children, *A Wonder-Book for Girls and Boys* and *Tanglewood Tales*, both of which retell the Greek myths, the one set of fantastical material that received college-level approval. Until the publication of *The Wizard of Oz* by Baum, however, American children had little fantasy to choose from; only later was there an explosion of material which leaned heavily towards the whimsical, kicked off perhaps by E. B. White's success with works such as *Charlotte's Web* (1952).

The period between the First and Second World Wars creates a uniquely coherent period in British fantasy, which we will explore in Chapter 4. However, while this coherence is political and cultural, in terms of the fantastic it is a period of wild experimentation with form and content. It includes such rich and diverse work as that of A. A. Milne, Walter de la Mare, Alison Uttley, Eleanor Farjeon, Roger Lancelyn Green, Enid Blyton, T. H. White and, of course, J. R. R. Tolkien. A number of these writers, although famous in the UK, were virtually unknown in the United States.

In the aftermath of war, there were drastic changes in both the structures and stuff of British fantasy. Chapters 5 and 6 discuss the changing landscape, social, political and literal, of post-war British and Commonwealth fantasy. War had been demanding of children, both on the home front and in the European and Asian war zones, and we see this reflected in the works of C. S. Lewis, Susan Cooper, Alan Garner, Lloyd Alexander and Margaret Mahy. It had also raised levels of fear, and we see this expressed both in the new quest narratives, and in the wainscot fantasies of Mary Norton, Tove Jansson, Carol Kendall and Patricia Wrightson, and to a degree in the trickster fantasies of Roald Dahl. The widening scope of children's actions in fantasy literature is noticeable and startling. In addition, we begin to see the coming together of the stuff of fantasy, as folklore, fairy and genre fantastic converged.

From the 1960s the diverse strands of fantasy seen in previous generations began to separate into clear subgenres. Chapter 7, 'Middle Earth, medievalism and mythopoeic fantasy', focuses on the strand that came to dominate the 1970s and 1980s, led by the mass-market publication of Tolkien's *The Lord of the Rings* in 1965. American authors such as Ursula K. Le Guin, Patricia McKillip, Robin McKinley, Tamora Pierce and Jane Yolen all moved into secondary-world fantasy, each making use of its traditional structures without necessarily accepting its traditional assumptions. Along the way the Americans also took on Garner's challenge to make use of the stuff of the world around them, from new arguments about medieval Europe to unfamiliar folklores and different religious traditions, while challenging and interrogating colonialist and class assumptions along the way. By the middle of the 1990s this was the dominant tradition, spreading across an international market.

Yet behind the scenes an urban and indigenous fantasy tradition, led in Britain by Diana Wynne Jones, Barbara Sleigh and others, still thrived, existing in the interstices of a publishing market dominated by social realism. In 1997 this tradition was revived by the publication of *Harry Potter and the Philosopher's Stone*, which transformed the children's book market into an international industry. The success of *Harry Potter* and its consequences are discussed in Chapter 8, along with another change, the clear emergence of a separate but linked teen market (where we have sited Phillip Pullman, for reasons we will make clear at that point). Books written for 'children' in the 1990s feel far more distinctly *children's* books, in that they are clearly aimed at the pre-teen to perhaps fourteen-year-old market. As the limited age range of the audience for such books became clear, and as the time the average spent in education increased into the late teens and beyond, the outward-bound trajectory of the narratives – towards the adult world of work – in much of the earlier children's fiction of all genres was undermined. Fantasy for teens emerged, shaped around their concerns.

The final chapter, Chapter 9, reflects two very different trends. One set of Young Adult fantasies, often set in *this* world and where the fantastic takes on the role of exotic and disruptive intrusion, is paranormal fiction. Although such tales are often hard-hitting and the characters may have real-world issues to deal with, these are ultimately consolatory fictions, which deal with finding groups to join, and gaining status, often through romance. Another set of Young Adult fantasies deals with what we describe as the fantasy of bitterness and loss: these are uneasy stories of outsider teenagers in hostile environments, and we as critics believe that this subgenre includes much of the finest fantasy for any age group currently being written.

## CHAPTER I

# How fantasy became children's literature

Historians of children's literature begin their narratives in a variety of time periods, and with a specific range of texts, but these choices are not value neutral: each choice, for period or genre, tells the reader something about the historian's or critic's understanding of what childhood is, or what children's literature is. Children's fantasy has far stronger roots in tales of the fantastic than it does in tales for children: the history of children's fantasy is essentially one of appropriation, both children appropriating texts, and those who have written for children in the last three centuries appropriating and adapting their material for children. The close relationship between these processes may be one factor in the disproportionate representation of fantasy among those children's book titles which retain their popularity – beyond nostalgia – into the reading lives of adults.

Seth Lerer, in *Children's Literature: A Reader's History, from Aesop to Harry Potter* (2008), begins with the ancients and identifies children's literature less as a body of texts – which was generally shared with adults – than as a mode of delivery: the children of educated classical Greeks and Romans would have been introduced to the *Iliad* and the *Aeneid*, but would have been taught in excerpts, with an emphasis on memory, recitation and quotation, so that the well-rounded citizen could draw on a common culture of citizenry.[1] This tradition lasted well into the twentieth century in the great British public schools and is well portrayed in that classic of children's literature, *Tom Brown's Schooldays* (1857) by Thomas Hughes. In this model of children's fiction, fiction is a thing *for* children, but not *of* them. It is a route out of childhood and into the adult world which does not treasure the child or childhood as something precious, and in which children's reading is contiguous with that of adults: it is primarily moralistic and therefore, as with Greek and Roman education, primarily civic.

This approach is valuable to the student of children's fantasy literature because much of what has become the matter (the themes or substance) of children's fantasy, particularly in the British tradition, is drawn from a core of texts never intended for children. One such text is the beast fable. The beast fable was intended for all: it did not socialize people into the *civitas* in the way Greek and Roman education might, nor into the religious and social order as did the transmission of biblical stories, but it did teach children the arbitrariness and cruelty of the world, and taught them the moral values that they were to share with the adults who told the stories. The beast fable came to the British from the Greeks via the Romans: Aesop's fables were first translated into English by William Caxton in 1484. Despite the pre-Christian origins of Aesop's fables, they were absorbed into the English canon, their classical antecedents granting them respectability.[2] In *Aesop's Fables* we see the taproot of many modern tales: 'The Tortoise and the Hare' and 'The Shepherd and the Wolf' are just two of the more popular fables that have become regulars in cartoons and picture books. The fables capture two of the qualities that come to be associated with stories for children: the moral lesson, and the anthropomorphization of animal characters. The latter allows the poor to laugh at their superiors and the child at adults without threatening the social order while gaining a moral perspective on irrational behaviour: 'The Fox and the Stork', for example, is an early lesson in spite and status-seeking. We can see this rather brutal understanding of the adult world later in the work of Hans Christian Andersen, as in 'The Tale of the Ugly Duckling' (1843), in which in order to get on, you must reject the people who cared for you; in many stories in which rightful inheritance beats striving or self-education every time; or in Rudyard Kipling's *The Jungle Book* (1894), in which the animals share the pleasures and pains of human servants.

A beast fable, *Reynard the Fox*, appeared in an English translation by William Caxton in 1481. Here, the trickster clearly represents something darker and more subversive than in *Aesop's Fables*. The fable opens with the declaration that the book is for the good of readers, 'as far as they in reading or hearing of it shall mowe understand and feel the foresaid subtle deceits that daily ben used in the world, not to the intent that men should use them, but that every man should eschew and keep him from the subtle false shrews, that they be not deceived'.[3]

They weren't and we are not. This is clearly a cover story, unlikely to convince anyone of any age with an ounce of common sense. As the fable begins, Noble the Lion – portrayed as a medieval king – calls everyone to the court to bear witness against Reynard the Fox. Reynard declines the invitation, conscious that all have complaints against him. Beginning with the Wolf, each animal then enumerates the various ways that Reynard has done them wrong: everything from pissing on the Wolf's children and sleeping with his wife to murdering Chanticleer the Rooster's daughter. The Fox's nephew, the Badger, defends Reynard, insisting, not very believably, 'that he is a gentle and true man. He may suffer no falsehood. He doth nothing but by his priest's counsel.'[4]

Unconvinced, the Lion sends a series of animals to bring Reynard in, forewarning each of them of the Fox's trickery. Reynard nevertheless succeeds in making a fool of each animal, playing on their vanity, gluttony or other vice. At one point Reynard agrees to make confession and recounts a long list of sins in delicious detail (one of the first examples we have of the gallows confession narrative, itself the beginnings of a new genre), but he soon returns to his immoral ways. Condemned to death by the King, the Fox, in his own defence, tells a long, involved and frankly preposterous tale in which he is positioned as the hero, attempting to save the King from the treachery of Bear and Wolf, and disclosing the location of a supposed treasure. Noble pardons Reynard and makes him an officer of his court. The tale continues at some length, with a series of variations on what has come before, and ends with the Fox triumphant, recounting his deeds to his wife and family.

This, as Roald Dahl demonstrated in his modern version, *Fantastic Mr Fox* (1970), is a tale designed to encourage emulation of the subversive; it teaches people to live in the world not through obedience, but through cleverness. Reynard tales vary, from simple trickster tales to ones of class warfare, and have proven far less tameable than the more realistic stories of Robin Hood. They point out and condemn vice, but they also show the sinner triumphant, using his golden tongue to talk his way out of trouble. These stories take pleasure in the subversion of the social order: the fifteenth-century German tale, *The Historie of Frier Rush*, first published in 1620 in England, which recounts the many comic high jinks of a devil who masquerades as a monk and wreaks havoc at a monastery, falls into a similar category: it is near the knuckle and is acceptable only because of its anti-Catholicism. The book's cover, which claims the work is 'full of pleasant mirth and delight for young people', reminds us that the accessibility of this material to the young was designed to inculcate in them *all* adult values, many of which involved hatred and contempt for others.

It seems clear that by the late sixteenth century, and well into the eighteenth century, virtually all the important works of literature available to adults were also being read to or by children of a surprisingly young age. Among these was a variety of literary works in many genres, sometimes heavily redacted and modernized to make them suitable for contemporary audiences of various sorts, sometimes presented in abbreviated form in inexpensive chapbooks. These included romances, Christian allegories like John Bunyan's *The Pilgrim's Progress* (1678), legends, fables, ballads, histories and fairy tales (*The History of Tom Thumbe* was published as early as 1621 and *Jack and the Gyants* in 1708) – indeed, any literary work with significant fantastic or adventure elements that might attract children. Worth mentioning here is even such a sophisticated work as Edmund Spenser's epic poem *The Faerie Queene* (1590) as well as the less complex (and now less well-known) *The Seven Champions of Christendom* (1596) by Richard Johnson. The first English-language translation of *The Arabian Nights* (1705), with its tales of Sinbad and Aladdin, was another among the many adult books quickly adopted by children.

The fantasy in many of these works may have been primarily intended (by those who made the books available to children) to be read as allegory or at least to be taken as morally serious, but it also seems probable that younger readers viewed Spenser's and Johnson's knights and dragons, and even the adventures of Bunyan's Christian, in a manner not all that different from how their modern counterparts see comparable characters in the work of J. R. R. Tolkien or Lloyd Alexander or in the deeply allegorical fantasies of C. S. Lewis. Renée Kennedy writes of Richard Johnson's *The History of the Seven Champions of Christendom* (1596): 'Although each of the Champions is accorded a title of sanctity, his heroic deeds and acts of virtue place him more in the company of knights and troubadours than among the beatified.'[5] It is no surprise that Johnson's St George kills a dragon, but there is also a complex origin story for the saint that involves a Caesarean birth and kidnapping by a 'famous Enchantress', who raises the infant St George and later attempts to seduce him, and then gives him magical gifts before he uses his 'inchanted Wand' to trap her in a rock. The killing of the dragon is recounted with significant gusto:

> Now as St. *George* entered the Valley, and came near to the Cave, the Dragon espied him, and sent forth such a terrible Bellowing as if all the Devils in Hell had been present. St. *George* was never a whit daunted, but spurred his Horse and ran outrageously at him; but his Scales being harder than any Brass, he shivered his Spear in a thousand Pieces; and withal smote St. *George* so hard with his Wings and Tail, that he struck him down from his Horse, and bruited him fore.[6]

The other saints, including Andrew of Scotland and Patrick of Ireland, have almost as much fun rescuing maidens in distress, killing monsters and the like. *The Seven Champions of Christendom* was published as an inexpensive chapbook available to a wide variety of readers, including children.

John Bunyan himself confessed a guilty love for *The Seven Champions* in his childhood, along with the equally exciting tale of *Bevis of Hampton*: 'Give me a ballad, a news-book, George on horseback, or Bevis of Southampton; give me some book that teaches curious arts, that tells of old fables; but for the holy Scriptures I cared not.' Admittedly, he made this confession in the work *A Few Sighs from Hell, or The Groans of the Damned Soul* in which, while admitting that fantastical tales appeal to children, he did not consider this a good thing.[7] To the religious of his sort, books written for children were acceptable only if they were aimed at either the development of basic literacy skills or the teaching of Christian morals. Yet the Puritans did retain a taste for the dark and fantastic, as in Milton's *Paradise Lost* (1667), and for the allegorical, as in John Bunyan's *The Pilgrim's Progress* (1678), as well as a sense of wonder, as seen in the nature-worship poems in Isaac Watts's *Divine Songs Attempted in Easy Language for the Use of Children* (1715). *The Arabian Nights* on the other hand may have been seen as without redeeming moral value, which may have speeded its way into English culture, first through chapbooks and later in the racy and lower-class entertainment of the pantomime.

## Perrault, fairy tales and the French court

Despite, or perhaps because of the rational turn of the Renaissance, a formalization and elevation of the folk tale began in the middle of the sixteenth century and carried on into the Enlightenment, first in Italy and then France. The great French historian Philippe Ariès points to the tremendous popularity of folk tales with the French nobility.[8] Among the most significant collectors were Giovanni Straparola, whose *Le Piacevoli Notte* (1550–3) includes well-known variants of 'Puss in Boots' and 'Iron John'; Giambattista Basile, whose *Il Pentamerone* (1634–6) includes the first published version of 'Rapunzel'; Charles Perrault, whose *Tales and Stories of the Past with Morals* (1697), subtitled *Tales of Mother Goose*, includes well-known variants of 'Little Red Riding Hood', 'Sleeping Beauty', 'Puss in Boots' and 'Cinderella'; Madame D'Aulnoy, whose *Les contes des fées* (1697), many of which appear to be both her own creations and very clearly intended for adults, featured the first use of the term 'fairy tale'; and Charles-Joseph de Mayer, whose forty-one-volume

Charles Perrault (1628–1703) was born into wealth and opted for a career in government service. In 1669 he advised King Louis XIV to include more than three dozen fountains with sculptures of characters from *Aesop's Fables* in the new gardens at Versailles, thus beginning his association with the literature of the fantastic. Perrault is credited with initiating the long-running argument over the relative quality of ancient versus modern writers that was still being fought in Tolkien's day. He sided with the moderns. Perrault's *Tales of Mother Goose* made him famous beyond court circles and, although many of his stories are based on earlier published 'folk tales', it is his versions, along with those of the Brothers Grimm, that have come down to us in the present day. Among his best-known tales are 'Sleeping Beauty', 'Little Red Riding Hood', 'Puss in Boots' and 'Cinderella'.

*Le cabinet des fées* (1785–9) anthologized most of the significant tales published in the two previous centuries.

At one time such collections (with the exception, perhaps, of Madame d'Aulnoy's *Les contes des fées*) were regarded as comprising largely traditional tales, the result of the collectors having taken careful notes from the (generally) poor folk who had transmitted the tales down through the years in various supposedly authentic forms. However, most of these collectors rewrote their stories to varying degrees to make them more appealing to their primary audiences – in Perrault's case, an upper class that was in part bourgeois and in part aristocratic, and, in the Grimms' case, an almost exclusively bourgeois audience. Lerer suggests that the first published French fairy tales were 'exemplary fables for the courtier adults. They taught ideal behaviour … They contributed to the mythology of courtliness and kingship'; he describes Perrault as 'the best and most widely read of these tale-tellers'.[9] By the eighteenth century these collections were seeping into the English market: Perrault first appeared in English in Robert Samber's 1729 translation, while Madame d'Aulnoy's fairy tales were translated in 1752.

The prominent fairy tale scholar Jack Zipes argues that as the bourgeoisie gained increasing economic power in the sixteenth and seventeenth centuries in both France and England, and as their interests gradually merged with those of the aristocracy, fairy tales were one of the tools that proved useful in what was, in part, an educational process.[10] Perrault sought to merge bourgeois and aristocratic ideas and produce a somewhat more homogeneous and controllable national culture (although evidently such merging could not bridge the class divides that culminated in revolution).

As part of this process, by the end of the seventeenth century, child-hood was conceived of as a state of natural innocence, and therefore potentially corruptible, and the civilizing of children – a process of social indoctrination through anxiety-provoking effects and positive reinforcement – operated on all levels in manners, speech, sex, literature and play. Instincts were to be trained and harnessed to sociopolitical values. The supervised rearing of children was to lead to the *homme civilisé*. Thus it was 'not by chance that Perrault and the women writers of the 1690s created their fairy tales for the most part to express their views about young people and to prepare them for roles that they idealistically believed they should play in society'.[11] This is of central importance. This role for the fairy tale helps to explain why it became an entry point for women into literature, as the perceived responsibility for the moral education of children was gradually shifting from men to women.

Although Perrault often appears as the towering figure engaged in this work in France, of equal importance were the aristocratic women who created and popularized fairy tales in the salons of the seventeenth century. Among those now largely forgotten women are the above-mentioned Madame d'Aulnoy, Madame de Murat, Mademoiselle L'Héritier and Mademoiselle de La Force. Zipes (citing Renate Baader) points out that while the tales of Perrault and other male fairy tale producers generally emphasized wifely obedience, women 'commonly refused to place themselves in the service of social mobility. Instead, they put forward their demand for moral, intellectual, and psychological self-determination.'[12] In doing so, they operated in the one sphere that was theirs, child-rearing.

Ariès writes that even as fairy tales were gaining popularity in the French court in the late seventeenth century, there was significant debate over the extent to which such stories were appropriate for adults or for children. Perrault's tales, Ariès insists, were, at least in principle for children, though widely loved at court, while other collections were 'more serious work meant for grown-ups, from which children and the lower orders were excluded'.[13] Yet there is a clear sense in the collections of Madame Leprince de Beaumont that children – or at least older children – *were* the intended audience. De Beaumont, then living in England and working as a governess for the children of the Prince of Wales, first published 'Beauty and the Beast' in her *Le magasin des enfants* in 1756 (it appeared in English in *The Young Misses Magazine*, 1765), a publication specifically aimed at upper-class girls, and it was intended to teach good manners.

The tale itself was not original. It had already taken on a recognizable shape in Madame Gabrielle de Villeneuve's 'Beauty and the Beast' (1740), which served as the basis for de Beaumont's tale. In de Villeneuve's version of the tale Beauty is but one of six children of a wealthy merchant. Her two sisters are less beautiful than she is, and less sweet-natured, though little is made of this. In de Beaumont's retelling, however, we are specifically told that Beauty's sisters are not as good as she is because they are beset by pride. 'They gave themselves ridiculous airs, and would not visit other merchants' daughters, nor keep company with any but persons of quality. They went out every day upon parties of pleasure, balls, plays, concerts &c. and laughed at their younger sister, because she spent the greatest part of her time reading good books.'[14] The older sisters snub appropriate suitors, telling them that they will marry no one beneath the rank of earl, whereas Beauty thanks her suitors, but 'correctly' tells them that she is as yet too young to consider marriage. When the merchant loses almost everything, his older daughters forsake him, mistakenly assuming that their lovers will still marry them without their wealth, and the narrator tells us that 'every body' castigates them, saying 'we are very glad to see their pride humbled; let them go and give themselves quality-airs in milking the cows and minding their dairy'.[15] Beauty, however, is pitied by that same 'every body', because she is 'a charming, sweet-tempered creature' who speaks 'kindly to poor people'.[16] She continues to refuse suitors, who would happily marry her though she is poor, and goes to live with her family in a small 'country-house'. The merchant, although much reduced, is still far from destitute, even owning a harpsi-chord, which Beauty plays, though only after all of her chores are done. Her sisters, of course, will do nothing but complain and the tale continues in this manner at some length. Beauty has her expected romance with the Beast and the story concludes with her visit home – where she discovers her sisters happily married – the delay of her return to the Beast, and her resolve: 'It is true, I do not feel the tenderness of affection for him, but I find I have the highest gratitude, esteem and friendship; and I will not make him miserable: were I to be so ungrateful, I should never forgive myself.'[17] De Beaumont thus sets forth the ground rules for making decisions about marriage; 'tenderness of affection', what we would call romantic love, is not necessary, nor are wits or good looks, so long as one feels gratitude, esteem and friendship.

De Beaumont's 'Beauty and the Beast' is set within a larger, more or less realistic narrative or framing device in which a governess, Mrs Affable, tells stories or teaches lessons to a group of girls under her care, Lady Charlotte, Lady Witty and others. After she finishes telling them 'Beauty and the Beast' the girls discuss the tale, going over and agreeing with its lessons, and one of them, Miss Molly, notes in support of the story and apropos of ugliness that when her father 'first took a little black to be his foot-boy, I was afraid of him, and hid myself when he came in; but by little and little I grew used to him, and now he lifts me into the coach when I go abroad; I never so much as think of his face'.[18] Although popular in its day, de Beaumont's tale was also criticized for its focus on feminine virtue and its willingness to let children be children: the idea that fairy tales were *for* children was still somewhat uncomfortable.

## A Grimm business in Germany

Which brings us at last to the Brothers Grimm. It may come as no surprise to any experienced teacher of children's literature that, when asked to discuss the original version of many fairy tales (or *Märchen* in German), from Cinderella to Snow White to Sleeping Beauty to The Little Mermaid to Beauty and the Beast, most college students taking children's literature classes will automatically assume that the teacher is referring to the Walt Disney versions of those tales. So deeply has the Disney dream-machine infested Western culture that the actual creators or collectors of these stories, from Perrault to de Beaumont to the Grimms to Andersen, are seen by most non-scholars as secondary creators. Our students have usually heard of the Grimms and may vaguely

Jacob (1785–1863) and Wilhelm Grimm (1786–1859) had what might be the ideal childhood for men bent upon literary success. Raised in moderate wealth by a hard-working lawyer father, they received a classical education. Then their father died abruptly when Jacob, the eldest of six children, was just eleven, leaving the family in dire poverty and forcing both him and Wilhelm to grow up rather quickly. Two years later, however, a well-to-do aunt secured them a place in a prestigious *Lyzeum* as well as financial support for the family. Contemporary evidence shows that the boys were under great pressure to succeed. Mistreated as scholarship boys, they developed, moreover, a keen appreciation of class differences and political oppression. Because of their low social status, they were only allowed into law school at the University of Marburg by special dispensation, despite outstanding grades. There they once again faced discrimination. Although both brothers had studied law, they also had a predilection for literature and in 1806, at the request of Clemens Brentano, a well-known author of the time, they began collecting both oral and literary tales. In a few years both men had established themselves as scholars of folk literature with significant publications, and in 1812 came their first volume of collected tales, *Kinder- und Hausmärchen*, complete with copious scholarly annotations.

be aware that they predate Disney, but for most of them this is irrelevant. Yet there was a time when the Grimms bestrode the world of fairy tale every bit as much as Disney does today, and were given the credit they deserved – sometimes more than they deserved – for their work.

The Germany in which the Grimms grew up was fragmented into many small principalities, some of whose rulers were despots, and the country suffered much from the violence of the Napoleonic Wars. Jacob and Wilhelm were deeply invested in the idea of a unified and peaceful Germany and Jacob was politically active as early as 1814, when he became a member of the Hessian Peace Delegation. Later both brothers became professors at the prestigious University of Göttingen where they carried on their careers as important scholars of folklore and linguistics, though both were forced to resign for their part in a political protest in 1837. This pattern continued for much of their lives: scholarly success and liberal political activism, followed by political repression as a consequence. Both brothers saw their work on German folklore and linguistics as patriotic, part of an effort to foster a just and united Germany.

Popular belief has it that the Grimms went out into the countryside like modern collectors, taking accurate dictation from the common folk. This, however, is not the case; they invited both amateur and professional storytellers to visit them and tell their tales. Most were well-educated young women who told stories they had heard from their servants or nursemaids. The Grimms were thus, more often than not, collecting at at least one remove from the actual folk. Some related tales that they had read in their childhood – stories at least two generations removed from their oral roots. Further, the Grimms took some of their narratives from already published materials, which they rewrote to their own satisfaction.

The enthusiasm with which the tales have been received by children, however, may reflect precisely the degree to which they are *not* suitable but rather transgressive, at least in the minds of their child readers, touching on matters that adults may think are naughty or taboo. One example of this inappropriateness is 'The Story of the Youth who Went Forth to Learn what Fear was'; this story, of a boy seeking to learn how to shudder, could be the ancestor of all scout campfire tales as well as R. L. Stine's *Goosebumps* series (1992–7). 'Hansel and Gretel', with its tale of abuse and abandonment and the dangers of having a stepmother, is rooted in a commonplace situation, due to the period's high childbirth mortality (higher than in previous eras thanks to the participation of doctors with multiple patients). The German *Märchen* seem to delight in a studied brutality and remorselessness. The daughter in the Grimms' version of Cinderella (Aschenputtel) is brutalized by her father as well as her stepmother.

## English fairy tales, Mrs Teachum and Mrs Trimmer

Turning away from stories that were not created with children in mind, we will now discuss literature which was specifically *designed* for children. Jack Zipes argues that 'it is absurd to date the origin of the literary fairy tale for children with the publication of Perrault's tales'.[19] Zipes instead references the later publication of inexpensive chapbooks of fairy tales in the 1720s as the true origin of published work of this sort for young audiences. Yet the texts discussed so far, however much they were enjoyed by children, were not child-directed texts but written for adults; and sometimes they were not texts at all but oral narratives accessible to all. As reading became an increasingly important skill in the sixteenth and seventeenth centuries – moving from a professional skill to an indication of elite status, then to a key requirement for accessing the new Protestantism and artisan or middle-class status – the tools of teaching became more formalized.

The first tools of literacy with which most English children of the sixteenth century would have become familiar were hornbooks, containing their ABCs, or perhaps what were known as 'abcie books' which might contain not just the alphabet and basic numbers, but a catechism. Eventually a variety of books designed to teach proper grammar began to appear, starting with John Hart's illustrated primer *A Methode, or Comfortable Beginning for All Unlearned* (1570). Works of educational theory, in some cases using that term very loosely, were also increasingly common, most importantly Roger Ascham's influential *The Schoolmaster* (1570), which centred on the teaching of Latin but emphasized the necessity for teachers to be firm and persuasive rather than abusive in their methods.[20]

A century or so later educational theory reached a high point with John Locke's *Some Thoughts Concerning Education* (1693), which became the most influential English-language book on educating children in the late seventeenth and eighteenth centuries. Locke's book, although written for gentlemen and not entirely original in its ideas, presented the notion that we are all *tabulae rasae*, blank slates, at birth, thus implying that anyone, even a commoner, has the ability to learn and be successful. Further, writing in clear, easy-to-understand English, he popularized the idea that other things besides the classics were worth reading and learning. Finally,

Locke emphasized that even small children should be treated as rational beings. Thus there was a gradual change in the mid seventeenth century from material exclusively aimed at children who could read Latin to works like James Janeway's pioneering, pre-Lockean *A Token for Children* (1671), which told didactic stories about good children in English, and William Ronksley's *The Child's Weeks-Work* (1712), which featured a variety of verses, riddles, jokes and short fables. Locke's philosophy was increasingly reflected in such works.

A candidate for the role of first popularizer of fairy tales directed at children, at least in English, is Robert Samber, whose 1729 English-language version of Perrault's work, *Histories, or Tales of Past Times told by Mother Goose*, helped transform public opinion on this issue. Sarah Fielding's *The Governess; or The Little Female Academy* (1749) was the first novel written expressly for children and contains within it 'The Story of the cruel Giant Barbarico, the good Giant Benefico, and the pretty little Dwarf Mignon', a beauty-and-the-beast type of story which predates the publication of de Beaumont's 'Beauty and the Beast' by more than a decade. In Sarah Fielding's work we encounter what would become a nineteenth-century trend, the remaking of fairy tales in the interests of children's literature. In a closed narrative or club story (a tale told within a frame story), Mrs Teachum allows the fairy tale to be told by Jenny, a student, as a reward for her good behaviour. In the tale the giant Barbarico is totally evil, a murderer and a cannibal, while his smaller compatriot, Benefico, despite being a giant, is entirely good, and has devoted his life to trying to repair the damage Barbarico does. Coming upon a pair of lovers, Fidus and Amata (a gesture by Fielding towards the pastoral tradition), Barbarico scares the latter to death and carts the former off to his cave for torture. Fidus soon meets the giant's kind slave, Mignon, who consoles him with the promise that both will one day escape Barbarico's clutches. Eventually Mignon discovers a magical fillet (or headband), which he manages to tie around the giant's neck, rendering him helpless before freeing the giant's many other prisoners and sending for the good Benefico to cut off Barbarico's head.

After hearing the tale, Mrs Teachum insists that 'giants, magic, fairies, and all sorts of supernatural assistances in a story, are only introduced to amuse and divert: for a giant is called so only to express a man of great power; and the magic fillet round the statue was intended only to shew you, that by patience you will overcome all difficulties'.[21] The fantastical, it seems, is only valid as a teaching device, and has little or no legitimacy or moral value in its own right. This warning is also repeated later, for, as

Mrs Teachum insists, 'if the story is well written, the common course of things would produce the same incidence, without the help of fairies'.[22] Thus the use of the supernatural should be seen as amusing but, at the same time, as an indicator of the storyteller's immaturity or lack of skill. What is noticeable, however, is the shift from the random and malicious punishment in the earlier stories to something much more controlled and set within the social order. This taming of fairy stories became a trope in the nineteenth century as a clear trend to turn the fairy tale towards a discrete child audience.

Benjamin Tabart's *Collection of Popular Stories for the Nursery* (1804) was the first volume of such tales specifically advertised as for children; Tabart also published the first known version of *Jack and the Bean-Stalk* (1807). Like Tabart, later collectors and eventually Andrew Lang (beginning with *The Red Fairy Book* in 1890) tended to shape their tales in ways either more likely to appeal to children or, perhaps, less likely to make the parents of child readers nervous. Thus nineteenth-century folk and fairy tale collections meant for children were written in somewhat simpler language and with less emphasis on romance and abstractions, while at the same time reflecting the middle-class morality of their day. The Victorians themselves had an explanation which seems correct as far as it goes, but which doesn't go far. They said it was simply a reflection of moral progress in the real world.

A new group of censors was arising, the most influential of whom were the conservative and prolific children's writer Sarah Trimmer (1741–1810); Thomas Bowdler (1754–1825), who published a *Family Shakespeare* (1807) carefully edited to remove all obscenities, leading to the term 'bowdlerize'; Maria Edgeworth (1768–1849), who also had a major impact on American children's literature; and Mary Sherwood (1775–1851), who produced an edition of Fielding's *The Governess* in 1820 which increased its religious content while revising its fairy stories to more closely reflect the morality of the day. Although these writers and editors differed in their views on the fantastic (not to mention in their actual literary talent), their tendency to disapprove of it is clear. Fielding may have felt that the development of the imagination played a legitimate role in the education of the young, but others, particularly the self-appointed guardians of children's literature, disagreed. The influential (and aptly named) Mrs Trimmer, the first critic to review children's books on a regular basis, and in fact the first to attempt to set up a canon of children's literature, did not entirely despise fairy tales, if they avoided violence and had properly Christian morals, but very few such works fulfilled her criteria. She was unable to 'approve of those [tales] which are only fit to fill the heads of children with confusing notions of wonderful and supernatural events, brought about by the agency of imaginary beings'.[23] Although she could remember the interest with which she read or listened to 'Red Riding Hood' and 'Blue Beard' in her 'childish days', she wanted to save future generations from this experience because 'the terrific images which tales of this nature present to the imagination, usually make deep impressions, and injure the tender minds of children, by exciting unreasonable and groundless fears'.[24]

Mrs Trimmer was even more hostile to the excesses of *Cinderella*, which 'paints some of the worst passions that can enter into the human breast',[25] and she was deeply critical of the fairy tale collections of Perrault, d'Aulnoy and Tabart. Despite the growth of Romanticism in the literary culture of her day, Mrs Trimmer's stated goal was to replace the fairy tales that even she remembered fondly with only the most moral and non-violent of fables and Bible stories. Paradoxically, however, her viewpoint, which tended to denigrate the fantastic as inappropriate for both children and adults but never actually forbade it, still left it available (if sometimes in what the French sometimes called *livres châtrés* or castrated books) for those of all ages who were less worried about being appropriate in their reading. Some years later, the ever-so-practical Society for the Diffusion of Useful Knowledge, founded in 1826, did its best to eradicate the Gothic in children's literature for all social classes.

## Defending the imagination

For every Mrs Trimmer or Thomas Bowdler, terrified that children's minds might be damaged by the dark and the fantastic, there were other, perhaps less respectable, voices raised in defence of the imagination. It seems probable that fantasy literature in the modern sense, whether written for adults or children, comes mostly from Romanticism and its interest in various folk traditions.[26] *Lyrical Ballads* (1798) by Coleridge and Wordsworth, and Coleridge's *Christabel and Other Poems* (1816), are particularly significant texts. In Germany, Ludwig Tieck, Wilhelm Hauff and other Romantics began to write their own literary folk tales, aimed primarily or exclusively at an adult audience but, again, available to and of interest to children. Writers as diverse as Samuel Johnson and Thomas Carlyle remembered their youthful reading of fairy and folk tales with great and unrepentant pleasure and Samuel Taylor Coleridge in a letter to Thomas Poole, dated 16 October 1797, strongly defended the value of the fantastic, writing that 'from my early reading of fairy tales and genii, etc., etc., my mind had been habituated *to the Vast*'. He then went on to state rhetorically, 'I know no other way of giving the mind a love of the Great and the Whole. Those who have been led to the same truths step by step, through the constant testimony of their senses, seem to me to want a sense which I possess. They contemplate nothing but *parts*, and all *parts* are necessarily little. And the universe to them is but a mass of *little things*.'[27] For Coleridge the reading of fantastic literature was quite literally necessary, both for children and adults, to open their minds to the most important metaphysical and presumably religious issues of all.

Unfortunately, by the mid to late eighteenth century the increasing demand for literature acceptable to parents had led to the denaturing of challenging adult works in versions specifically for child readers (rather than, as before, in versions for a more refined class). This practice was not entirely new, of course; abridged editions of *The Pilgrim's Progress* had been commonly given to children to read for many years. Literary works like Daniel Defoe's *Robinson Crusoe* (1719) and Jonathan Swift's *Gulliver's Travels* (1726, amended 1735) became available not only in condensed chapbook form but in shortened, expurgated editions, deemed safe for children's more susceptible minds.

Perhaps the most notable example of the denaturing of a classic work of the fantastic imagination occurred with *Gulliver's Travels*. In its original form the book is a barbed, often obscene and sometimes very dark satire on the politics of Swift's day and on human nature in general. Recognized as a classic soon after its publication, *Gulliver's Travels* managed to avoid bowdlerization for many years: it went through some sixty editions between its initial publication in 1726 and the end of the eighteenth century, none of which were expurgated or amended. But in the early nineteenth century, this all changed. Between 1800 and 1900 it went through another 150 editions, more than half of which were cut, mostly to expurgate the satire and the scatological humour, until in the twentieth century many children only encountered the first two of Gulliver's voyages, in contexts which suggested that both were intended as parables of childhood.

Shakespeare was as significant a purveyor of fantasy as Swift, and at the beginning of the nineteenth century he too was bowdlerized. Charles Lamb (1775–1834) and his sister Mary Lamb (1764–1847), in the much-loved *Tales from Shakespeare* (1807), toned down, rendered obscure or removed entirely all of Shakespeare's explicitly or implicitly violent or sexual elements. The result is that as we enter the nineteenth century both children's literature and the fantastic were becoming shaped by ideologies of confinement: both were being restricted to the domestic sphere and to a narrow moral compass.

Yet the movement was not all in one direction. The Gothic novel began its rise to popularity in Britain at exactly the same historical moment as the fairy tale: even as fairy tales were being expurgated to make them suitable to a new notion of the child as innocent – as needing shelter from premature exposure to adult society – the rise of the Gothic, some felt, was undermining the purity of the teen reader, and in particular the emerging girl reader, as literacy rates among women began to climb. As Anna Jackson and her co-editors argue in *The Gothic in Children's Literature*, despite all attempts to suppress such stories and provide more edifying substitutes, 'Children ... have always had a predilection for what we now categorize as the Gothic, for ghosts and goblins, hauntings and horrors, fear and the pretence of fear.'[28] The Gothic novel has its schlock classics, like Horace Walpole's *The Castle of Otranto* (1764) and Mrs Radcliffe's *The Mysteries of Udolpho* (1794), but also its Great Classics, such as Mary Shelley's *Frankenstein* (1818), Charlotte Brontë's *Jane Eyre* (1847) and Emily Brontë's *Wuthering Heights* (1847). In place of the brutality of folk tales it offered corruption; in place of moral guidance it proffered temptation.

## CHAPTER 2

# Fairies, ghouls and goblins: the realms of Victorian and Edwardian fancy

For much of the nineteenth century the development of children's fantasy beyond the European fairy tale was a British concern. Although Nathaniel Hawthorne's *A Wonder-Book for Girls and Boys* was published in 1852, it was to be the end of the century before American writers became extensively involved in the development of children's fantasy, and while fairy tales continued to develop in continental Europe, the more fantastical tales which departed from fairy were increasingly likely to be British.

Why the British should have developed the fantasy mode is unclear. Selma Lanes argues for an 'often unacknowledged longing on the part of adults for celestial fare for young children',[1] but this still leaves the question of *Why Britain*? One factor may be that for much of the late eighteenth century the British were both cut off from the rest of Europe, thanks to the Napoleonic wars, and expanding into the Far East. The appeal of the exotic, from continental Europe and elsewhere, clearly fed a desire for *something else*, which can be seen in the art of the period: from the Boydell Shakespeare painting project (predominantly of *A Midsummer Night's Dream* and *The Tempest*) begun in 1786 as part of an attempt to foster a school of British historical art, to the much later paintings of the Pre-Raphaelites and the visionary artists like Richard Doyle, Richard Dadd and John Anster Fitzgerald, images of fairies and their cruelties have shaped many modern fantasies.

Victorian fantasy and fairy developed in Britain almost precisely alongside the great cultural shift which took place at the start of the nineteenth century, from a Britain which envied the civilization of others (from the French chef to the Chinese rooms in the Brighton Pavilion) to one which came to regard the cultural as well as material riches of the world as somehow British by right of innate superiority. Omnivorous collection of source material is one of the early hallmarks of the British children's fantasy in a period of intense cultural appropriation. The belief of many

British writers and folklorists that their own folk and fairy culture had been dissipated by industrialization, and the relative scantiness of the English tradition, may also have encouraged them to look elsewhere for source material, although one of the remarkable things about fairy is that in all historical periods it is *just* in the process of departing or has departed within living memory: where there are exceptions these tend to be regional folk tales from isolated locations such as the Fens.[2]

The writers of the Romantic movement had always been enthusiastic for fantasy, and even as the realism of the Victorian novel began to hold sway over British culture, this love for fantasy remained, if mostly on the periphery of culture, such as in children's literature. The children's fantasy writers of the early to mid Victorian period were thus conscious of writing against a realist tide. A number of them, such as Charles Dickens (1812–70) and Mary Louisa Molesworth (1839–1921), understood fantasy as able to carry moral messages, while others such as George MacDonald (1824–1905) and Charles Kingsley (1819–75) – both Church of England ministers – were eager to enlist to their cause the Protestant tradition of allegory in arguing for a form of fantastical fiction that (in a defence still heard today) offered a deeper reality.

Alongside this conscious attempt to stay within a pedagogical tradition of children's entertainment, however, many sought quite deliberately to create a new kind of *fiction* and it is for this reason that Victorian children's fantasy became so essential to the development of the fantasy genre as a whole.

### A market for children's fantasy

In this chapter we will explore the change in mood in the ideologies of literary realism and the ideology of childhood which took place in the mid nineteenth century, so that by the end of the century there was a clear market for children's literature, and a clear understanding that certain types of fantastic adventure – fairy tales, treasure hunts and quest narratives – were for children.

The reasons for the spread of the fairy tale were in part material: the literacy rate may have sagged at the start of the nineteenth century as many of the traditional modes of schooling sponsored by local philanthropists or in private dame schools failed to keep up with urban conditions and changing rural relations, but by the mid to late nineteenth century the factory schools, the spread of Sunday schools, radical working men's organizations, small private schools and from 1870 the new board schools led to a steady rise in literacy rates in England and Wales. The Registrar General's census suggests that between 1830 and 1870 male literacy rose from around 67 to around 80 per cent, female literacy from around 50 to 70 per cent. Revolutionary innovations such as the steam press, stereotyping and new techniques of paper-making reduced the cost of books, and while new books were not yet in the housekeeping budgets of the working poor, there was a thriving second-hand book and magazine trade that speeded up the dissemination of print as the century rolled on.[3]

Transport improvements (water transport is a risky way of moving paper, and trains are rather good places to read) also facilitated the expansion of the print industry, and as is ever the case in publishing, the ability to print more pages faster demanded ever more content so that the presses would not remain idle. Many of the new magazines (anxious to avoid news in order to avoid the newspaper tax) found in the older fairy tales – and in the new tales hastily written to well-understood formulae – copy to fill their pages. (It is no coincidence that some of the earliest writers of children's magazines were the printers themselves.) Distribution too improved markedly. By the mid eighteenth century, booksellers had emerged clearly as shopkeepers, agents and retailers. As retailers of luxury goods, they were in a position to benefit from the expansive economy of industrializing Britain. To give just a couple of examples, Newcastle had two booksellers in 1700, between ten and fifteen in the years 1736–71, and thirty-eight recorded in 1787. In Bristol there were thirty-three booksellers in 1775, and forty-two in 1793. Liverpool had ninety-eight booksellers by 1800.[4] In addition there were coffee houses, book clubs and, later, subscription libraries run by working men's combinations or private enterprises. By the mid nineteenth century, Mudie's circulating library dominated the book trade. As an added incentive the 1842 Copyright Act gave protection to authors for their lifetime and for forty-two years after their death.

When the number of literary works published expands, new genres and subgenres are bound to develop. Two elements destined to become the stuff of modern fantasy came to the fore in this environment: the court fairy tales of the seventeenth and eighteenth centuries, revised for new purposes; and later, a growing awareness of the native stuff of the fantastic. The nineteenth century was marked by a growing consciousness of the 'nation'. Fairy tale collectors paid attention to the works of scholars like Francis Cohen, who championed a scholarly antiquarianism, 'a practice that promises to tabulate and record the last vestiges of folk innocence',[5] and who linked the fairy tale directly to concepts of racial and cultural infancy. This antiquarianism drew on the 'Indo-European' thesis of Sir William Jones (1786) – that European and Indian languages emerged from a common root – and was the bedrock of racial thinking in the nineteenth and early twentieth centuries. This development was to have a far stronger influence on fantasy in the twentieth century, but it needs to be marked here, for one of the elements that was to create the modern fantasy reader as well as writer was an awareness and appreciation of folklore.

In the nineteenth century, the construction of didactic folklore served both to inspire nationalism and to direct it. Both the Right (German fascists) and the Left (English pacifists and conservationists) sought to appropriate folklore in their search for authenticity. Shared by both sides was the belief that a country acquires its *reality* or truth from an acknowledgement and incarnation of its indigenous fairies. This notion carried over into the twentieth century and was reincarnated in the Western understanding of postcolonial magic realism and fantasy.

Although a late contributor to this trend, Irish poet and cultural nationalist W. B. Yeats (1865–1939) is one of the best-known collectors of this type, influenced heavily by the antiquarian movement and the growing desire to document folk culture. In his *Fairy and Folk Tales of the Irish Peasantry*, Yeats was anxious to claim an authenticity for the tales he amassed (most of which actually came not from the scholarly Folk Lore Society or its journal, but from the *Dublin and London Magazine* and the *Dublin University Magazine* as well as other cheaper titles), for their authenticity was essential in the reconstruction of an Irish nationalism along the ethnographic lines which were increasing in importance. Yeats was as keen to use Irish folk and fairy tales to create young Irish men and women as others were to use English folk and fairy tales to create young English men and women. He asserted both that the Irish peasantry *did* believe in these tales, and that, because they had not been exposed to them, the Irish people as a whole had been cut off from their roots.[6]

Yeats's belief that the English fairies were mere extensions of French fancy, and that only the Irish fairies had authenticity behind them, is an attitude and ideology that has continued to be fought out among both authors and critics and is central to understanding the ways in which fairy has been constructed in modern fantasy. There is a direct link between, on the one hand, the antiquarians and the revivalists of folk tale and folk song in the early twentieth century, such as Cecil Sharp, and on the other Rudyard Kipling's *Puck of Pook's Hill* (1906) and

*Rewards and Fairies* (1910), which recreated fairy as an intrinsic part of England, and of the story of England. Writers such as Kipling, inspired perhaps by the Shakespeare revival of the 1870s and 1880s, cast the fairies themselves as intrinsically *English* in a way which has reverberated down through modern fantasy. There is a kinship with L. Frank Baum's search for an authentic American fantasy, with the émigré fairies of Charles de Lint, Emma Bull and Neil Gaiman, and more recently the indigenous supernatural beings of authors such as Hiromi Goto, Nnedi Okorafor and Karen Lord.

## Putting the fairy in folk tale

Perhaps most important, it was the folk tale that put the 'fairy' in fairy tale, for in the eighteenth and nineteenth centuries the presence of fairies was not a prerequisite in the work of Perrault, Grimm, Andersen or many other collectors, retellers and originators. Andrew Lang, in an article in the *London Illustrated News* in 1892, included Norse tales in the genre while pointing out the absence of fairies. The roots of the nineteenth-century 'fairy tale' were various, from folk traditions of the supernatural as well as the specifically fairy, to what might be called the new folk tale of the anthropologist. Beast tales descended from Aesop; tales of enchantment from the Arabian Nights and from Grimm; enchanted objects straight from the legendary Land of Cockayne, where beer runs in rivers and roasted birds grow on trees; traditions of Gothic fiction from the turn of the century; and pantomime traditions from the middle of the century: all these, along with allegorical neo-Christian quests, were grouped together as 'fairy'.

The medium of the nineteenth-century British fairy tale was in flux. At the start of the century the traditional tale was most often found in chapbooks – crudely printed, anonymously written articles traded by ped-lars to children and the barely literate. In the mid century, fairy tales trans-muted into both the subject of antiquarian study and a vehicle for moral guidance. The book market in the nineteenth century was structured in such a way that the new type of fairy tale, infused with Christian allegory, could be considered as what today we would call crossover publishing: it aimed to resonate with the previously disregarded nursery tales and raise them to be suitable parlour fare for both children and adults of the mid-dle classes. By the mid century new urban folk tales such as the tales of Spring-Heeled Jack (1837) and Sweeney Todd (*The People's Periodical*, 1846) were appearing, and the rise of the cheapest of the periodicals, such as John Maxwell's *Halfpenny Journal: A Weekly Magazine for All Who Can Read*, encouraged a search for recycled material, such as reprints of the Arabian Nights and, as a part-work, a serialized version of *Grimm's Goblins*.[7] This downward class shift in the audience was part and parcel of the age shift which was clearly taking place by the end of the century, for as the market for fairy and fantasy came to be seen as less elevated in terms of class, it was also understood to be less ambitious in maturity. It is rarely discussed but material dismissed as juvenile is frequently the same material dismissed as only suitable for, or desired by, the uneducated.

The fantasy writers of the nineteenth century established the language and shape of modern fantasy. They took the fairy tales of the eighteenth century, and where their predecessors had attempted to reclothe them, polish them and render them suitable for contemporary mores and manners, the writers of the nineteenth century embarked on a different project, to create new tales and a new kind of fairy. This was not necessarily a collective project, although many writers were involved, however peripherally, with the Pre-Raphaelite school (including writers as diverse as Christina Rossetti and Rudyard Kipling), but it was a communal endeavour in terms of shared journal markets, publishers, a frequent willingness to be directly inspired by others and a growing body of mutual criticism.

The writers discussed in this chapter were attempting a number of new things. First, they wished to create convincing alternative worlds for a culture in which realism increasingly required a separation of spiritual and secular realms – no longer could the miraculous event easily be portrayed as a realistic happening whether in a folk tale or a religious story. Second, they wanted to create new fairy tales, although Dickens in his essay 'Frauds on the Fairies' (1853) expressed his fear that these new stories might lack the authenticity and purity of the old tales.

As retellings were produced for the new literary magazines, the nature of both praise and criticism reflected this ambivalence, as readers noted the crudity yet liveliness of the original tales, and the literary yet often anaemic nature of modern retellings. Fairy tales became *material* which could be adapted at need: the Labour Churches and the Labour press, such as Robert Blatchford's children's magazine, *The Cinderella Supplement*, positioned the fairy tale – with some difficulty, Caroline Sumpter argues – as presenting an alternative economic morality to the new market system. Similarly, the aesthetes who followed Wilde saw in the fairy tale ways to code alternative sexual moralities.[8]

Some author of this period were also attempting to write for a relatively new niche audience: children. Children were the cutting-edge fiction market of the mid to late nineteenth-century publishing industry. Unlike adults they were not required to read primarily for educative purposes (indeed, this was a period when much education took place without textbooks); and in a world which was already regarding non-fiction as appropriate to men and fiction to women, small children were gendered feminine in ways which permitted fiction for their entertainment. In addition (and this has been under-researched) the circulating libraries did not cater for children, in contrast to their lock-hold over the adult market that forced adult fiction into certain shapes, such as the three-volume novel.[9]

At the same time the late eighteenth and nineteenth centuries saw a growing interest in the nature of childhood, and in educational pedagogy, so that fantasy writers were very much engaged in a discussion about the nature of childhood, perhaps most markedly in Kingsley's *The Water-Babies* (1863) but very visibly elsewhere.

Humphrey Carpenter argues that the precipitous decline in the middle-class birth rate (he uses as his indicative examples the writers themselves, often children of large families in the 1850s, but themselves having very small families), and later the respectable working-class birth rate, allowed both for the sentimentalization of childhood and for the concentration of material resources on the few children parents did have, in which education was an important factor and the children's gift book only one aspect.[10] As fashion caused the fairy story to spread downward, the expanding market created a new category, the gift book, initially aimed at adults but, with their pictures and illustrations, becoming a popular item in the children's market. *Aunt Judy's Magazine* (1866–85), edited by Margaret Gatty, the daughter of a chaplain and the wife of a vicar, *Good Words for the Young* (1868–77), edited by Norman Macleod, and *The Monthly Packet* (1851–99), edited by Charlotte M. Yonge, were the three leading titles published for children. The readers were assumed or hoped to be infants to teens, but there is evidence that most boys had departed the magazines by their early teens. All three of the magazines aimed for a combination of the informative and the entertaining but cast an eye to the parent as the arbiter of taste, Gatty by preferring to avoid tales of sensation, while *Good Words for the Young* balanced the very popular serialization of George MacDonald's novels with scholarly articles on King Arthur.

Of the three journals, only *The Monthly Packet* survived until the end of the century, overtaken by new gender-specific titles, such as *The Girl's Own Paper* (1880–1956), Samuel Beeton's *Boy's Own Magazine* (1855–90) and *The Boy's Own Paper* (1879–1967). These were less inclined to publish what we might call fairy, but the boys' titles in particular were influenced by a branch of fantasy developed by Rider Haggard: the fantastical adventure in exotic lands. By the 1880s, the effects of the 1870 Elementary Education Act had filtered through and magazines for children were increasingly seen as part and parcel of education, provided by Sunday schools and passed along through enthusiastic second-hand trade.[11]

### The first great era of fairy stories

While fairy tales might have come to be acceptable as stories for children, the process by which stories suitable for children were becoming 'children's stories' was still under way. This was a period in which, while there was a concept of 'stories for infants', attitudes towards later age groups were more nebulous; and where fantasy was concerned, a market understood as the young of all ages was a very real thing. Even to deconstruct this market as dual may be to impose a binary which Victorian readers would not have recognized. Lewis Carroll (1832–98) referred to his texts as suitable for the childlike of all ages, and there is no reason to doubt that, at least later in the century, many of the best-known texts, from *The Water-Babies* (1863) to *Alice's Adventures in Wonderland* (1865), and even a lesser-known text such as Jean Ingelow's *Mopsa the Fairy* (1869), offered delights for the adult reader in terms of knowing references, and, as we shall see, delight in the observation of children.

Fairy tales increased in popularity as a choice for children, precisely because they came to embrace the didactic, rather than because children were permitted more frivolity. Something of a publishing outlier, and perhaps the first Victorian fairy tale of any importance specifically intended for children, was John Ruskin's *The King of the Golden River*, which appeared in book form in 1851 (and promptly sold out three printings). Ruskin was primarily a critic, and *The King of the Golden River* has the feeling of a manifesto for a belief in the fantastical world as a powerful mode for learning. It had been written a decade earlier for the then twelve-year-old Effie Gray, who would later become Ruskin's wife. Based very loosely on tales from Grimm – via the translator/bowdlerizer Edgar Taylor whose 1823 and 1826 volumes of *German Popular Stories* remained the main English version of the Grimms' tales in the English market through the nineteenth century and beyond – Ruskin's tale is infused with the Gothic (it features priests and bishops and the theft of holy water), but it is also highly political and concerned with the ecology of the landscape.

The tale concerns three brothers, the older two avaricious, the youngest kind and open-hearted, who compete to create a river of gold in a waste land which is itself the result of the older brothers' mistreatment of the personified Southwest Wind, Esquire. To succeed, they must carry holy water to the source of the river and throw in three drops. In classic fairy tale fashion, however, the avaricious brothers each refuse to give water to three thirsty strangers. The elder brothers fail in their quests and are then turned into black rocks in the river, while the youngest, Gluck (whose name means 'good luck'), takes pity on the three in need of water, shares it, and gains wealth beyond his dreams by reforming the agricultural economy of his valley and purifying the river, so it becomes the golden river of the title. His deed brings prosperity to all around.

The process of fashioning fairy tales into material for children was in part the process of reshaping the ideology of childhood. As the image of children moved from souls born in sin who needed to be tamed, to innocent *tabulae rasae* on whom the adult world would write, both traditional and new fairy tales underwent a shift, from the fairy tale as near horror to the fairy tale as conveyor of clear moral guidance. Perrault's 'Sleeping Beauty' concludes with the Prince's mother attempting to dine on her grandchildren, and, when defeated, being forced to dance in red-hot shoes. Hans Christian Andersen mutates the story into 'The Red Shoes' (1845), in which the sin of vanity is punished by the loss of feet. The inconsistencies of characterization in George MacDonald's *At the Back of the North Wind* (1871), which tells of a saintly small boy and his oppressed father (a hansom cab driver), stem in part from the ideological appropriation of fantasy for the toolbox of the didactic. Little Diamond, for all of his adventures with the North Wind, is a didactic and moralistic character, a stand-in for Christ perhaps, whose readers and whose *companions* within the text can attain salvation through the entertainment of fancy. MacDonald does not use fancy to release us from realism (which in his understanding includes the spiritual world); he uses it to draw us closer to the real. Charles Kingsley's *The Water-Babies* (1863) wears its didacticism on its sleeve as Tom the chimney sweep undergoes a spiritual journey and meets Mrs Do-As-You-Would-Be-Done-By and Mrs Be-Done-By-As-You-Did. Similarly, Mary Louisa Molesworth's *The Cuckoo Clock* (1877), in which Griselda escapes the oppression of her aunts' care through travels to fantastical lands within the house, is concerned with the inculcation of obedience and passivity perhaps more than it is with the wonders of a porcelain mandarin's palace seen from the outside.

By the end of the century we can see in Lucy M. Clifford's 'The New Mother' (1882) how bad behaviour by children leads to the usurpation of the maternal role by a demon and a splitting off of the horror/punishment tale into a new form. This tendency in fantasy should not be seen as one that was to be outgrown. *The Cuckoo Clock* anticipates the trajectory of much twentieth-century children's quest fantasy in requiring the fantastic to deliver a contextual lesson in moral growth: Griselda's cuckoo is less transparently a parent figure than is the North Wind, but rather it is an early mage, guiding adventure and encouraging the protagonist to explore the lesson.

While writers such as MacDonald, Kingsley and Molesworth concerned themselves with spiritual growth, Charles Dickens, Oscar Wilde and F. Anstey were occupied with more temporal concerns. Dickens's 'The Magic Fishbone' (1868) has much to say about domestic economy and the virtues of calm prudence; Wilde's 'The Happy Prince' (1888) is all about the material nature of poverty; Anstey, in *Vice Versa, or Lessons to Fathers* (1882), focuses on parental hypocrisies; Julianne Ewing, in 'The Magician's Gifts' (1872), on the danger of husbandly bad temper; while H. Buxton Forman was happy to advocate girls' education in 'King Wiseacre and the Six Professors' (1867). Yet this is not a clear split: all of these authors saw the two realms as linked. Kingsley's concern for the moral well-being of the chimney sweep was also a concern with the physical well-being of each small soul and was translated into political action through, for example, his involvement in both Christian Socialism and the 'muscular Christianity' movement and his authorship of realistic novels like *Alton Locke* (1859) which was specifically intended to bring to light the horrifying situation of London's working poor. Each of these texts helped shift the focus but not the weight of moral concerns in children's fantasies in ways that shaped the modern children's fantasy precisely into the powerful vehicle for moral discussion that it remains today. However fantastical the creatures in their worlds, moral lessons were intrinsic to the construction.

Lewis Carroll is an interesting case that proves the rule: although *Alice in Wonderland* and its sequel can be considered as nonsense tales, both are didactic – there are things they wish to teach, whether it is the absurdity of modern manners or the absurdity of chess – but both are relentlessly, irresistibly destructive of the social order to the extent that they push societal and fantastical conceits to absurd extremes. So too does Edward Lear's nonsense verse: it is subversive of the social order, frankly rejectionist and escapist. Verses such as 'The Owl and the

Pussycat' and 'They Went to Sea in a Sieve', argues Humphrey Carpenter, 'consist largely of explorations of the possibilities of Escape'; 'In these and other rhymes, published from the 1870s to the 1890s, Lear is stating a theme that becomes central to the great children's writers: the search for a mysterious, elusive Good Place.'[12] Yet the verses are filled with the accoutrements of morality; the Owl and the Pussycat, for example, run away to get married. The realization that fantasy could be as effective as realistic stories in imparting moral education, if not more so, was one element in the appropriation of fairy tale and fantasy into the realm of fiction for children.

Not all the fairy tales we now associate with children's literature are focused entirely on the child. The works of George MacDonald frequently stand back and address a presumed adult audience. Charles Kingsley's *The Water-Babies*, although it has delighted children, was written for adults – and intellectuals at that – and is a moral and reforming tract aimed at children's elders. However, if we understand the choice of a child protagonist, and the presentation of that protagonist as either an equal or just a step up from the audience, as one aspect of what makes a children's book a book for children, then we can begin to see a children's fiction emerging from the body of experimental fantasy. (There are exceptions where authors chose to use child protagonists because they were fascinated by childhood rather than because they were writing for children – Lewis Carroll's *Sylvie and Bruno* is an obvious example.)

The child protagonists who appear in the earliest Victorian fantasy stories such as those by Dorothea Kilner are but faint creatures, who are treated and mistreated by fantasy in direct proportion to their good behaviour. They are objects upon which fantasy acts. But one of the key shifts in the second half of the century is the instability of the childish body, subject to transformation into bird, fish or water baby, and at the same time the degree to which the child's role is to move through this fantastical world, channelling his or her fresh-eyed observations to the (adult?) reader. The child is becoming not just object but subject.[13]

The innocence that Kingsley, MacDonald, Carroll and Ingelow constructed was important to understanding the ideology of fairy tales, as it was the ideology of childhood. These writers emerged from a tradition in which folk tales and fairy tales themselves were reflections of the childhood of the species or the race, so that in writing new tales of fairy they asserted their youth and the youth of their culture. Where those hostile to fairy tale might call it childish, the writers might have preferred *childlike*. This is perhaps expressed best in Ingelow's *Mopsa the Fairy*, in which a kiss from Jack gifts to Mopsa the most precious of experiences, a true childhood; and in Kenneth Grahame's *The Wind in the Willows* (1908) in the chapter 'Piper at the Gates of Dawn', during which the animals become childlike in the face of Pan. Of the characters in *The Wind in the Willows* C. S. Lewis wrote, in 'On Stories': 'the life of the characters is that of children for whom everything is provided and who take everything for granted. But in other ways it is the life of adults. They go where they like and do what they please ...'[14] They are a child's fantasy of adulthood.

## Changing attitudes towards childhood

Humphrey Carpenter's *Secret Gardens* pays particular attention to modes of portraying childhood in nineteenth-century writing. For him, there is a distinct shift among writers such as Molesworth, Ewing and Frances Hodgson Burnett towards the 'Beautiful Child', the child so innocent as to appear, at times, positively simple. Molesworth's Griselda (*The Cuckoo Clock*) and Burnett's Dickon (*The Secret Garden*, 1911) are portrayed as attaining or striving for a naivety and beauty of spirit that does not fit them for the world but that leads adults (or other children) into the next.[15]

George MacDonald's *At the Back of the North Wind* exemplifies this trend and presents itself as a book *about* a child, *for* adults. Even conceding that the protagonist Little Diamond, 'God's Baby', might be more appealing to a piously reared child of the mid nineteenth century than to a modern one, he is presented as an ideal. He is not, once we move into the second half of the story, in which Little Diamond wanders as the Christ Child through the city, a real child. He is a child to be admired, to be played with and petted, but not one who can possibly be allowed to grow up (as indeed he doesn't). But Diamond's companions Nanny and Jim, street children rescued by God's Baby, have all the virtues and vices of normal children. These children are not the stiff, unrealistic characters of most contemporary children's fantasy: they are an adult's observation and they are written in such a fashion as, in modern parlance, to allow children to identify with them (even while, as street children, they are very different from the intended readers).

We can see something very similar in J. M. Barrie's *Peter Pan*: although a play written for children, its humour is constructed around an adult mockery of children's misunderstandings (the opening night audience was predominantly adult). But it may also be a mockery of the 'Beautiful

Child' tradition, for although Peter is excluded from the world by virtue of his innocence, Neverland is an expression of Eden as malicious and unthinking, not a version that understands innocence as wholly good. This understanding renders Carpenter's perceptive comments rather sinister:

> Barrie's audience is meant to realise that the Never Land is entirely untrue. The 'secondary world' in *Peter Pan* does not exist except in the children's imaginations. The play is constantly hinting at this … in *Peter and Wendy* Barrie describes it as simply 'a map of a child's mind', the ideal adventure-land, 'not large and sprawly, you know, with tedious distances between one adventure and another, but nicely crammed'. There is no question about it being real.[16]

It is for this reason that Carpenter suggests there is a 'terrible whimsy' about the work, a mocking of the audience. 'His whole self is not engaged in the creation of his stories.'[17]

Perhaps the most striking aspect of mid to late nineteenth-century children's fantasy is the degree to which the fantasies seem contained and bounded. Furthermore this containment is presented as desirable. Colin Manlove argues that the character of British fairy tale gave to British children's fantasy one of its major characteristics, domesticity: 'a strong practical streak and an emphasis on working things out; a domestic and often house-based action; concern with family relationships rather than with romantic ones; small interest in advancement to royal rank; and a recurrent penchant for putting miniature people beside giants'.[18] Many of these points, particularly the love of the miniature, will be explored in Chapters 4 and 5, because domesticity is a theme that becomes stronger by the 1940s and 1950s. But the 'house-based action' is a striking feature of nineteenth-century fantasy: it can be argued that even Never-Never Land is situated in the bedroom. Well into the mid twentieth century, perhaps the most important of English-language children's fantasies, C. S. Lewis's *The Lion, the Witch and the Wardrobe* (1950) begins its adventure with a game inside an old house, and contains its fantasy world within an old wardrobe, an essentially ordinary, domestic piece of furniture. In *The Lion, the Witch and the Wardrobe*, the fantastic is *contained*, and containment itself – later, in *The Last Battle*, extended into the containment of a larger, heavenly Narnia, both in a shed and behind a wall – is constructed as marvellous.[19]

Containment can be literal or metaphorical. In literal examples the fantastic is accessed within the house, or is actually contained within the house. Molesworth's *The Cuckoo Clock* is one of the earliest examples, and one of the most extreme. Griselda goes to live with two elderly aunts while her family is abroad. After a few nights she discovers the cuckoo in the cuckoo clock, and, as we come to expect in children's fairy tales, the cuckoo takes her on adventures, which take place entirely within the house. The first magical journey is to the palace of the nodding mandarins, which is actually a china model in the house; the second journey is to the land of the butterflies, which has every appearance of the old ladies' own garden. In real life Griselda does not enter the garden until very late in the adventure, and there meets a young boy whose desirability as a playmate rests in part on his desire to come into the domestic sphere first of the garden, and then of Griselda's home.

Containment is not just a girl thing. MacDonald's *At the Back of the North Wind* is fascinated by the construction of domesticity and within that the central figure of domesticity, the mother. In most of these texts, mothers are Wendys; like *Peter Pan*'s Wendy, they live to serve. The North Wind is a glorious and capricious mother figure who changes shape and mocks Diamond for asking for things inappropriate for his shape and size. There are times when this seems almost cruel to modern sensibilities, yet the aim seems to be to inculcate sweetness and humility in Diamond; certainly these are the values we are told he expresses, and MacDonald continually emphasizes that what makes Diamond special is both that he is (overwhelmingly) contained within the home, and that his passions and emotions are contained. For he is not rough like other boys, and in this and other texts there is a real sense that the authors are writing for the boys they were, the boys who did not enjoy boyhood as it was being modelled elsewhere. The texts become the space in which arguments over boyhood are made.

Diamond is at his best, and is most influenced by the fantastic, when he is at his most domestic and most feminine. The book sees magic as belonging to the infant mind, but advocates the preservation of the infant mind, in death if necessary. And even within what is by contrast clearly a boys' book, where boyhood is seen as growing up and going out, the domestic is the locus of the fantastic: F. Anstey's *Vice Versa* (1882) might seem an odd choice for this argument in that it is set, at least in part, in a minor boys' public school, but this is no *Stalky & Co*. While Kipling's *Stalky & Co* (1899) and other school stories of the period have a clear idea that boys should be boyish and spend lots of time outdoors, *Vice Versa* is almost entirely set indoors: the use of the house and the space in the school is very much status-marked, and it is status within the space that is the source of conflict between father and son;

the fantastic and the issue of territoriality within the domestic sphere is a central argument of the text. George MacDonald's *The Princess and Curdie* (1883) has two threads: the invasion of the goblins and Irene's relationship with her grandmother. The goblin invasion is precisely about a fantastical challenge to the home and hearth; the magical nature of the grandmother is contained and yet not contained (in the way we saw in *At the Back of the North Wind*) within the household itself. The grandmother is a goddess figure, but she is also a *mother*, a representation of Mary, and she both isolates the fantasy and emphasizes that the true fantastic is found at the heart of the home. From Lewis Carroll, the obvious contained fantasy is *Through the Looking Glass*. Classic commentary on this book emphasizes the subversive nature of Alice's relationship with the characters through the glass and the way in which the book challenges domestic manners so that it is a fantasy of domesticity gone askew. Furthermore, Alice never leaves the house in which the adventure begins: if the other world is through and inside the glass, then it shares topographical space with the real world. In our last example of literal containment, Edith Nesbit's *The Magic City* (1910), Philip builds a portal to the fantastic on a table, using primarily domestic objects. Furthermore, throughout the entire journey he and his stepsister make, it is continually reiterated that he has not left the domestic sphere: when he finds himself on an island that no one but he has been able to land on, he is joined by his sister Helen, for this island is the fantastical counterpart of the island they built – as a game – together. When Julius Caesar appears towards the end, the conclusion sees him *realized* as Lucy's father.

Some containments are more metaphorical. Charles Kingsley's *The Water-Babies* (1863) takes Tom out of the external world of the street and of chimney-sweeping (in the nethers of the house) into a river which could not be more external, but the images of civilization are of houses and the inside of houses, and the most fantastical scene Tom confronts is not the water-babies, but the pristine white room into which he falls. Similarly, although Diamond, the 'God's Baby' of MacDonald's *At the Back of the North Wind*, travels abroad, there is a continual emphasis first on the safety and security of his own home, however poor, and on the construction of domesticity as the desired outcome of the fantastic: the resolutions to the adventures in this story include the recreation of a domestic partnership with the daughter of Diamond's father's employer, and the reconstruction of an employment–familial relationship for Diamond's father and his new employer: the employer buys the family horse (also called Diamond), and brings the family, together with the beggar girl and her best friend, to live with him in what feels like a recognizably late eighteenth-century household, in which master regards man as his responsibility. Diamond makes a number of trips outside the home but they are all problematic: one surveys the wickedness of the world, another surveys the desperation in the world, and the third is a trip to the back of the North Wind, which is described as a garden – another contained place – and both is and isn't fairyland.

Ingelow's *Mopsa the Fairy* is one of the few of these early fantasies which allows the protagonist out: Jack gets trapped in a tree in the garden where he meets fairies, and the fairies and he are taken to fairyland by an albatross. But Jack's liberation into the wild comes to a crashing halt when one of the fairies, the one he kissed, turns into a baby girl, and Jack finds himself a surrogate parent. For much of the rest of the adventure, Jack is looking after Mopsa, until he is liberated by *her* adulthood. Fairyland is a nursery: the one adult character is an old apple-seller who, having found her way into fairyland, is occupied as a nursemaid to the fairies, which she prefers to the destitution she experiences in the real world. Again, like Diamond's father, and like the nurse in Nesbit's *The Magic City*, entering the household of another reinforces the message of domesticity – although Nesbit does allow the nurse to be resentful of her status and limited prospects in the fantastic world. In Lewis Carroll's *Sylvie and Bruno* much of the narrative takes place in the domestic sphere of what at times feels like the back garden of the house in which the narrator is staying, or the garden of the house which he is visiting. It is no surprise that the liminal figure whose nonsense poems are the portals into fantasy in this book is a gardener: he is both the route out, and the patroller of borders.

For most of these writers, safety is clearly the household and the garden, but the garden extends the possibilities of the imagination and of reach: thus fantasy and fantasy play take place in the garden. A. A. Milne's *Winnie-the-Pooh* (1926) may take place in the Hundred Acre Wood, but the wood is at the bottom of the garden. A text that is occasionally – by those interested in the pagan mythic – referenced as fantasy is Frances Hodgson Burnett's *The Secret Garden* (1911) and here the domestication of the fantastic is key to the story, for while Dickon, symbol of the High Wild Magic, is allowed to roam the moors, his role is not to take Colin and Mary into that fantastical space, but to bring the fantastical space into the hidden garden: Mary and Colin never actually leave Mistlethwaite Manor. Even Kenneth Grahame's *The Wind in the Willows* (1908) is oriented always to the discovery of home. The Wild

Wood may be scary, but the four most fantastical places in the novel – in the sense of inducing various kinds of awe – are the residences of Rat, Mole and Badger, and that of the Piper at the Gates of Dawn which, for all its evocation of pagan gods, is a scene of intimate domesticity in which a small otter-child is found asleep at the feet of Pan. The Wild Wood itself is described in mundane terms compared to the fantastical wonder of the farmed (domesticated) landscape:

> To all appearance the summer's pomp was still at fullest height, and although in the tilled acres green had given way to gold, though the rowans were reddening, and the woods were dashed here and there with a tawny fierceness, yet light and warmth and colour were still present in undiminished measure, clean of any chilly premonitions of the passing year.[20]

Then there is Kipling's *Puck of Pook's Hill* (1906), a fascinating novel of time travel and historical fantasy in which two children gain access to the past through Puck, one of the last of the faery. The story itself can be understood as the domestication of the English and of England. But it is the past that travels to *them*, which might seem puzzling to modern sensibilities. For nineteenth-century readers, however, it is congruent with their experience: in this period an English person was much more likely to meet, say, a person from India when the Indian travelled to England than the other way around (this may still be the case) so that for most people, the foreign was something that was brought into the domestic space through travellers' tales, souvenirs, trade goods and new foods. Elsewhere was not a place to which you went, but a place that changed your world.

This construction is still there in Edith Nesbit's *The Phoenix and the Carpet* (1904) but it is noticeable that with *Five Children and It* (1902) and *The Story of the Amulet* (1906) the tradition is ruptured. It is Nesbit's new structures – in which children go out to adventure and very decisively experience the fantastic in the great outdoors, with the outdoors depicted as a safe space in which to explore the fantastic – that come to dominate fantasy in the twentieth century. The 'return home' is a common motif in the modern fantastic, but to return home one has to leave it, and many of the early fantasies do not.

We can see a very clear shift in point of view within children's fantasy over the course of the nineteenth century. The earliest fairy tale writers used an omniscient narrator: these were tales told *about* characters from some distance. But by mid century two modes became the norm: a formal address *to* children, which we can see in the work of Kingsley, and a focus on the depiction of the child as a young person. This second aspect is what frequently renders the work of nineteenth-century writers twee to modern eyes. For all that we understand these books as children's books, they frequently cast the child protagonist, whether MacDonald's Princess Irene or Kingsley's Tom, as *younger* than the reader. This is often understood as talking down to the reader, but might be better understood as lacking the dialectic of identification between reader and protagonist. The construction of the fantasy story as a story played out on the stage, watched by the audience – rather than participated in, as in many modern tellings – encouraged what Maria Nikolajeva called the narrated monologue, in which the voice of the author directed the reader to sympathize with the protagonist but frequently undercut the structures of identification and empathy.[21]

## Moving away from the fairy tale

Through the nineteenth century and well into the twentieth, much children's fantasy continued to understand the child protagonist as a rather passive figure, a blank slate shaped by environment in as much as he or she has not yet been redeemed. In early fantasy this redemption is through Christianity; in later fantasy it is often achieved with magic. Charles Kingsley's *The Water-Babies* epitomizes the trend: in this book Tom's motivation, as Carpenter observes, comes pre-shaped.[22] If he is un-Christian in all the senses that this means, it is because he has not been educated as a Christian. He must be stripped back to the innocence of birth and reborn through the baptismal and magical waters of the river into a life shaped by Christian teaching. This is a salvation by Grace, consistent with Kingsley's Protestantism. In more complex fashion in George MacDonald's *The Princess and the Goblin* (1872) and *The Princess and Curdie* (1883), motivation is precisely not what does not need to be explored, for Curdie and the Princess demonstrate their *innate* goodness in their behaviour to goblins, grandmothers and monstrous (but good) creatures. In Carlo Collodi's *Pinocchio* (1883), the titular puppet is motivated by a lack of education (environment) but it is salvation by Grace that underpins the magic: the blue fairy forgives him because he loves his father, but also because she has the Grace to forgive.

By the end of the nineteenth century there were glimmers of a shift. In discussing childhood, and its construction in fantasy texts, Carpenter argues that the key text that informs the work of the Edwardian writers is Richard Jefferies's *Bevis: The Story of a Boy* (1882).[23] Jefferies had

previously produced *Wood Magic* in which 'Bevis has the power of understanding the speech of birds and animals, even of the trees and the wind,
apparently just because he is a child, with his child's perception and
vision still unfaded' – clearly an antecedent of the Pan worship of P. L.
Travers and an extension of Carpenter's Beautiful Child syndrome (the
Victorian tendency to depict children as almost supernaturally perfect).[24]
*Bevis*, in the opening chapter, portrays children as self-absorbed, con-
centrated and yet easily distracted, experimental and engaged with interrogating their surroundings. Crucially, Bevis is a child engaged with
childhood and other children. Unlike previous child characters (even
Alice), his focus is not on adults, but on the world he and his friends
create.

The shifts in mode take some time to bed into the form. In *The
Princess and the Goblin* this manifests in an unevenness of tone. The overall narrative is the conventional distanced *telling* of the fairy tale, but
once Curdie walks on, we are into a much more immediate, participa-
tory tone in which the child reader is expected to identify with Curdie.
The distanced mode is also dominant in Kingsley's *Water-Babies*. The
majority of the story is an *observation* of Tom, with very little inter-
nal monologue of any kind. It offers up an account of Tom, much as
MacDonald does of little Diamond in *At the Back of the North Wind*.

But there are voices that offer a distinct shift in address. Charles
Dickens's 'The Magic Fishbone' (1868) shifts the focus onto the child,
Alice, by writing the story from the point of view of her father, thus
solving the difficulty of getting into the mind of a child, and uses this
shift in perspective to allow the (presumed child) reader to look at a king
with the equality of a cat. The result is a direct, friendly, demotic address
that moves the fantasy towards a more casual language, which Edith
Nesbit was to make her own in *The Story of the Treasure Seekers* (1899),
*The Wouldbegoods* (1901), *Five Children and It* (1902), *The Phoenix and
the Carpet* (1904) and *The Story of the Amulet* (1906). The importance of
this shift in voice can be seen in the most uneven of Nesbit's works, *Wet
Magic* (1913). A relatively late book, it begins with magic intruding into
the children's visit to the sea. While the children are on land, the narrative voice is close and personal, with much use of the quoted monologue
and a certain amount of what Nikolajeva calls psycho-narration, in which
the mind's thoughts are recited in a rather disjointed fashion. However,
when the children go under the water, we are thrown back to a narrative
style reminiscent of Ruskin's *The King of the Golden River*, in which exter-
nalized and distanced description and the attempt to describe the fantasy

land, rather than the children's experience of the fantastic, reduce the story to a travelogue.

The rhetorical shift which takes place in children's fantasy across the nineteenth century also changes the conception of the child from a slate to be written upon to a protagonist bringing to the adventure his or her own understandings and needs. For all that Nesbit's characters may at first appear interchangeable, within their ensembles a clear sense eventually emerges of different interests and personalities. In *Five Children and It* and its sequels, Robert takes the lead, Anthea is the brave but cautious one, Jane is much shyer, and these characteristics shape their adventures. Similarly, Barrie's Michael and John have clearly different responses to Peter, as do each of the Lost Boys, who are more differentiated than one might expect, but most interesting perhaps is Wendy, who is a complex study, displaying feminine delight in house-making and irritation at being taken for granted or mistreated. Wendy, for all that she horrifies modern feminists, is *not* the contented 1950s housewife but rather is a person trying to impose order on the disordered, and to carve out space for herself in a world actually dominated by Peter. Wendy's desires become crucial to the end of the text, which is about the conscious choice to leave magic behind, unlike many later texts in which it is magic which deserts.

Finally, if we see the emergence of books for children within the body of fantastic literature more generally as those books written with the assumption both of entertaining children and asking children to identify with the characters (as opposed to presenting children as entertainment for adults), this helps to embrace at least one anomalous text. Christina Rossetti's *Goblin Market* (1862) is seen by some critics as a poem for children, but by others as for adults. Its overt sexuality seems to put it beyond the possibility that it was meant for children in late Victorian England, and its intended destination was the adult *Cornhill Magazine*, though it came out instead in *Goblin Market and Other Poems* as a Macmillan Christmas volume. Yet, with its teenage protagonists and its concerns with addiction, drugs and sex, it can make a fair claim to be the ancestor of modern Young Adult fantasy.

By the end of this period we can see some distinct strands of fantasy emerging. Early nineteenth-century fantasy is clearly rooted in the fairy tale: it takes place in a nebulous other world, neither here, nor in what we will come to understand as a full fantasy. By the 1860s and 1870s, what we now call portal fantasies dominate, linked to the real world, Manlove argues, by the 'it was really only a dream' conclusions that later come to be seen as clichéd.[25] Victorian interest in the symbology and innate realism of dreams allows a double reality to be created in texts as diverse as *The Water-Babies*, *Alice* and *The Cuckoo Clock*. What seems a weakness today, in its time can be understood as deepening the immersion in fantasy. An aspect of fantasy that remained as yet underdeveloped, or under-appropriated, for children's fantasy, was the fantastical Gothic. Although a number of authors such as Frances Hodgson Burnett produced clearly rationalist-Gothic-inflected tales such as *The Secret Garden*, the ghost, vampire or terror story was yet to provide material for those writing conspicuously for the new market.

There are also moral shifts: it can be argued that the stories become less moral, as in Kingsley's amoral fantasies and Carroll's subversive challenges, but it might be better to see the shift as away from the moral *lessons* of Ewing and MacDonald, in which the fantasy hews closely to allegory and parable, and towards fantasy as a ground for working out moral problems, as we see in *Through the Looking Glass*, in *Peter Pan in Kensington Gardens* and in the work of Nesbit. By the end of the period, the child protagonist – now dominant – has become a moral actor/agent in the world.

What stands out is what is not there. The consistent full fantasy world as popularized by Tolkien is absent from most of these texts (*Goblin Market* is an interesting exception in that it clearly has rules that the sisters must obey). The quest fantasy, although already developing in the adult market through MacDonald's *Phantastes* (1858) and William Morris's *The Well at the World's End* (1896), does not yet have a match in children's fiction: adventure away from home is still predominantly for adults and children are very definitely children, not teens (David Balfour in Robert Louis Stevenson's *Kidnapped*, 1886, is seventeen, older than any of the protagonists in these fictions). In as much as the Victorian children's writers have a common guiding principle, it is that *anything* can happen, whether rendered absurd as in the works of Lewis Carroll, a reflection of the spiritual in the world as in MacDonald, or a presentation of the world as permeable and changeable as (in different ways) in the works of Kipling and Nesbit.

CHAPTER 3

# *The American search for an American childhood*

Most of the great American children's classics of the nineteenth century, of course, are based in the realist tradition. Nineteenth-century American readers, writers and critics generally felt a very real antipathy to the fantastic. Maria Edgeworth (1767–1849), an Irish writer who was enormously popular in the United States, emphasized the current and the practical in her fiction, and had no truck with fairy lore. In his Preface to her *Moral Tales*, her father, the educational reformer Richard Lovell Edgeworth, praised her for showing how her protagonist's 'romantic eccentricities' get her in trouble and cause her to be 'ashamed to acknowledge her former friends'.[1] In 1839 the American educator Jacob Abbott, best remembered today for his realist and didactic children's books in the Rollo Holiday series, wrote with great feeling about the worthlessness of the shortcuts to happiness provided by such magical objects as Aladdin's lamp, indicating that he had not entirely understood the message of the story, which also taught the reader not to squander good fortune. Some years later, Samuel Griswold Goodrich (1793–1860), who, as Peter Parley, was the bestselling children's writer in America during the nineteenth century, declared that he despised fairy tales, Mother Goose and all things fantastic in children's literature, going so far as to argue that 'much of the vice and crime in the world are to be imputed to these atrocious books put into the hands of children, and bringing them down, with more or less efficiency, to their own debased moral standard'.[2] And yet, the United States was not devoid of fancy, nor did all writers and readers regard fancy as the road to dissolution; for some, as we shall see in this chapter, fancy and fantasy were part of the essential heritage of the American child.

## Distrust of the fantastic

The folklore of the Europeans who settled in the New World was rich. Stories of fairies who moved to America along with the immigrants

49

they had lived with and bedevilled in the Old Country are quite common. The descendants of immigrants from the Scottish Highlands were particularly likely to hold on to such stories and, in those areas most isolated from the homogenizing tendencies of US development, they thrived. Appalachia was particularly fertile soil for such tales. However, despite these imports, as Brian Attebery argues in *The Fantasy Tradition in American Literature*, there was a general tendency for colonial and American storytellers to play down the fantastic, either rationalizing the tales, that is, finding non-fantastic explanations for what in the original story was a clearly supernatural event, or including the supernatural but retaining a European setting, so that 'fairyland – that is the entire realm of faërie or enchantment has become distant and abstract, no longer the glittering hall under the next mountain'.[3]

The difficulty was that from its inception European-American culture had a strong tradition of outright opposition to the fantastic. There was a little breathing room for allegory, as in the works of Milton and Bunyan – John Bunyan's *The Pilgrim's Progress* (1678) was a particular favourite – but these works were valued for their moral precepts rather than their fantastical imagination. One consequence was, as Attebery puts it, the transportation to the early Puritan colonies of 'a fundamental bias against fantasy in the folklore of this country'.[4]

Attebery's argument is supported by the contents of the standard collection for teaching Colonial American literature, the *Norton Anthology of American Literature*: in its first volume there is very little of the fantastic. In the published fiction of the period (as opposed to ongoing oral folk tradition), there was an accompanying paring away of the supernatural in such examples of that folk tradition as actually saw print: ballads, tales and legends. Many of the folk tales that had their origins in America, the Paul Bunyan and Pecos Bill cycles, for example, or some of the tales associated with real people like Davy Crockett and Mike Fink, were told with a satirical edge as something closer to traditional travellers' tales. These mutated into a new form, the 'tall tales', epitomized in the movie *Big Fish* (2003): stories that all but the most naive listeners or readers were expected to assume from the outset to be founded in exaggeration or outright lies but which yet might be thought to contain a nugget of truth. In the Western tradition, this form has remained distinctly American, and is strongly connected to the American traditions of boosterism, showmanship and sideshows that shaped late nineteenth- and early twentieth-century popular culture.

A writer who wished to produce something both American and fantastic, and to root his creation, as did the British fantasists, in his native lore, had to move against the current, restoring what had been lost over the years or finding eddies of tradition that had resisted the general erosion of the marvellous. One consequence was that traditional American versions of European folk tales were not only often conveyed with less fantastic content than were their British or German or Scandinavian predecessors, but, when they contained fantasy elements, they were sometimes explicitly told in such a way as to keep them from being taken seriously. Selma Lanes points out that the magic of the ghosts playing at ninepins under the Catskills in Washington Irving's *Rip Van Winkle* (1819) 'is not nearly so marvelous as the changes that come about in American life in the years of Rip's nap';[5] in 'most home grown American fairy tales, no magic is ever more powerful than the overriding reality of the American life experience'.[6] In many cases, as epitomized in the work of Mark Twain, magic in American fantasy is actually another name for ingenuity. Even in Oz, writes Lanes, 'the magic does not really reside in persons, not even the Wizard, but in the material abundance of the land and the relatively smooth-running machinery of a government in which all the inhabitants fully believe'.[7]

However, while outright *fancy* was frowned on, the literature of American high culture had a variety of fantastic strains from quite early on. The rationalized fantastic of the Gothic tradition, where the fantastic yields to a non-supernatural explanation, was practised by Charles Brockden Brown in *Wieland, or the Transformation: An American Tale* (1798) and in *Arthur Mervyn* (1798–9). Washington Irving, who was particularly influenced by Sir Walter Scott and the German Romantic Johann Karl Musäus and who is widely regarded as the father of the American short story, published at least one classic fantasy tale, 'Rip Van Winkle', in which a young Dutch colonist wandering in the Catskill Mountains runs into the ghosts of the explorer Henry Hudson and his crew playing nine pins, drinks with them, and falls asleep for twenty years (a variation perhaps on the medieval tale 'The Seven Sleepers of Ephesus', although, thinking of European fairy tradition, he might well have been *taken away by the fairies*), before waking to be reunited with his now grown-up daughter. Irving seems to have been more comfortable with rationalized fantasies such as 'The Legend of Sleepy Hollow' (1820) in which the supernatural element of the story turns out to be a hoax. His celebration of the Yankee preference for the rational may have bolstered his popularity: a number of his tales, including 'Rip Van Winkle' and 'The Legend of Sleepy Hollow', came to be regarded as American children's classics.

## Nathaniel Hawthorne and Company

Yet, the supernatural had its place: the best of the next generation of American fiction writers were heavily influenced by the frankly supernatural tales of the German Romantics, for example Johann Friedrich von Schiller's *Der Geisterseher* (1786), which became available in English translation as *The Ghost-Seer* (1795), and Lawrence Flammenburg's *Der Geisterbanner* (1792), which was translated as *The Necromancer* (1794). Irving and, a few years later, Nathaniel Hawthorne, Edgar Allan Poe and Herman Melville – all of whom wrote a significant number of fantasy stories of various sorts – were familiar with the full range of fantastic, often Gothic literature being produced in England and Europe at the time.

Poe, whose early poetry was influenced by Coleridge and Byron, and whose early fiction was most influenced by the Gothic writers and E. T. A. Hoffmann, published numerous masterpieces of fantasy such as 'The Fall of the House of Usher' (1839) and 'The Masque of the Red Death' (1842), works produced for an adult audience but eventually much appreciated by younger readers as well. Hawthorne's masterpieces, from 'Young Goodman Brown' (1835) to *The Scarlet Letter* (1850) to *The House of the Seven Gables* (1851), may never have had as much resonance with young readers as did the stories of Irving and Poe (despite having been introduced to generations of often unwilling schoolchildren), but Hawthorne became the first major American author to write fantastic tales specifically for children, with two highly successful collections retelling the Greek myths, *A Wonder-Book for Girls and Boys* (1852) and *Tanglewood Tales for Boys and Girls* (1853).

Hawthorne was married and had three small children when *A Wonder-Book* first appeared. The volume contains five stories, each a child-friendly retelling of one of the classic Greek myths – Perseus and the Gorgon, King Midas and the Golden Touch, Pandora, among others – and each framed by the episodic story of a group of small children who are being minded by Eustace Bright, an eighteen-year-old student on vacation from Williams College in Massachusetts. They are thus framed as educative, and also as stories for children that an adult might overhear. Eustace is a very American young man – Hawthorne refers to him as 'slender and rather pale, as all Yankee students are'.[8]

Hawthorne wrote that he had 'long been of the opinion that many of the classical myths were capable of being rendered into very capital reading for children' and readily admitted that he had both 'imbued' them with the morality of his age and allowed them to assume what he called 'a Gothic or romantic guise'[9] or, to put it another way, he rewrote them as something very much like fairy tales. Attebery criticizes Hawthorne for making his versions of these classic tales 'too prosaic', and suggests that the best of them 'are not high fantasy, not grand or heroic or deeply moving, but low and comfortable fantasy, childhood and household tales like the Grimms' – which rather misses the point that this was precisely what Hawthorne set out to achieve.[10]

An example of this prosaic style can be found in Hawthorne's 'The Golden Touch', in the use of direct speech and the naming of characters ('I choose to call her Marygold'),[11] creating a cosier relationship than traditional oral narrative. After Midas has turned the roses in his garden to gold, his daughter is disconsolate:

> 'Ah, dear father!' answered the child, as well as her sobs would let her; 'it is not beautiful, but the ugliest flower that ever grew! As soon as I was dressed I ran into the garden to gather some roses for you; because I know you like them when gathered by your little daughter. But, oh dear, dear me! What do you think has happened? Such a misfortune! All the beautiful roses, that smelt so sweetly and have so many lovely blushes, are blighted and spoiled!'[12]

Portrayed as a man who drinks coffee in the morning and worries about his daughter eating a healthy breakfast, it is impossible for Hawthorne's Midas to rise to the level of the original legend, but his pain upon accidentally turning his daughter to gold is touching, and that he is motivated as much by a desire to bring her back to life as to save his own life, humanizes him. Hawthorne draws attention to one of the defining features of American fiction for children in this period, which stands in stark contrast to the British tradition, and that is the absolute vitality of the relationship between parent and child. In the books discussed in Chapter 2, the absence of the parent relationship in British children's fantasy (and other fictions) of this period is immediately noticeable.

Hawthorne's British contemporary, Charles Kingsley, disliked the sequel, *Tanglewood Tales*, thinking it rather vulgar, and published his own collection *The Heroes* (1856) in response, but we must be clear that this is a period in which *vulgar* was a term which had a polar opposite meaning to that which it carries today. What would now be considered distressingly showy, over-decorated or distanced from its origins would in the mid to late nineteenth century have been considered elegant, that very distance from its origins being the test of elegance. *Vulgar* was a term used for what we might now call the demotic: a form of base realism that took the reader or the viewer of art too close to the realities of life. So Hawthorne's offence is to make the story of King Midas both familial and familiar. Hawthorne dissented. He insisted, 'Children possess an unestimated sensibility to whatever is deep or high, in imagination or feeling, so long as it is simple, likewise. It is only the artificial and complex that bewilder them.'[13]

Despite their popularity among contemporaries, it is clear that after mid century the influence of Irving, Poe, Hawthorne and Melville – at least that part of their work closest to the Gothic romance and the fairy tale – largely disappeared from what came to be seen as the mainstream of American literature. It was almost entirely replaced by realist narratives. When major American writers chose on occasion to touch upon the fantastic, their genres of choice were generally either the often ambiguous ghost story (Henry James and Edith Wharton) or dystopian literature (Samuel Clemens, Edward Bellamy and Jack London).

Fairy tales, however, have enormous staying power and, despite the early American hostility towards the genre, particularly on the part of moralists and educators like Abbott and Goodrich, they continued to have some popularity. This increased when English-language translations of the Brothers Grimm became available in 1825, and as German immigration to the United States rose dramatically from the 1820s, reaching an estimated total of 8 million by the end of the nineteenth century.

## A Danish import

The most immediate significant response to the rising popularity of fairy tales came from James Kirke Paulding (1778–1860). A sometime collaborator with Washington Irving, he produced *A Christmas Gift from Fairyland* (1838), which included such tales as 'Florella, or the Fairy of the Rainbow' and 'The Nameless Old Woman', featuring traditional fairy tale plots and characters placed in specifically American settings.

Less than a decade later, in 1846, appeared the first translations of some of Hans Christian Andersen's tales. Andersen's stories, with their heavy moralizing, appear to have eminently suited Victorian and particularly American readers. Andersen offered the very reverse of the temptation and reward offered by Aladdin's lamp. In Andersen's tales the magical object – the red shoes or the ice mirror – are the source of horror or, in the case of the match-girl's tinder box, the source of relief from earthly toil in a much more final way. To succumb to temptation in an Andersen story is to seek out one's own punishment: the little girl with red shoes loses her feet, the mermaid who sells her tail loses her life and any chance at an immortal soul. Those stories which end with reward – 'The Ugly Duckling' for example – celebrate innate qualities and Christian humility which, while at odds with the Yankee ethic, were in tune with mid-nineteenth-century, pre-Gospel-of-Wealth American evangelical Christianity.

Andersen had a number of imitators. Horace Scudder (1838–1902), a prolific editor and author, briefly gained recognition as the 'American Hans Christian Andersen'. Julian Hawthorne (1846–1944), Nathaniel's son, who was six years old when *A Wonder-Book* was published, was also influenced by Andersen: he went on to have a highly successful career as a biographer, novelist and short story writer. A significant amount of Julian Hawthorne's fiction for adults, such as the novel *Archibald Malmaison* (1879) and the short story 'Ken's Mystery' (1883), involved the supernatural. Four of his novella-length fairy tales for children were eventually collected in *Yellow-Cap* (1880), which included the rather traditional title story and the oddly allegorical 'Calladon', which concerns a young boy, the title character, who lives in a single room at the centre of a circular structure called Abracadabra. His life seems perfect and, because his needs are modest, he wants for nothing. Calladon's life changes, however, when the Master who has been with him his whole life simultaneously gives him a little girl to be his friend, and leaves for parts unknown, counselling the boy that he must regularly check himself in a small mirror that the girl carries in order to be aware of his moral state. The story, of course, is a retelling of the Fall from Grace, the expulsion from the Garden of Eden and eventual Salvation, albeit using characters that might easily have stepped out of 'The Snow Queen' or some other of Andersen's fairy tales. Its most refreshing moment, perhaps, comes when the Master emphasizes to Calladon that if the boy does wrong, it will be because he chooses to do so, not because the girl, Callia, has tempted him.

Other more traditional works of children's fantasy also appeared around the mid to late nineteenth century, all essentially minor but many of them readable: some were retellings of folk tales, such as Verplanck's *The Fairy-Book* (1836) and C. B. Burkhardt's *Fairy Tales of Many Lands* (1849); others were literary tales, among them Louisa May Alcott's juvenilia, *Flower Fables* (1855), Jane G. Austin's *Fairy Dreams; or Wanderings in Elfland* (1859) and Silas Weir Mitchell's *The Wonderful Stories of Fuzbuz the Fly and Mother Grabem the Spider* (1867). Two fantasists who wrote with great humour were Laura E. Richards (1850–1943), author of the animal fantasy *The Joyous Story of Toto* (1885), along with numerous nonsense poems, some of which are still popular today; and Charles E. Carryl (1841–1920), whose *Davy and the Goblin; or, What Followed Reading Alice's Adventures in Wonderland* (1885) is funny and highly energetic, if less creative and intellectually complex than its model.

### L. Frank Baum and the American fantastic

Most children's books published in the United States in the eighteenth and early nineteenth centuries, whether realistic or fantastic, were essentially English or European in content. However, as Gillian Avery points out, traces of an American idiom were beginning to make themselves known in the work of Abbott and Goodrich, along with such volumes as *Peter Parley's Puppet Show, Part the Second* (1821) – which shows an illustration of 'Johnny Bull from England come, / Who boasts of being a sailor, / But yankey tars will let him know / He'll meet with many a failure' – and William Cardell's *The Story of Jack Halyard, the Sailor Boy* (1824), the first volume in a popular series of realistic sea stories about a boy from New Jersey.[14] The mid century saw the first publication of collections of folk tales from (or ostensibly from) America's various other ethnic groups, including *The Indian Fairy Book* (1856), retold for children by Henry Rowe Schoolcraft and Cornelius Mathews; May Wentworth's *Fairy Tales from Gold Lands* (1867), which contains tales set in California, many of them taken from the folklore of the local Spanish, Indian and Chinese peoples; and, most famously, Joel Chandler Harris's collection of trickster tales, *Uncle Remus* (1881), which was originally intended for adults, but soon became a children's favourite.

Christopher Cranch and Samuel Clemens (better known as Mark Twain) are the strongest Americanizers in this period. Christopher Pearse Cranch (1813–92) wrote specifically for children and has a fair claim to be the first American fantasy novelist. His uniquely American fairy tales, *The Last of the Huggermuggers* (1855) and *Kobboltzo* (1856), feature a race of gentle giants, the Huggermuggers, living on an island in the Indian Ocean, and a plan to display them in the United States. A poet and artist of some talent, Cranch was a member of Emerson's Transcendentalist circle and later associated with the Hudson River school of painters. His tales, which are something of a cross between *Robinson Crusoe* and *Gulliver's Travels*, concern a sailor named Jacky Cable, who is shipwrecked on an island inhabited by both giants and a group that self-identifies as dwarves, even though they are taller than normal humans. The Huggermuggers, something like 80 feet tall, can speak English (and actually seem to prefer it to their native language). Their culture is also similar to that of Europe and the United States. Unfortunately, they are on the verge of extinction, with only one middle-aged married couple still alive. The dwarves, who tend to be jealous and venal types, are more numerous. After being rescued by an American trading ship, Jackie meets a Yankee named Zebedee Nabbum, who has been sent to find and bring back strange animals for Barnum's museum in New York. Motivated by profit, the two at first plot to capture a giant against his will, but then, realizing that 'They were not savages', decide that they will instead attempt to convince the giant to come with them and display himself.[15] As was common in early abolitionist thinking, it is the Westernized culture and sensibility that preclude enslavement, not an objection to slavery per se: in these terms *The Last of the Huggermuggers*, while not an anti-slavery tract, was clearly part of the growing Northern hostility to slavery in the 1850s in the wake of the Dred Scott Decision.

Longer lasting has been Mark Twain's *A Connecticut Yankee in King Arthur's Court* (1889). Originally published as a children's book, it has been variously described as science fiction, fantasy, satire or, as Attebery suggests in *The Fantasy Tradition*, 'a book which all by itself demonstrates the strong hostility between American thought and pure fantasy', combining as it does time travel, a humorous send-up of the conventions of chivalry (which could still be espoused with full seriousness by the author, editor and critic Howard Pyle some decades later) and what starts out as a near-utopian paean to progress, before it transforms itself into a devastating jeremiad on the dystopian horrors of the American Civil War.[16] The Yankee hero of Twain's book might easily be the sharp Yankee businessman Zebedee Nabbum from Christopher Cranch's *Last of the Huggermuggers*.

Fantasy literature for children became more common after the advent of such legendary publications as *The Riverside Magazine for Young People* (1867–70), edited by Horace Scudder, and *St. Nicholas Magazine* (1873–1943), edited for many years by Mary Mapes Dodge, which between them included original fiction by Hans Christian Andersen, Rudyard Kipling and American authors Julian Hawthorne, Frank R. Stockton and Howard Pyle. Horace Scudder spent years wooing Andersen, and his hard work paid off handsomely as seventeen of the Dane's children's stories appeared in *Riverside Magazine* over a period of three years, many of them before seeing publication in Denmark.[17]

Frank R. Stockton (1834–1902), an enormously popular writer in his day, is now best known for 'The Lady, or the Tiger' (1882), a non-fantastic work for adults. His earliest fantasies for children, a series of tales reminiscent of the *Arabian Nights*, concerning the adventures of a fairy named Ting-a-ling, began appearing in *The Riverside Magazine* and were published in book form as *Ting-a-Ling* (1870). In 1873 he became Dodge's assistant editor at *St. Nicholas Magazine*, where all of his later children's fantasies appeared, including the classics 'The Griffin and the Minor Canon' (1885) and 'The Bee-Man of Orn' (1887). Stockton's later tales were notable in that they avoided explicit moralizing and strayed from traditional fairy tale motifs, sometimes resorting to what Gillian Avery calls 'burlesque and knock-about farce'.[18] In 'The Griffin and the Minor Canon', for example, the last griffin in the world comes to a town in order to admire the sculpture of itself on the local church. The townspeople are terrified of the beast, but, in a repeat of the meme that what counts is civilization, the humane and thoughtful minor canon whom they send to deal with the griffin, discovers that it is both kind and learned, confounding all expectations to the contrary. The two become fast friends.

Howard Pyle (1853–1911) was best known in his day as one of the late nineteenth century's finest book illustrators and art educators (his students included Maxfield Parrish and N. C. Wyeth), but he was also the author of a number of mostly traditional short fantasies, first published in *St. Nicholas Magazine* and then compiled in *Pepper and Salt* (1885) and *The Wonder Clock* (1887), plus several powerful full-length works of historical fiction, some of which moved into the realm of fantasy. These included *The Merry Adventures of Robin Hood* (1883) and much later *The Story of King Arthur and His Knights* (1903), which was heavily influenced by Malory's *Le Morte d'Arthur* (1485). Although less well known, Pyle's most original contribution to children's fantasy is *The Garden Behind the Moon* (1895), in which a boy who is a misfit in his own community, a mooncalf teased by all the other children, has adventures after crossing the moon-path where he meets the god-like Moon-Angel. It is a bittersweet tale, inspired by the death of Pyle's own child, with similarities to William Blake's *Songs of Innocence and Experience* (1789, 1794), Charles Kingsley's *The Water-Babies* (1863) and George MacDonald's *At the Back of the North Wind* (1871). Not a traditional fairy tale, and frankly allegorical, Pyle's novel says much about death, astronomy and biology, and also portrays the 'most wonderful, beautiful, never-to-be-forgotten garden that the mind can think of. In it live little children who play and romp, and laugh and sing, and are as merry and happy as the little white lambs in the green meadow in springtime.'[19]

The first truly important American fantasy writer for children was L. Frank Baum (1856–1919), and his *The Wonderful Wizard of Oz* (1900) is perhaps the most American of all early children's fantasies, what Katharine M. Rogers calls 'an American version of the pastoral ideal'. 'Manners in Oz,' she suggests, 'are those of rural America at its best.'[20] When Dorothy is transported from Kansas to Oz, she may leave the United States behind, but her concerns and the book's underlying themes continue to be those of a relatively new nation just entering a new century, a nation still defining itself in opposition to the traditions of Europe.

Baum allowed witches into Oz, but he consciously eliminated most other traditional fantasy characters and created Munchkins, winged monkeys, a tin woodman and an animated scarecrow, among many other inventions, to replace them. Although his novel is not without adventure and occasional chills, he consciously decided to avoid both the darkness of the traditional European fairy tale and the explicit didacticism of much European and American children's literature. Baum's background had been in creating window displays for stores, which reached a high art at the end of the nineteenth century, and his wonders are as likely to be modern mechanical automata (for example the tin woodman or Tiktok, the windup mechanical man from *Ozma of Oz*, 1907) as they are to be magical. Further, both his characters and his plots tend towards scepticism and have no patience for humbug. As did Swift and Carroll before him, Baum probably sprinkled his text with disguised political and social commentary (although exactly what this commentary was is still a subject of much debate). *The Wonderful Wizard of Oz* sold well, immediately

The Oz books did not immediately receive universal praise. In fact there is evidence that Baum and his illustrator, W. W. Denslow, may have had to agree to pay for the printing and binding before his publisher George M. Hill would take on the project. Appearing in August 1900, the book received positive reviews, although it was not an immediate bestseller. Unfortunately for Baum, whose life had involved previous financial disasters, George M. Hill went into receivership in 1902, with all of its assets, including Baum's books, being put up for sale. Bowen-Merrill bought the plates for and rights to *The Wonderful Wizard of Oz* but Baum was not particularly happy with this publisher and in 1904 he signed a contract with Reilly & Britton for subsequent books in the Oz series, beginning with *The Marvelous Land of Oz* (1904), with John R. Neil replacing Denslow as the illustrator for the remaining books in the series. In that same year, Baum sold his first story to the prestigious *St. Nicholas Magazine*, thus achieving increased literary credibility.

engendering a successful musical (as well as several not all successful film versions prior to the Judy Garland hit of 1939), and Baum went on to write thirteen more books in the series, plus numerous other children's fantasies.

In the latter half of the nineteenth century rapid industrialization and movement from the country to the city caused a crisis in the American family, with many children simply being abandoned. A rapid growth in children's aid societies and the orphan train movement led to significant numbers of children being sent back to the countryside and placed as farm workers. As Marilyn Holt observes: 'The idea was that the values of independence and self-sufficiency that these children had learned on the city streets would benefit these rural areas. Baum's Dorothy is a construction of one such child.' Such attitudes towards independence – in *The Wonderful Wizard of Oz* Dorothy, the Scarecrow, the Tin Man and the Lion work together 'solely because their mutual purposes intertwine' rather than out of friendship or a traditional Christian ethic of care – made the book unpleasant for some readers.[21] Still, as the series continues, the main characters do become genuinely fond of each other and, though Dorothy remains a remarkably self-centred heroine when compared to, for example, Gerda in Andersen's 'The Snow Queen' (1845) or Jo in Louisa May Alcott's *Little Women* (1868, 1869), she is far from being a selfish child.

Baum died in 1919 having written fourteen Oz novels, with three of them appearing posthumously. He also authored a comic strip, *Queer Visitors from the Marvelous Land of Oz* (1905), a collection of short stories, *Little Wizard Stories of Oz* (1913), and a variety of other books, several of which, for example the fantasies *The Master Key: An Electrical Fairytale* (1901) and *Queen Zixi of Ix* (1905), are still quite readable. Baum had hoped to end the Oz series after *The Emerald City of Oz* (1910), and in 1911 brought out *The Sea Fairies* as the first volume in a replacement series, but neither it nor its sequel sold particularly well and Baum once again found himself in serious financial difficulties, so he returned to Oz with *The Patchwork Girl of Oz* (1913) and produced volumes in the series on a regular basis for the rest of his life.

The enormous popularity of the Oz books can be seen not only in their continuing sales, but also in the popularity of the many post-Baum sequels, including nineteen volumes by Ruth Plumly Thompson, beginning with *The Royal Book of Oz* (1921), all of them illustrated by John R. Neil, three more volumes by Neil himself, six further novels that are considered canonical, the most recent of which is *Merry Go Round in Oz* by Eloise Jarvis McGraw and Lauren Lynn McGraw (1963), and numerous non-canonical take-offs. Some, like Sherwood Smith's *The Emerald Wand of Oz* (2005), which was authorized by the Baum estate, were designed for children, while others are adult novels, most significantly Geoff Ryman's magnificent *Was...* (1992) which follows two characters, the supposed real-life Dorothy behind Baum's fiction, who is being destroyed by abuse, and a gay man who is dying of AIDS. Gregory Maguire's best-selling *Wicked* (1995) and sequels, which tell the history of Oz prior to Dorothy's arrival, is equally directed at adults, offering a coruscating satire on the ease with which we accede to oppression and injustice.

Speaking of *The Wonderful Wizard of Oz*, Gillian Avery admits that 'Of all American classics this is the most difficult for a foreigner to appraise', and she criticizes the book for both its optimistic attitude and a blandness that European readers find unappealing.[22] Baum's willingness to avoid emotional complexities, and the fact that in a sense he aligns himself with Samuel Goodrich's disdain for the darkness of traditional fairy tales, has been widely held against him. Nevertheless, while prior to Baum most of the best American fantasy for children – the work of Stockton and Pyle, for example – was essentially in the European tradition, after Baum a more American style, or several more American styles, could blossom. His literary reception was mixed, with many libraries refusing to carry Oz books until years after the author's death. As Rogers observes, even at the height of Baum's success, and despite sales to *St. Nicholas Magazine*, 'high-prestige publications treated him as a run-of-the-mill writer whose books happened to sell well'.[23] Baum's influence on American children's literature was nevertheless immediate. Just months after *The Wonderful Wizard of Oz* appeared, Eva Katherine Gibson published *Zauberlinda the Wise Witch* (1901), a tale set in the Black Hills of South Dakota, and a clear (if pale) imitation of Baum's work.[24]

Other, more significant writers who demonstrate Baum's influence to a greater or lesser degree are Carl Sandburg, whose *Rootabaga Stories* (1922) mix elements of the folk tale with Baum's playfulness and his aggressively American attitude; Carl Grabo, whose *The Cat in Grandfather's House* (1929) concerns the adventures of a little girl living in a house where all of the furniture is sentient; Ruth Stiles Gannett, whose *My Father's Dragon* (1948) and sequels tell the story of a little boy's adventures on a fabulous island full of talking animals; and Ray Bradbury, who references Baum with regularity, as in the short story 'The Exiles' (1950), or in his Mars stories, which share as much with Oz as they do with Edgar Rice Burroughs's Barsoom (to which we will return). Bradbury specifically salutes both Burroughs and Baum, 'two gentlemen of no talent whatsoever ... who changed the world somewhat more than they ever dreamed ... once their books came to be published and moved in the minds and blood of 8 year olds, 10 year olds, 12 year olds'.[25] That change, however, took some time.

Relatively little fantasy was published for children in the United States before the Second World War. The US children's book market was driven very much by the public libraries (librarianship as a profession emerged early in the United States, at the end of the nineteenth century) and, in particular, by the towering figure of the head of the New York Public Library's children's collection, Anne Carroll Moore. Also influential was *The Horn Book Magazine*, founded in 1924, which began as a newsletter from Bertha Mahoney Miller and Elinor Whitney Field, proprietors of The Bookshop for Boys and Girls which opened in 1916 in Boston as an outgrowth of the Women's Educational and Industrial Union. The connection with the WEIU gave the magazine a strong educative tinge. While these organizations were not hostile to fantasy, it would be fair to say that they were not enthusiastic: working in many cases to support the assimilation of immigrants, they were concerned with the Americanness of literature, and whimsy could seem if not wrong, then a luxury. This attitude shaped the career of E. B. White, the pre-eminent US children's fantasy writer of the period.

## E. B. White and the rise of urbane children's fantasy

Anthropomorphism has always been an important part of fantasy literature. The great late nineteenth- and early twentieth-century British tradition of literary animal fantasies – from Rudyard Kipling's *The Jungle Book* (1894) to Beatrix Potter's *The Tale of Peter Rabbit* (1902) and A. A. Milne's *Winnie-the-Pooh* (1926) – has no equivalent in American children's literature. The animal tales of Joel Chandler Harris (1848–1908), such as those collected in *Uncle Remus: His Songs and His Sayings* (1880), although highly regarded, were essentially Americanizations of traditional West African tales. The numerous children's novels of Thornton Burgess (1874–1965), such as *The Adventures of Reddy Fox* (1913) and *The Adventures of Danny the Field Mouse* (1915), although written for a slightly older audience, are obviously derivative of Potter and, although popular in their day, are overly didactic and not of equal quality.

Perhaps the first significant example of the extended animal fantasy written by an American is *To and Again* (1927), the initial volume in the wonderfully realized *Freddy the Pig* series, later republished as *Freddy Goes to Florida*, by Walter R. Brooks (1886–1958). Freddy is a very American pig, who drives a car and takes vacations in Florida. Other important American animal fantasies include Robert Lawson's *Rabbit Hill* (1944), a Newbery Award-winner, George Selden's *The Cricket in Times Square* (1960) and Randall Jarrell's oddly philosophical *The Animal Family* (1965), both Newbery Honor books, as well as Beverly Cleary's popular *The Mouse and the Motorcycle* (1965). But the most successful American animal fantasist of all was E. B. White.

The most prestigious American book award for children's literature is the Newbery. Authors of fantasies who have won the Newbery include:

- Hugh Lofting (1923)
- Rachel Field (1930)
- Kate Seredy (1938)
- William Pene du Bois (1948)
- Madeleine L'Engle (1963)
- Lloyd Alexander (1969)
- Robert C. O'Brien (1972)
- Susan Cooper (1976)
- Robin McKinley (1985)
- Lois Lowry (1994)
- Louis Sachar (1999)
- Neil Gaiman (2009)
- Katherine Applegate (2013)
- Kate Di Camillo (2014, 2004)

Many, though not all, of these authors are discussed in this book. Authors who won Newbery Honors, essentially runners-up for the award, whose work we will also be discussing, include:

- Ruth Gannett
- E. B. White
- Carol Kendall
- Lloyd Alexander
- Natalie Babbitt
- Ursula K. Le Guin
- Virginia Hamilton
- Laurence Yep
- Megan Whalen Turner
- Gail Carson Levine
- Nancy Farmer
- Shannon Hale
- Grace Lin
- Holly Black

E. B. White (1899–1985) gained early fame as the author of witty, stylish essays for *The New Yorker* and as the co-author of the spoof *Is Sex Necessary?* (1929) with fellow *New Yorker* regular James Thurber. White had toyed with the idea of writing children's fiction since the 1920s and had actually had a draft of *Stuart Little* (1945) rejected as early as 1938. Stuart, who is born to a normal New York couple named the Littles, has a more or less human body, but a mouse's head and tail, and is only two inches tall. This, naturally enough, leads to a variety of humorous experiences, as for example when Stuart's parents place him inside their piano so that he can play a malfunctioning piano key as needed, which was 'no easy job … as he had to crouch down between the felt hammers so that he wouldn't get hit on the head'.[26] According to Leonard Marcus, *Stuart Little* 'calmly took aim at two of the more widely shared preoccupations of postwar Americans: the wish for "perfect" babies and the fear of being judged "abnormal"'.[27] Eventually Stuart heads out on a quest, using a miniature motor car, searching for his best friend, a bird named Margalo. The story ends with Stuart feeling hopeful, but we are never told whether or not he finds his friend. This open ending bothered some initial reviewers but the book was an instant success with both children and adults.

*Charlotte's Web* (1952), White's masterpiece, is right on the very edge of what we are including as fantasy in this book. Although the animals talk, they never talk to humans and they never exceed the capacity of their animal bodies. The story concerns a young pig named Wilbur who is saved from being drowned as the runt of the litter by an eight-year-old girl named Fern. Eventually, through Fern's care and that of the farmer she must eventually sell him to, Mr Zuckerman, Wilbur becomes such a 'terrific' pig that he wins a ribbon at the county fair and is thus saved permanently from being slaughtered for ham and bacon. The brightest of the animals is the eponymous spider of the title, who not only improves Wilbur's vocabulary and teaches him much about the world, but also saves his life by spinning webs in the barn doorway that include words pointing to the pig's excellence, such as 'Some Pig' and 'Humble'.[28] Unusually among children's books but perhaps no surprise after *Stuart Little*, *Charlotte's Web* ends on a melancholy note, with the spider's death, a natural result of White's commitment to include as much realism as possible. That sadness is mitigated both by Wilbur's eventual discovery that some of the spider's many children will stay with him, allowing him to parent the baby spiders much as Charlotte had parented him, and the book's extraordinary last line: 'It is not often that someone comes along who is a true friend and a good writer. Charlotte was both.'[29]

Eudora Welty, writing in *The New York Times Book Review*, called it 'as a piece of work … just about perfect, and just about magical in the way it is done'[30] and such well-known figures as Bennett Cerf, David McCord and Jean Stafford also praised the book. Anne Carroll Moore, writing in *The Horn Book Magazine*, castigated *Charlotte's Web*, however, for what she saw as its unsuccessful attempt to fuse realism and fantasy. Moore had a long-standing feud with White's editor at Harper's, the great Ursula Nordstrom, and it may not have been coincidence that no book edited by Nordstrom had ever won either a Caldecott or a Newbery.[31] Still, White's book was eventually chosen for a Newbery Honor.

Like E. B. White, James Thurber (1894–1961) had a significant reputation as a writer for adults long before he gained renown as a children's author and, like White, the bulk of his work is more or less in the realist tradition, albeit a realism transformed by a sense of humour, sometimes zany, sometimes mordant, often misogynistic, that clearly shows Thurber to be Mark Twain's direct descendant. Attebery, however, suggests that, at least in his children's fiction, not only was Thurber influenced by Baum, he was 'the fullest flowering of that tradition'.[32] Thurber himself testifies to Baum's influence on him as a child in his essay 'The Wizard of Chitenango', in which he discusses Baum's determination to leave out traditional fairies and keep his stories from being too scary for children:

> I am glad that, in spite of this high determination, Mr. Baum failed to keep them out. Children love a lot of nightmare and at least a little heartache in their books. And they get them in the Oz books. I know that I went through excruciatingly lovely nightmares and heartaches when the Scarecrow lost his straw, when the Tin Woodman was taken apart, when the Saw-Horse broke his wooden leg.[33]

He goes on to insist that after the first two books in the series, *The Wonderful Wizard of Oz* (1900) and *The Marvelous Land of Oz* (1904), Baum lost his way. 'I think that the fatal trouble with the later books (for us aging examiners, anyway) is that they became whimsical rather than fantastic. They ramble and they preach.'[34] Ironically, these comments on Baum's work can also be applied to Thurber's children's fantasies, representing both their strengths and their weaknesses. *Many Moons* (1943), for which illustrator Louis Slobodkin won the Caldecott Award, *The White Deer* (1945) and *The Thirteen Clocks* (1950) are the best of them.

The Caldecott Award is the most prestigious American award for picture book art and has frequently gone to stories with fantastic content, many of them folk or fairy tales. Among those who have received the Caldecott for fantasy-related work in recent years are:

- Trina Schart Hyman (1985)
- Chris Van Allsburg (1986, 1982)
- Richard Egielski (1987)
- Ed Young (1990)
- David Macaulay (1991)
- Peggy Rathmann (1996)
- David Wisniewski (1998)
- Paul O. Zelinsky (1998)
- Eric Rohmann (2003)
- David Wiesner (2007, 2002, 1992)
- Brian Selznick (2008)
- Jerry Pinkney (2011)

As Attebery points out, Thurber's own works (at least superficially) owe far more than Baum's to the European folk tale. *The White Deer* and *The Thirteen Clocks* are filled with 'castles, enchanted forests, dukes, and wizards all much as we might find them in works of the literary followers of the brothers Grimm'.[35] The fact is, however, that Thurber's backdrops, and for that matter his plots, are relatively unimportant, the former only developed to a sketchy degree, the latter more or less the same from book to book, two problems that sometimes make these stories less than satisfying to modern fantasy readers raised on Tolkien's verisimilitude. Attebery argues that Thurber's interest is centred on individual details and language play.[36] His protagonists are imaginative and artistic; further, they, or at least the narrators who tell their stories, have some self-awareness, an understanding that their worlds and their tasks are artificial. Thurber's voice in these fantasies periodically implies that he, as a sophisticated twentieth-century satirist, is playing with a more primitive genre, not to look down upon it perhaps, but to have fun with its imaginative potential. Each tale features a problem: a sick princess in *Many Moons* (from 'a surfeit of raspberry tarts'),[37] concern in *The White Deer* over whether or not a princess is human or deer, the sadness that has gripped a kingdom due to the reign of a cold and loveless Duke in *The Thirteen Clocks*. In each case, the important people of the kingdom, royal advisors and such, cannot deal with the problem, making ridiculous suggestions that fail to get anywhere. Where the tales are particularly American is that there is no hereditary right to succeed or any sense of destiny: in each tale, the hero who wins the day is some mild-mannered but imaginative fellow, a typical Thurber protagonist.

It is ironic that the most talented of Baum's successors in the world of American children's fantasy was Edward Eager (1911–64), who owed very little to Baum's approach but instead was rooted firmly in the British tradition. Eager set out explicitly to emulate the grande dame of British fantasy, Edith Nesbit. In *Seven-Day Magic* (1962) the author makes his literary antecedents clear when he has his child protagonists insist that E. Nesbit is their favourite author, 'though Fredericka liked the Oz books nearly as well'.[38] Deborah O'Keefe lists Eager, along with Nesbit and Mary Norton, as one of the 'three classic creators of children's magic fantasy'. Each of these writers, she says, wrote about 'cheerful children in an ordinary, stable world who stumbled into adventures caused by magic'.[39] In *Half-Magic* (1954), for example, four such children discover a magic wishing coin that only grants *half* of what you wish for, with sometimes hilarious consequences. Thus when they wish that their mother were home, she finds herself teleported halfway there, and when they ask to go to a desert island, they find themselves in the middle of the Sahara. In order to get what they really want the children must ask for exactly twice what they need, for example requesting that the coin give them two keys when they really only need one to unlock a door.

In such commercially successful novels as *Half-Magic* and *Seven-Day Magic*, Eager provides his child protagonists with a series of fast-moving, exciting adventures, but without ever placing them in what feels like serious danger, and, as in Baum, with no serious moral attached. Eager was funny, and humorous fantasy was a new thing in the US tradition. Although some of the humour in his books stems from the truly wonderful illustrations of N. M. Bodecker, much stems from Eager's critical awareness of what Nesbit had achieved. This quotation from the beginning of *Half-Magic* is clearly a send-up of Nesbit, and of the tradition of saintly children common to the realist tradition in both countries.

> Jane was the oldest and Mark the only boy, and between them they ran everything.
>    Katharine was the middle girl, of docile disposition and a comfort to her mother. She knew she was a comfort and docile because she'd heard her mother say so. And the others knew she was too, by now, because ever since that day Katharine *would* keep boasting about what a comfort she was, and how docile, until Jane declared she would utter a piercing shriek

and fall over dead if she heard another word about it. This will give you some idea of what Jane and Katharine were like.

Martha was the youngest, and very difficult.[40]

Taking a page from E. B. White, perhaps, Natalie Babbitt (1932–) wrote a series of introspective rural fantasies that feature quiet humour and complex moral dilemmas. In such tales as *Tuck Everlasting* (1975) and *The Eyes of the Amaryllis* (1977), young people must deal with serious human dilemmas that have been made more difficult by the presence of magic. In *Tuck Everlasting*, one day in 1881, while wandering in the woods beyond her home which she has specifically been forbidden to enter, eleven-year-old Winnie Foster meets Jesse Tuck, son of Angus and Mae Tuck, a family who in 1794 discovered and drank from a spring which gave them eternal youth, but also froze their moral and emotional development. Jesse, although a nice enough fellow, has in effect been a teenager for 104 years, and he quickly develops a crush on Winnie. The story becomes more complex when an outsider, the 'man in the yellow suit', discovers the nature of the spring and plots to exploit both it and the Tucks. Immortality, of course, is one of humanity's dreams, but Babbitt, like so many writers, sees it as being as much a curse as a blessing. The Tucks, although good working-class people, are both emotionally exhausted and terminally bored with their lives, but they can't change. The book's crisis occurs when the man in the yellow suit threatens Winnie and Mae Tuck kills him to protect her and, secondarily, keep the secret of the spring. Babbitt invites her readers to consider whether or not such a murder might in fact be morally necessary. She also provides Winnie with the choice of waiting until she is a bit older and then drinking from the spring in order to become immortal and marry Jesse (which she decides not to do, conferring immortality, instead, on a toad). These complex moral issues and their possibilities for class discussion have made *Tuck Everlasting* a long-time favourite of middle-school teachers.

Although quiet, often bucolic fantasies like those of White and Babbitt continue to be published to this day, the mainstream of children's fantasy in the United States was changed irrevocably by the work of one non-American writer. J. R. R. Tolkien's *The Hobbit* appeared in 1937, but for a number of years was no more than a moderate success in the United States. The first volume of his adult fantasy *The Lord of the Rings* appeared in 1954, and, although it took a few years to catch on, changed everything for both adult and children's fantasy. However, while Tolkien was a turning point, a clue that there was another strand on which to draw was already there, in a branch of fantasy not yet considered as for children.

## The pulps

One of the contentions of this book is that what is understood by 'children's fantasy' is in part shaped not just by ideological ideas of children's behaviour but also by a much simpler definitional criterion, the age at which schooling ends and children enter the adult world. As children began to stay in school longer and the concept of childhood was thus extended in the mind of the public, a new literature developed to satisfy the needs of these older children, one that, in part, took up the genres that such older children had already been enjoying as post-educational younger adults. Massachusetts limited the working hours of children in 1836, mandating at least three months of education a year for children under fifteen, but it was not until 1892 that the Democratic Party adopted a platform to ban children's employment in factories under the age of fourteen years, and only in 1916 that Congress adopted a child labour law which forbade the movement of goods across state lines if minimum age laws were violated. Not until 1938 did the Fair Labor Standards Act actively control child labour, so for many children 'childhood' was a fairly brief period. This was not only a working-class phenomenon: Americans assumed that children would begin earning money quite early on in most social classes; running errands, selling newspapers, acting as messenger boys or clerks. In the depression of the 1930s only a minority of working-class and lower middle-class groups, most notably Jewish immigrants, tried to keep their boys in school. The streets of US movies of the 1930s are populated with working children, particularly boys. Some areas of work – newspaper sales, messenger boys – created entire teams of older children and young men who spent large amounts of time together and who had – once they had contributed to the household budget – money of their own. One of the things they spent it on was pulp fiction.

Developing in the 1830s and 1840s (descended from other forms of popular literature going back hundreds of years earlier) was a tradition of sub-literary fiction or heavily sensationalized non-fiction aimed primarily at the increasingly literate working classes in both Great Britain and the United States: these works included the penny dreadfuls, lurid and sensationalized tales of supposedly true horror, and the slightly later and slightly more upscale dime novels. Although written for adults, such works found their way into the homes of teen readers and were much beloved by that age group.[41]

Enormously popular, though held in contempt by librarians and other pillars of the literary establishment in the United States, the penny dreadfuls and dime novels in particular became some of the best-selling works in the English language. A small but significant minority featured primitive forms of fantasy, such as the British *Varney the Vampire, or the Feast of Blood* (1845–7), variously attributed to Thomas Preskett Prest and James Malcolm Rymer, or, more often, science fiction (which appealed to the practical sensibilities of many working Americans), such as the American Edward Ellis's *The Steam Man of the Prairies* (1868) and the various Frank Reade and Frank Reade Jr stories (beginning in 1876). Some fantasy and science fiction likewise appeared in the later serials produced specifically for children by the Stratemeyer Syndicate (founded in 1905) and numerous other publishers of the type.

Many fans of the later incarnations of the penny dreadfuls, dime novels and serials eventually graduated to what came to be called the 'pulps'. These fiction magazines, produced on cheap pulp paper and aimed largely at a working-class audience, specialized in genre fiction (mysteries, westerns, the fantastic, romance) and, although ostensibly for adults, were once again much beloved by teenagers. Many famous writers got their start in the pulps, including Raymond Chandler and Dashiell Hammett, along with a number of authors of fantasy fiction. Few histories of children's literature devote space to pulp fiction because, strictly speaking, it wasn't written for children, and because it has been widely condemned as sub-literary. Nonetheless it was one of the most powerful influences on children's fantasy literature, particularly for older readers.

Edgar Rice Burroughs (1875–1950) is the key figure: although his most famous character, Tarzan, is a British lord raised by apes in Africa, Burroughs's fiction is intensely American, featuring characters who are

Created by Edward Stratemeyer (1862–1930), the Syndicate churned out hundreds of cheaply made volumes in many popular series for children, all but the earliest produced by ghostwriters using house names. Most of the best-known series, *The Hardy Boys*, *The Bobbsey Twins* and *Nancy Drew*, were largely realist, if often rather implausible. *The Rover Boys* and particularly *Tom Swift* centred on new technologies, with the latter gradually moving into science fiction. The *Great Marvel* series was also science fiction. *Nancy Drew*, the popular series about a girl detective, occasionally included Gothic or borderline fantasy elements. Other series with stronger fantasy content included *Make Believe Stories* and *Bomba, the Jungle Boy*.

self-reliant, paradoxically self-made despite noble ancestry, and intensely egalitarian. Burroughs's two most famous series, *Tarzan* and *Barsoom*, which begin with *Tarzan of the Apes* (1912) and *A Princess of Mars* (1917) respectively, sit on the border between science fiction and fantasy. In terms of popularity and sales, Burroughs was probably the most successful and influential author in the American fantastic pulp tradition, receiving, along with the much less prolific A. Merritt, the highest magazine payment rates in the field.[42] Other successful pulp fantasy writers of the first half of the twentieth century, like H. P. Lovecraft, Merritt, Robert E. Howard and, somewhat later, Ray Bradbury, were also popular with adolescent readers and it is clear that the new American pulp magazines – such as Frank A. Munsey's *The Argosy* (1882–1988 in various formats), *The Popular Magazine* (1903–31), *Weird Tales* (1923–54 and intermittently thereafter), *Amazing Stories* (1926–2004, 2012–), *Astounding Stories* (later *Analog*, 1931 to the present) and *Unknown* (1939–43), along with many others – attracted a strong adolescent following.

Although even those magazines that specifically identified themselves as science fiction did frequently publish fantasy, *Weird Tales* and *Unknown* are perhaps the central publications here. *Weird Tales*, whose best-known editor was Farnsworth Wright, printed a variety of orientalist fiction, Gothic horror and what came to be called sword-and-sorcery. *Unknown*, edited by John W. Campbell, Jr, better known as the editor of *Astounding Science-Fiction*, specialized in stories in which the supernatural elements ran according to clearly defined rules – fantasy for engineers and a latter-day extension of that early American distrust of the fantastic discussed above. Burroughs, Howard and Lovecraft in particular had many literary descendants and had a significant influence on children's fantasy. Burroughs was a strong influence on Andre Norton, whose *Witch World* (1963) had many sequels, and also on Ray Bradbury. Howard, due largely to the renewed interest in and republication of his work in mass-market paperbacks in the 1970s, was widely imitated and became, with Tolkien, a major influence on the original Dungeons and Dragons role-playing fantasy games. In the United States at least, he may be the greatest influence on modern fantasy literature prior to Tolkien. By the end of the period and into the early 1950s, for many older children and younger teens *this* was what American fantasy looked like.

## CHAPTER 4

# British and Empire fantasy between the wars

'Inter-war' is a politically coherent period in Europe: not a term usually used by American critics, it has a very specific cultural meaning. European history of these years feels bracketed by the two world wars. The period between 1918 and 1939 begins with depression, emerges into frivolity and optimism, crashes into the Depression, and ends with the sense from 1936 on that another European war is inevitable. It feels not like a period of peace, but a lull in which, for some, old certainties were to be clung to, while for others they were to be examined and rejected. The period saw the beginning of the end for Britain's Empire. By 1922 most of Ireland was independent of Britain, and became a full republic in 1948. In 1947 India would declare independence. But in the world of children's books this period remained predominantly an export-driven culture in which British books were sent to the colonies.

For a colonial author to be published in the UK in this period required them to be part of the UK community, as was the Australian P. L. Travers. Although a small number of books did travel from Canada and Australia to Britain, American books were yet to arrive in either Britain or the Empire, and for much of the twentieth century a child in New Zealand or Hong Kong was more likely to have read a British author than was an American child. Until very late in the period, the contained feeling of many of the fantasies discussed in this chapter reflects the period's unease, and so too does the sense conveyed in many of the texts that 'out there' is a dangerous place. But some of the crucial issues of the war years also appear: nationality, identities and origins, class antagonism, even the servant shortage that left many middle-class children to roam free relatively unsupervised. Yet, by the end of the nineteenth century a Canadian tradition and hints of an Irish tradition were emerging separately from the British tradition – traditions that were distinctly more rural, less contained and more engaged with the landscape than was the fantasy of Great Britain in the inter-war years.

The inter-war period is discrete in publishing terms: between 1910 and 1917 there is but one title in our bibliography. A. A. Milne's *Once on a Time*, a Thackeray-esque pantomimic parable, was published in 1917, but it was a significant exception and, as Milne wrote in the Preface to the 1925 edition, it 'died quietly, without seriously detracting from the interest which was being taken in the World War, then in progress'.[1] Indeed, the whole field of children's fantasy appears to die quietly during the Great War.[2] Angela Brazil's *A Patriotic Schoolgirl* (1918) is clearly more in tune with the tenor of the times than the leftward-leaning politics of writers such as Nesbit, while fantasy itself might have appeared frivolous to a period not yet accustomed to the great war epics of post-Tolkien fantasy. Not until the 1920s do we have more than two titles per year. Similarly, as the world enters another war and book publishing is crippled by paper rationing, production of fantasy for children again slows down: two titles in 1939, four or five titles for the whole of the 1940s. C. S. Lewis's Edmund, it seems, was starved not just of Turkish delight but of the delights of the fantastic.

There are distinct critical problems in considering this period. This is not a time in which there is a coherent sense of what fantasy *should be*: the authors discussed in this chapter, while clearly influenced by Nesbit, were each exploring for themselves how to write fantasy. A thread of influence links some authors, such as Ida Renthoul Braithwaite and Margaret Lodge, to the Victorian fairy tales. Another link goes back to Thackeray's *The Rose and the Ring* – not a children's book but one highly influential on children's writers such as A. A. Milne and Edward Wyke-Smith – which has been frequently repackaged for children. And there are also links to folklore. There is little, however, to tie together a body of perhaps sixty texts. There are tales of toys and animal companions, and tales of adventures on flying carpets, beds or boats, but what each author does with this material is distinctively different from the others. There are no subgenres as we will understand them in the second half of the twentieth century, and yet, what makes this time so fascinating is precisely that we can see quite clearly a number of elements emerging which, by the end of the period, will have formed the stuff of children's fantasy and its major traditions.

There is a rather weak sense of a children's market in the inter-war period. Much of what we have described as children's literature is clearly satire, with a dual audience. The resulting tension can be seen in three texts: A. A. Milne's *Once on a Time* (1917), Esther Boumphey's *The Hoojibahs* (1929) and the first version of T. H. White's *The Sword in the Stone* (1939). The preface to the second edition of Milne's book states, 'I shall say boldly that this is a story for grown-ups'; and in doing so looks back to Thackeray's *The Rose and the Ring*.[3] It is a modern fairy tale, an elaboration of the formula 'once there was a magic ring'. Although the creation of a secondary world is convincing, it is told utterly tongue in cheek. A King is persuaded into war by a conspiring Countess, while his daughter is baffled, and a small child's magic ring drives the plot. The narrator claims to be writing a new history of the Euralian–Barodian war, which contradicts the seventeen tomes of Roger Scurvilegs, and belief in the tale is both created and compromised by this narrative voice, for the story is told as a long series of jokes, poking fun at the two Kings, the Prince and the Countess for their conceit. The jokes are essentially adult ones about pomposity in love and war.

In *The Hoojibahs* there is a sense of laughing *at* rather than with children. When a painter fails to complete a road sign, the road extending from it rolls up, hiding the village from everyone. Left to themselves, the houses and trees in the village start to play, until, that is, the Hoojibahs turn up. The Hoojibahs want to be human but don't know how: they have often figured out only bits, for example that policemen direct traffic. So the Hoojibahs kidnap Lucy to explain the world to them. She organizes them (by size) into Mummies, Daddies and children (one of the children has a beard) and sends the Daddies to make bread and butter in an office and the children to school where she teaches them letters they already know, and to read, which they already do better than she does.

The most famous of the satires of this period is T. H. White's *The Sword in the Stone*. It has a complex publishing history that takes it out of the realm of the children's fantastic, so for the purposes of this book we will stick to the very first iteration, which is not a novel but a series of distinct stories, linked loosely within a narrative of the education of a boy. While some stories – such as that where Wart is turned into a fish – are clearly fantastical, contemporary satire is foremost. Kay and Wart do not go to Eton because a giant is blocking the route; when Wart joins the birds of prey for a night, he finds himself in an officers' mess, in which there is at least one very badly shell-shocked senior officer; there are continual references to contemporary institutions. Alongside this are references to viruses, economics and war. For all of the book's whizz and frivolity, it is both didactic and adult. Children get great pleasure out of *The Sword in the Stone*, but if we omit the discussion of Kay's career as a bully, then this is a book whose concerns are modern politics, in which the fantastic is an amusing access route. Not until the later books in White's

*Once and Future King* tetralogy – aimed primarily at an adult audience – does he engage deeply with fantasy, and this is through the growing tradition of the heroic romance.

Along with satire are books of the absurd. J. B. S. Haldane's *My Friend Mr Leakey* (1937) is a collection of tales of whimsy rather than fantasy. 'The Story of the Rats', for example, recounts increasingly absurd attempts to deal with clever rats at the Port Authority. Eric Linklater's *The Wind on the Moon* (1944) is best thought of as a novelization of a Hilaire Belloc naughty child poem. When Dorina's and Dinah's father goes away, they become fed up with good deeds going awry and resolve to be bad. This ranges from eating themselves into round balls (and later crying off the fat) to using magic potions from a witch to bring the pigeons on the wallpaper to life. All the other characters are distinguished by Happy Families nomenclature (Catherine Crumb the baker's daughter) and the tale's tweeness sometimes grates. At the end, the magic stops after they rescue their father from a dungeon and the witch goes to the Sahara for her rheumatism. The Australian Norman Lindsay's *The Magic Pudding: Being the Adventures of Bunyip Bluegum and his Friends Bill Barnacle and Sam Sawnoff* (1930) is a nonsensical caper, in which humans, anthropomorphized animals and a talking pudding engage in Laurel and Hardy-style adventures. Childish language and wilful misunderstanding combine with Land of Cockayne-style fantasy and Gilbert and Sullivan-style songs, illustrated with extraordinarily vibrant cartoons. Brenda Niall argues that it is a trickster tale: 'It has no moral lesson. The struggle for possession of the magic pudding ... has nothing to do with rights. The adversaries are all tricksters and victory goes to the more ingenious strategists', which may actually be an indication of its very Australianness, embodying the concept of the free life, unfettered from constraints, which underpinned the marketing of Australia.[4] As literature, the book stands alone: it has no emulators and is part of no fantastic tradition, even within Australia, and reads today as a fireside tale rather than a children's book. As we shall see in later chapters, most Australian fantasy for older children has developed within the European tradition.

## Is children's fantasy worth writing about?

Another factor in the study of inter-war children's fantasy is that we have little in the way of contemporary criticism: unlike the nineteenth century, there is no group of writers discussing their work in letters, and the infrastructure of literary criticism of children's fiction was in its infancy. The first books that we have are from the USA: Anne Carroll Moore's *Roads to Childhood* (1920), *New Roads to Childhood* (1923) and *The Three Owls* (1925); in addition there are Frenchman Paul Hazard's *Children, Books and Men* (1944) and New Zealander Dorothy Neal White's *About Books for Children* (1946); but none of these has strong concerns with fantasy. Of the most immediate post-war commentators, Roger Lancelyn Green, an important collector and reteller of hero tales, published *Teller of Tales* in 1946, but none of the fantasy authors he discusses (Carroll, MacDonald, Nesbit, Barrie, Grahame and Kipling) are important to the inter-war period. There are interesting discussions by C. S. Lewis in his essay 'On Stories' and by J. R. R. Tolkien in 'On Fairy-Stories', in the collected *Essays Presented to Charles Williams* (1945), but these are very general.

The first book from the UK to consider *contemporary* children's fiction in depth and to make a significant attempt to consider fantasy (and one which influenced this book enormously) was *Tales Out of School: A Survey of Children's Literature* (1948) by Geoffrey Trease. Trease was a writer of children's historical fiction, a genre which was to travel alongside fantasy in the immediate post-war period, but in the inter-war years appears to have had little interaction with it. He was reviewing for *The New Statesman* (a left-wing publication) when he was approached by the New Education Book Club to write a book about contemporary children's literature. Trease as a radical writer was engaged with a growing argument that the Empire's children needed to be educated in very different, more collaborative and more liberal values than those inherited from the nineteenth century. Frequently this led the Left to revivalism, and he identifies the folk revival that took place in the late nineteenth and the early twentieth centuries as one of the strongest elements influencing the shape of the English-language children's fantasy story, both in this period and beyond.

Trease as a critic was not particularly keen on fantasy: too much of it was 'sob stuff', by which he may have meant the sentimental nineteenth-century tales of fairies, aimed increasingly at the younger child. Trease thought the best children's fantasy was to be found in dragon stories (he himself had written a play, *The Dragon Who Was Different*, 1938) – stories rooted in myth and legend. Although he praised the originality of Mary Norton's *The Magic Bed-Knob* (1943) and *Bonfires and Broomsticks* (1945), his real interest was in what he saw as the *matter* of British fantasy, the earthy folk and fairy tale. He lists Padraic Colum, Charles J. Finger, Rachel Field, Eleanor Farjeon and Elsie Byrde among others, but essentially misses many of the names that have come to typify the period to post-war readers.[5]

Finally, one problem for the critic is that there is a false coherence to the inter-war period because it is bracketed by two fantasy writers – one before and one after – who are significant not only because they are excellent but also because each in turn handed on a set of ideas of what fantasy for children should look like which continues to structure fantasy for children to this day. At the beginning of the century we have Edith Nesbit, and much of the fantasy of the inter-war period operates within the traditions she established: fantasies in which children discover an element of fantasy intruding into their world, or in which they go on adventures facilitated by magical conveyances. Shortly after the war, in 1950, comes the publication of C. S. Lewis's *The Lion, the Witch and the Wardrobe* which was to position religion, immanence, destiny and other worlds at the centre of fantasy for children, and radically change what we understand children's fantasy to be. One of the difficult things when discussing inter-war fantasy is to avoid under-rating those few fantasies that do not emulate Nesbit or else do not conform to post-war and post-Lewis expectations.

## Spinning new strands of fantasy

If we are to find any coherence, we need in this chapter to begin considering children's fantasy not as a homogeneous whole, but rather as strands that were beginning to spin off into the distinct threads of subgenres that emerged after the war. These strands roughly comprise folk tales, fairy-oriented fantasy, 'new fairy tales' satire and magical adventures with toys, animals or gods. In several of these forms we also see the first stirrings of the portal fantasies. We will begin with the rise of folklore, its absorption into the stuff of fantasy and the development of a new fairy tradition.

For the most part, once we move into the modern fantasy period, this book does not concern itself with the collection or retelling of folk and fairy tales, but so many of the Irish,[6] Empire and Commonwealth authors of the 1950s through the 1970s were profoundly immersed in the collections and retellings of the nineteenth and early twentieth centuries that it is necessary to be aware of the richness of material that was emerging to understand the sense of depth that many critics have observed in their work. Furthermore, while the collectors of folk and fairy tale may have seen their work as distinct, the readers of stories of the fantastic extended their interest to these tales. One of the consequences of the integration of folklore into the children's fantastical tradition, is that the concerns of folklorists with national identity and international commonality became part of children's fantasy, shaping distinct national traditions, and embedding in it a set of ideas that had strong ideological positions whose consequences became visible in the second half of the twentieth century.

The heyday of folk tale collection ran from the 1870s through to the beginning of the Great War and into the early 1920s, with a revival in Ireland and Germany as a consequence of those countries' nationalistic projects, and also in Canada as nation-building got underway in the inter-war years. The period discussed here saw the translation of many of these tales into popular works for children and their embedding as part of the British child's literary and national education.[7] The first significant example may be Kipling's *Puck of Pook's Hill* (1906). Many children would also have read collections intended for adults and often understood by the authors and collectors as being anthropological or antiquarian studies. Andrew Lang is perhaps the best-known example, his 'coloured' fairy books being staples on many children's shelves.

Andrew Lang (1844–1912) was a prolific author of numerous popular and scholarly works on anthropology, history and literature, including *Custom and Myth* (1884). His many novels include the fantasies *Prince Prigio* (1889) and *The World's Desire* (with H. Rider Haggard, 1890). He is best remembered today for his twelve beautifully illustrated collections of folk tales, beginning with *The Blue Fairy Book* (1889) and including *The Red Fairy Book* (1890) and *The Green Fairy Book* (1892). Like other intellectuals of his day, Lang was also involved in psychic research and in 1911 served as president of the still-extant Society for Psychical Research.

The major nineteenth-century collectors and retellers – Lady Wilde, Lady Gregory, W. B. Yeats, Douglas Hyde, James Curtin and Andrew Lang – saw themselves not as fiction writers but as observers and pre-servers of a culture in decline. The roots of this movement are complex and intensely political, linked to rising nationalism across Europe, to the restiveness of subject peoples from the Irish to the Hungarians, and also to new ideas about racial identities. One of the strongest cultural strands feeding into fantasy came from the Scandinavian collectors. Unusually, this was a movement from the centre, begun in 1630 when Gustavus Adolphus instructed parish priests to collect local folklore. Scandinavia, like the British Isles, comprised a number of nations anxious to assert cultural individuality, but it also, fortuitously for the Irish and Scottish nationalist collectors, shared a mythlore with those two countries, creating a pan-nationalist movement. In Ireland folklore and fairy tale eventually became a crucial element in nation-building in the 1930s, with the establishment of the Irish Folklore Commission in 1935 (a body with very strong links to Scandinavian folklorists). Although Welsh folklore as a whole seems to have received relatively little attention, the translations produced by Lady Charlotte Guest between 1838 and 1839 were significant contributions to the stuff of fantasy. One of the most important single texts was Sydney Lanier's *The Boy's Mabinogion* (1881).[8] This took Welsh myth beyond Arthurian tales (although the series to which it belonged included a *Boy's Arthur*, 1880) into the Matter of Britain, and was to have a profound influence on Kenneth Morris (who published *The Book of the Three Dragons* for children in 1930) and on post-war writers: Alan Garner, Susan Cooper and Lloyd Alexander, among others.

Fairy tales published in the period include James Stephens's *Irish Fairy Tales* (1920), W. J. Glover's *British Fairy and Folk Tales* (1920), George Douglas's *Scottish Fairy Tales* (1920) and Ruth Bryan Owen's *The Castle in the Silver Wood* (1939). The dominance of Irish stories in the new collections was fed in part by nostalgia among the prosperous children of Irish and Scottish émigrés in America and Canada. The fairy tale market, unlike the children's book market as a whole, was cross-Atlantic, with many American collectors and retellers writing for the Dublin and London publishers, and a number of simultaneous publications. By the 1920s Irish folk and fairy tales were influencing the new children's fantasy. W. W. Tarn's *The Treasure of the Isle of Mist* (1919) begins as a very traditional Irish folk tale, in which help given to a pedlar leads to a quest and entry into an animist world in which trees and rivers and mountains are the repositories of immanence. Patricia Lynch's justly acclaimed *The Turf-Cutter's Donkey* (1934) similarly begins with very traditional Irish fairy tale tropes, such as a silver tea pot left by tinkers, and an encounter with a leprechaun.

If these stories could bind nations, they could bind nations into empires. This period saw a rising number of fairy tales from the Empire translated into the English language and into British mores. Dewan Sharar's *Hindu Fairy Tales* (1936), Blanche Vaile's *Fairy Tales from New Zealand* (1928), Mary Frere's *Fairy Tales from India* (1926) and Edith Howes's *Maoriland Fairy Tales* (1913, but with several reissues during the period) all served British audiences as fanciful travelogues. In Australia the indigenous writer David Unaipon – also an inventor and lecturer – published a number of stories in the *Sydney Daily Telegraph*, later collected by the anthropologist William Ramsay Smith and only recently republished under the author's own name. These tales became the ur-material for many white Australian fantasy writers.

The folklore movement was imbued with an attitude of primitivism. Collectors – both native and outsider – saw the existence of folklore as a retention of the past, of the primitive. Elizabeth Andrews drew on the work of David MacRichie and Sir Harry Johnston – who conjectured that African pygmies might possibly have populated the outer reaches of Western Europe – in order to argue that the old Ulster tales referred to lost races. Ulster fairies, Andrews noted, were not the tiny fairies of Victorian fancy (and of this period of children's fantasy), but were instead child-sized or even larger, an idea that survives into modern fantasy. Eleanor Hull's *Folklore of the British Isles* (1928) quite noticeably relegates English folk tales to the distant past, placing the liveliest traditions in Ireland, Scotland and Wales, areas that English writers regularly portrayed in literature as simultaneously backward and romantic. Katharine Briggs's work after the war positions the local British stories she collected as very much part of a distant faded past. A result of this primitivism was that in the nineteenth century and well into the twentieth, many of the fairy and folk tale collections came from *elsewhere*, from places still supposedly closer to their primitive roots.

Thus there was a significant influx of folk material from those areas of the world already a focus for orientalist fascination. Japonisme was at its height in the late nineteenth century, as shown by Gilbert and Sullivan's *The Mikado* (1885). We can still see the influence of chinoiserie in the pantomime of *Aladdin*: traditionally Aladdin's mother, Widow Twankey, works in a Chinese laundry. For children, the publisher Philip Allan brought out a series of *Wonder Tales*, including *Wonder Tales of Old Japan* (1924). Grace James offered *Green Willow and Other Japanese Fairy Tales* (1923) and N. Kato published *Children's Stories from Japanese Fairy Tales and Legends* (1926). These tales are distinctive in their combination of moral messages – the role of humility for high and low – and their animism. Their world is casually magical. No one is surprised when a fox talks, or a dragon-serpent guards a bridge, nor when gods intervene in the lives of men, and many of the tales of the zodiac, translated into the loves of princesses for herdsmen, have the same quality of the here and now that the Greek myths contain.

The popularity of fairy tales, although linked to nationalism, was also linked to internationalism. For many internationalists (not automatically of the Left), the more one knew and understood others, the easier it would be to avoid the misunderstandings which lead to war. Thus we have A. J. Glinksi's *Polish Fairy Tales* (1920), Parker Fillmore's *Mighty Mikko: A Book of Finnish Fairy Tales and Folk Tales* (1922) and even Gerald Friedlander's *Jewish Fairy Tales* (1922), along with general collections such as Romer Wilson's series, *Green Magic, Silver Magic* and *Red Magic* (1928, 1929 and 1930 respectively), all subtitled *A Collection of the World's Best Fairy Tales from All Countries*. Russian tales had entered the British Isles in the seventeenth century, thanks to Samuel Collins, an Oxford doctor; and the work of Afanas'ev, the Russian ethnographer, had resulted in the publication in serial form of a range of tales between 1855 and 1864. The works of Pushkin and Gogol retelling, respectively, Russian and Ukrainian folk tales had sought to Westernize many of these tales and render them acceptable to the elites of their society. The Russian Revolution and the arrival of White refugees encouraged the favourable reception of retellings, among which the best known is Arthur Ransome's *Old Peter's Russian Tales* (1916). The Bolshoi ballet company's performance of *Swan Lake* in London in 1911 helped create a popular consciousness of romantic Russia, as did famous Russian ballet dancer Anna Pavlova, who settled in London from 1912.

There was a rising demand for education from the middle classes and the working poor, and the nationalist impulse behind the folk and fairy tale revival contributed to some of the material designed to meet it. In this period we see the repurposing, revival and retelling of Greek, Roman and early medieval European hero tales. After the war, Roger Lancelyn Green would dominate the retelling of classical tales, but before it a number of other authors stood out, especially Enid Blyton, who published *Tales of Ancient Greece* (1930), *Adventures of Odysseus* (1934) and *Tales of the Ancient Greeks and Persians* (1934), and Padraic Colum, who wrote *The Golden Fleece and the Heroes Who Lived Before Achilles* (1921).[9] In the 1920s and 1930s Britain was not a cohesive society; it was split by poverty, class warfare and competing national identities, and the interest in these classical legends reflected a growing desire to foster a greater sense of national identity in a contested space. They were intended to create a sense of common heritage in European culture.

The retellings of more local hero stories, however, may have been targeted at more particularist identities. As Stephens and McCallum discuss in *Retelling Stories, Framing Culture* (1998), of the range of possible hero stories from the British Isles the three that emerged as dominant were the Robin Hood tales, from the north of England, the Irish tales of the Kings, and Arthuriana. Although firmly non-fantastical for most of its history, the legend of the greenwood became itself a mystical trope in the work of later fantasy writers and thus needs to be included here. Robin Hood had received some attention from the writers and scholars of the early nineteenth century who had sought to appropriate him as a symbol of England and liberal nationalism, the Robin Hood of Walter Scott's hugely popular novel *Ivanhoe* acting as template for stories that were witty but essentially genteel. In the twentieth century, however, Robin Hood was reframed to reflect a land divided into rich and poor, in which the return of the King was not necessarily the solution to all ills. In 1933 Michael Tippett produced the ballad opera *Robin Hood* which contained the lines: 'So God he made the outlaws / To beat the devil's man / To rob the rich, to defend the poor / By Robin's ten year plan' – lines which have rather pro-Soviet implications. Geoffrey Trease's *Bows against the Barons* (1934) was even more forceful, linking him instead to a popular revolt, as too did Bernard Miles's version of Robin Hood performed at the Unity Theatre in 1938. These texts fed into new ideas of Englishness, stirring beneath the surface since *Puck of Pook's Hill*, and expressed in this period in Hilda Lewis's *The Ship that Flew* (1939). This was an Englishness that reached back to an Anglo-Saxon identity and with it a sense of commonality with the other peoples of the British Isles, and drew on tales of Hereward the Wake and other rebels to feed the new fantasy.

Arthur had been a popular source of romance in the sixteenth century, but had been banished in the seventeenth as being too secular. He and his court took part in the Gothic revival and then in the high tide of Romanticism, emerging as part of the iconography of Victorianism (Victoria and Albert had their portraits painted in the costumes of Guinevere and Arthur). 'Tennyson's *Idylls of the King* made the legends a household word in Victorian England';[10] they were popularized by Wagner's *Tristan* and *Parsifal*, and again by William Morris's poem *The Defence of Guenevere*, and also in Algernon Swinburne's *Tristram of Lyonesse*. Alongside all of this written and musical material was the work of the Pre-Raphaelite painters and artisans, like William Morris, Dante Gabriel Rossetti and Sir Edward Burne-Jones. They passed on the matter to their descendants but the image of Arthur as a holy warrior would not survive the Great War; Charles Williams, one of the Inklings, published the poem *Taliessin through Logres* in 1938 but by the inter-war period Arthur had become a more mundane figure. What he had not become is more Welsh; Welsh culture had been in decline since the final defeat of Owain Glyndwr in 1409; Welsh was excluded from the law courts in 1536, and from all offices of the kingdom.

The Inklings was a writing and literary discussion group centred on Oxford University from the early 1930s to the late 1940s. The two members of the group of most interest to students of children's fantasy are, of course, C. S. Lewis and J. R. R. Tolkien, but Roger Lancelyn Green was also a children's writer and scholar of some importance and Charles Williams was a significant author of religious fantasies. Inklings member Owen Barfield, a noted literary scholar, also wrote one fantasy novel. Among the classic works previewed in rough draft at Inklings meetings were Tolkien's *The Lord of the Rings* (which was not much liked by Lewis or Barfield), Lewis's *Out of the Silent Planet* and Williams's *All Hallows' Eve*. The American-born Mythopoeic Society, founded in 1967, is dedicated to the study of the work of the Inklings and gives annual prizes for both scholarly and creative work that either discusses or emulates the fiction of Tolkien, Lewis and Williams. The British Tolkien Society, founded in 1969, is a similar though more narrowly focused group. Both organizations sponsor events commemorating the Inklings around the world.

In the nineteenth century the spread of mass education brought the issue to the fore: a parliamentary commission (1847) produced a report, written by three Englishmen, which condemned the morals of the Welsh and blamed poor educational outcomes on English-language teaching to Welsh children. Unfortunately the recommended remedy was to ban Welsh in many schools. This, combined with the influx of English-speakers in the early twentieth century, meant that the language was in sharp decline by the 1911 census. The pushback began in the 1930s after the government refused to hear a Welsh-language deputation protesting a new air base, and by 1932 there was Welsh radio broadcasting. One reason for the rise of Arthuriana may have been an attempt to create a joint mythology for England and Wales during a period of deliberate nation-building, but the evidence is poor. The Welsh association with Arthur is utterly stripped from the period: he is a British hero, not a Welsh one, and this would not be corrected until Susan Cooper's *The Dark is Rising* sequence (1965–77).

In contrast, the Irish hero tales of old kings and of the Fianna were central to the constructions of Irish identity at the end of the nineteenth century. In his introduction to *Irish Myths and Legends*, W. B. Yeats placed these tales less as heroic in the nineteenth-century sense, but rather as being similar to Greek hero myth: tales of interactions between men and women and their environment, tales of love and loss, of warfare and death, revolving around the choice of good deaths, or ethical lives, but rarely around abstract longings or visionary imperatives. Theirs were very material gods, expressing bitterness and spite as humans do. In the twentieth century, as Ireland moved towards and into independence, and as the Irish-American migration developed the nostalgia that would be such a distinctive element of its diaspora, new voices such as Kenneth Morris, Charles W. Finger, Douglas Hyde and Padraic Colum began to retell the hero stories with an eye to more accurate translations or towards creating a different kind of audience. These retellings were vital to the post-Second World War development of Empire and Commonwealth fantasy, but they were not significant in and of themselves to the publication trends of this period.

The nineteenth-century stories with fairies, in which children meet fairies and are thus thrust into an adventure, were also declining. This may be linked to the loss of faith in the Cottingley Fairies, the fairy photographs created by two children, Elsie Wright and Frances Griffiths, in 1917, which Sir Arthur Conan Doyle, paradoxically a spiritualist as well as the author of Sherlock Holmes, foolishly publicized as real. These tales continued, but were for younger children. In 'On Fairy-Stories' Tolkien reserved much of his wrath for the modern tale in which a child met a fairy, usually smaller than herself, and was taken off on an adventure in which moral lessons were learned and in which the sweetness and delicacy of the fairy were somehow held up for the usually female child to emulate.[11] These tales were predominantly a late nineteenth-century phenomenon but their day was not yet past, although it was noticeable that they no longer had a dual-audience effect. They were definitely for children.

A good example of the kind of literature that Tolkien may have been describing is Ida and Genbry Outhwaite's *The Enchanted Forest* (1921), in which Anne rides her pony Dandy into the wood to find her rabbit, Peter Pottifer. She is thrown and, when she lands, it is to find herself a fairy with wings, accompanied by Peter, a little boy in fur-skin. The two children then have adventures with teddy bears and fairies, until they return to the real world, where Anne discovers that she has been missing all night and a baby seen in fairyland is her new brother. When she looks in the rabbit hutch, Peter Pottifer is back. In this vision, fairyland is an ideal playground. Similarly, Dearmer Mac Cormac's *Patty Who Believed in Fairies* (1928) is aimed perhaps at five-year-olds although it has clear links to the dual audience of *The Water-Babies*. Patty's mother writes fairy stories but she tells them to Patty beforehand, so Patty believes in fairies. The Dream Fairy begs for a wish: that her favourite mortal may spend a day and night in fairyland. Patty receives a guided tour whose general

theme is fairy babies in flowers and the care of baby bunnies by earth
fairies. A sea baby who leaves his nursery without permission becomes
ashamed for doing so, because obedience is the true source of happiness.
The Canadian writer Basil R. Campbell took a very similar tack with
*Tony* (1933), as Tony is also rewarded for his belief by a trip to fairyland,
but to make the story work, Tony had to be written *very* young. The
same is true of the Canadian Carol Cassidy Cole's *Velvet Paws and Shiny
Eyes*, a small hand-sized book published in Toronto in 1922, but also in
England in 1933 in an edition which is very much larger, both with animal cut-outs stored as inserts in paper pockets. In *Velvet Paws and Shiny
Eyes* Cole's small hero Eric is turned into an elf because he is unkind to
animals, and is educated by his adventures with the (named and com-
municative) animals around him. When he wakes from his dream he is
thoroughly reformed. Similarly, in Cole's *Little Big Ears and the Princess*
(1926), Princess Rosalie (who lives in Canada but is definitely a princess)
becomes friendly with a rabbit who introduces her to all the other animals of the forest from whom she learns moral lessons.

The dominant theme in Canadian children's books in the inter-war
period is clearly adventure in the wilderness and an awareness and knowledge of wildlife, sometimes merging the world of fairy with the world
of the forest. These tales might have been included further on in our
discussion of animal tales or toy tales but the animals in these texts often
appropriate the role of fairies as both moral guide and practical guide in a
magical world, though this magical world is often mundane, in the sense
that it is the real world of the forest.

A rare contribution to this genre from Australia was May Gibbs's
*Snugglepot and Cuddlepie*, which first appeared in 1918 but was collected
as *The Complete Adventures of Snugglepot and Cuddlepie* in 1946. These
anthropomorphic tales animated two gumnuts (the seeds of the Banksia
flower) as brothers and sent them out into the world to have the kind of
adventure usually enjoyed by small children.

## New fairy tales

What Trease recognized as the core of fantasy in the inter-war period
was the new fairy tales, real attempts to write new tales in the old form.
New fairy tales, as opposed to retellings, caught on for a range of reasons
in the nineteenth century. But the new tales of this period functioned
at the axis of folk, fairy and, in the case of Walter de la Mare, the supernatural. In *Broomsticks and Other Tales* (1925) de la Mare's stories have the

folk tale's characteristic bagginess and use of reported speech, but their content draws on Edith Nesbit's awareness that the magical is all around us, and their themes pass from the absurd to the eerie. In 'Pigtails, Ltd' a spinster convinces herself that she has lost a little girl, and after creating a home for thirty little girls who meet the right description, she herself begins to dwindle until she is the little girl she once imagined, while the other thirty never age. In 'Alice's Godmother' Alice is invited by her many times great-great-grandmother to join her in her house to evade Death.

Not all of the new fairy tales took the same form. Alison Uttley produced two collections in this period, *Moonshine and Magic* (1932) and *Candlelight Tales* (1936). The first of these collects beast fables and uses proverbs and sayings as the basis for fanciful tales. In 'The Bull in the China Shop', a sick woman sends her cat to find someone who can both mind the china shop and stand the teasing of bad Tommy. Finally, the bull offers to help in the shop, polishes the china and tosses Tommy out of the shop. Other tales in the collection have an eeriness descended from Grimm. In 'Tom Miller and his Shadow' a boy loses his shadow to one too many tricks, and finds it again in a circus in old age. In *Candlelight Tales* Uttley turned away from the fanciful to the almost deliberately mundane, as she took old nursery rhymes and sought to make them intimate through explanation. Unfortunately, the removal of fancy rendered them banal.

More successful than Uttley in reducing the fanciful while still staying within the realms of the fantastic, was Eleanor Farjeon's *Martin Pippin in the Apple-Orchard* (1921). As with Uttley, these are rationalized tales, stripped of their magic, but Farjeon's versions move us towards the revival of the courtly tale of knights, romance and great deeds that was to become a strong element of genre fantasy in the twentieth century. A more fanciful collection is her *Italian Peepshow* (1926) which mixes fantasy retellings of nursery stories and occasional new fairy tales such as 'Rosaura's Birthday' in which a young woman who wants to stay young is turned into a marionette, and 'The King of Tripoli Brings Pasta', a *pour quoi* or just-so story in which King Nero of Tripoli begs the sea for its shells, and the churches for their bells, and as he gives away this largesse to his starving people it turns to pasta.

In their best work, both Farjeon and Uttley developed a voice that we will later see developed further in the work of Joan Aiken – a kind of blithe sideways look at the world. Almost more 'Aikenish' is Richard Hughes's *The Spider's Palace and Other Tales* (1931), whose stories are often absurd and fantastical rather than fantasy. In 'Telephone Travel' a little girl answers a phone and travels down the phone line to a new house. There she is cosseted and makes a nuisance of herself until Fireworks Night when she is given a rocket which lifts her up and drops her in her own home again. In 'The Old Queen' a young king and queen help a fairy to make them magic cloaks in which they will live forever, but the fairy doesn't concentrate, and the king's is never made. The couple grow old together and the king dies, but the queen is ruling still. There is a darkness here that draws us back to the rootstock of the arbitrariness of the true fairy tale.

One of the most interesting strands of new fairy tales comes from Canada. Here there appears to have been a conscious attempt to blend Irish, Scottish, English, African and indigenous peoples' stories and to combine them with the specific landscape of Canada. Palmer Cox's *Brownie* series – elaborate pictures accompanied by epic poetry suitable for children – tackle such subjects as 'The Brownie and the Whale', and it is noticeable that there is always an Indian (First Nations) brownie among the group of otherwise rather Irish-looking characters.[12] The most notable of the collectors/remixers were Cyrus Macmillan, 'Maxine' and Howard Angus Kennedy. Macmillan's *Canadian Wonder Tales* (1918) and *Canadian Fairy Tales* (1922) came out in both Canada and England, a dual publication common in this period. The *Wonder Tales* are a mixture of fairy stories in Canadian settings and animal tales. The foreword describes the tales as 'gathered in various parts of Canada':

> The author's method resembles that followed by the brothers Grimm a century ago. He has taken down from the lips of living people, pretty much as they were given to him, a series of stories which obviously contain many elements that have been handed down by oral tradition from some far-off past.[13]

This was a very real attempt to create a Canadian folklore: they are blended stories, with a pick-and-mix approach to tropes and storylines. Although the stories treat Indians as one homogeneous group, they also do the same to Europeans.

Meanwhile, other writers were starting to use fairies in more subversive ways, which increasingly used fantasy to negotiate a route out of their lived world rather than enjoining children to accept their realities. Margaret Lodge, while still understanding fairy tales as for younger children, succeeded in reimagining the form for the 1920s. Lodge updated the tone of the tale and introduced as protagonist the kind of modern girl who populated the girls' stories aimed at older readers. *A Fairy to Stay*

(1928) is a practical and sensible fantasy that uses the common school-story trope of the period in which there is a clash between modern and old-fashioned child-rearing methods. Pamela lives with two elderly aunts. Her hair is kept in a long pigtail, she is educated at home, and only allowed out with the aunts or the maid. She longs to bob her hair, play outside, go to school and join the Brownies. Pamela meets a fairy just after the aunts have confiscated her fairy-book as being too childish, and shortly after, in a fit of misery, she cuts off her pigtail. The fairy offers to try to convince the aunts that they are wrong. Most of what the fairy does is naughtiness, but fascinatingly, it is couched as a pedagogical argument, giving to the aunts what they claim to agree with: discipline in the form of sharp punishment. However, this approach doesn't work and the aunts become more and more irritated with Pamela's fairy. In the end it is Pamela's final three wishes – to go to school, to be a Brownie and for the aunts to love her – which make the difference. She gets her wishes, but with the wish comes forgetfulness.

Lodge's later book, *The Wishing Wood* (1930), makes a similar argument about the nature of childhood. Two girls go to stay with their childless great-aunt and great-uncle. Great Aunt Susan is kind, Great Uncle James is gruff. The girls find a wishing wood and make a wish to be able to move around quickly. They get the gift of a sort of skim-skip, which will last as long as they don't wash their feet or until the end of the moon phase. Anxious to share their luck, they first tempt a rather plain, spoiled girl into wishing (she opts for beauty and becomes so impossible that it's a relief when she falls into a pond and her wish is over); then the chauffeur, who wants to go at sixty miles an hour; then their great-aunt, who wants them to behave like their grandmother did as a girl (very prim and sober – it is a painful day); then their great-uncle, who wants to feel like an eight-year-old boy. At the end everyone forgets everything. Lodge's concern with modernity produces an interesting marriage between the fairy story, Nesbit's sense of magical chaos, and the girls' adventure.

Some of the fairy tales mutate quite clearly into early portal fantasies. The Canadian Grant Balfour's *On Golden Wings through Wonderland* (1927) concerns two children, Robin and Mary, both below school age. The gender descriptions are a little unusual for their day. Robin, the boy, is described as kind, while although Mary is given the quality of gentleness, she is also described as more adventurous. Only when Mary is away does Robin meet the Queen of Fairyland who gives him the power to understand animals: this he uses to open a school for squirrels, which is then described in terms we have come to associate with doll-play. In contrast, when Mary is kidnapped by a giant, the Queen gives her wings, and it is she who has most of the adventures. The novel begins with a garden fantasy of the kind we discussed in Chapter 2, then moves out from the confinement of the garden into a wider and more exciting world to become a distinctly Canadian hybrid animal adventure in which hawks, bears and lions are vital participants, and the children – in a motif that will become very familiar – make friends with the indigenous people who are the rightful rulers of the areas contested by the giants. Finally the story moves into a late nineteenth-century moral tale in which a fairy grandmother turns out to be their mother, and the lion is transmuted into their father. The novel's adventures have accumulated in a rather ad hoc manner, but there is never any question that they are real; Canadian fantasy does not seem to have passed through a dream justification stage. What stands out, however, is how much it is assumed by early Canadian fantasy writers that adventure for children, whether in mimetic or fantastic literature, should take place in the outdoors. This stands in sharp contrast to the enclosed garden and house fantasies that were still, to a great extent, the norm in British fantasy of the same period, although they were yielding to a sense that there was a playground *over there beyond the portal* in which children might have adventures.

Douglas A. Anderson asserts that E. A. Wyke Smith's *The Marvellous Land of Snergs* (1927) inspired Tolkien's *The Hobbit*.[14] The positive inspiration is clearly confined to the Snergs themselves who look remarkably like hobbits (although without the charm) and who hold feasts at any excuse. *The Marvellous Land of Snergs* owes most to *Peter Pan* in its attitude to childhood, and anticipates White's *The Sword in the Stone* in terms of its structure and grab-bag approach to fantasy. It sticks to the common form in this period of retaining the child protagonists as the central focus of adventure and fantasy. The land of the Snergs is a Ruritanian island, which is reachable from here, and is timeless. The children are there as part of an experiment in child-rearing by the ladies of the Society for the Removal of Superfluous Children. Dressing all alike, they spend much of their day playing on the beach.[15] There are Flying Dutchmen resident on the island, and across the river are the Snergs. When Sylvia and Joe, the naughtiest children, cross the river, they meet a Snerg called Gorbo who is the usual faux parent figure, even though he is depicted as not very clever. They are forced to escape from an Ogre, they meet Sir Perceval and an Arthurian court, and eventually come home as heroes. Once again, fairyland is a place that is rather keen on young human adventurers. Where the earliest of the fairy stories tended to take humans into fairy so that they might be shown fairyland, these tales posit human saviours, a change from simple adventurers to colonial rulers of a sort first seen in the USA in *The Wonderful Wizard of Oz* but previously unknown in British Empire fiction.

In *Through the Enchanted Wood: Being Some Account of the Adventures of Peggy and Michael among Modern Fairies* (1931) by Hampden Gordon, the twins share a dream of an enchanted wood, but this is not the usual sort of dream because they can both control it and bring things out of it. In one instance, they persuade a giant to take a bath in a pool so that in the waking world a dam breaks and water is brought to their parched garden. When their uncle declares he needs inspiration, they visit the Nine Muses. When he needs a name for a character, they visit the character and trick her into giving them her name. And finally, they go on a treasure hunt and bring back a gold watch and a gold brooch. Although the adventures are real rather than mere dreams, they lack the context of the portal fantasy as it will emerge later: there is none of what science-fiction writer Ken MacLeod calls "learning the world," no feeling that a great mission is in the offing, no sense of tourism.

The same is not true of the book's indirect sequel *The Golden Keys: Being Some Further Account of Adventures with Paradoc, the Gnome, among Modern Fairies* (1932) which does begin to show these traits. The role of fairies begins to shift in these stories. Increasingly fairies take on a more ambivalent role, facilitating adventure but acting in concert: children acquire active roles rather than being objects of a fairy's whim or desire. One of the more interesting characters in *Through the Enchanted Wood* had been Paradoc, the page to the King of Gnomes. In this sequel, a boy known as Bosh rides his pony into the wood and at No Man's Corner turns to find he is somewhere else. There, he is recruited by Paradoc the Gnome to join him and the twins Peggy and Michael to search for five Golden Keys that are needed in fairyland. They proceed to have a series of adventures in what feels a lot like a treasure hunt. The keys are the keys to a magical gun, and must be turned by mortal hands. The gun fires out of the window at the castle of the monster, and that's it. Yet there is in *The Golden Keys* none of the sense of fear and immanence that we associate with Narnia and no *significance*. These are three children helping out a friend who, although older than they are, knows less and is less smart.

Although we don't usually consider P. L. Travers's *Mary Poppins* (1934) a fairy story, it has much in common with Lodge's *A Fairy to Stay* in that Mary's appointed role is as a corrective in an ill-run nursery, and her purpose is to disrupt. Mary Poppins contains within her much of the capricious vanity of the Elizabethan fairy. She is vain, must be flattered, is capable of great wonders, but turns on her charges at a moment's notice. Mary Poppins is sinister in her denial to her charges that anything fantastical has happened, and yet at times relentlessly ordinary. Landsberg has criticized the books for 'constantly playing to the adult audience'; Mary Poppins is 'extraordinarily vindictive with the disconcerting megalomania of a baby. Her magic is inconsistent and perverse.'[16] The books work in part because Mary Poppins is as seductive to the reader as she is to Michael and Jane, and as deceptive. It is Mary who is magical and Mary who is having the adventures. The children are almost never at the centre of the adventure; they are only guests in the conspiracy. The way magic works here reflects the real world: children are on the margins.

*Mary Poppins* may be one of the first real mutations of the fairy story into fantasy. The fairy story, as usually understood, was wearing out, but it was to have a last and highly successful outing in the work of Enid Blyton, one of the most prolific writers for children in the twentieth century and with a range which included boarding school stories for girls, adventure stories for both sexes and toytown fantasies for very small children. She created two classic fantasies, *The Adventures of the Wishing Chair* (1937) and *The Magic Faraway Tree* (1943 with sequels following). David Rudd notes that the books are, by the standards of modern fantasy, chaotic, drawing on many different tales, many different forms, and seeming to 'wilfully breach the barrier between the fantasy realms and that of everyday reality'.[17] Yet, she reinvigorates the fairy adventure through the sheer originality of the people with whom she fills her fairy worlds. There are far fewer traditional fairies. Instead there is a mixture of folk tale villains and toy story heroes, with wicked witches and wizards (whose villainy is demonstrated by the sin of serving milk-less cocoa). In *The Adventures of the Wishing Chair*, Molly and Peter are looking for a present for their mother in an antique shop when weird things start happening. They seek refuge in a chair and when they wish they were at home, it takes off and flies them back. They think of returning it but the magical wings have gone. From now on, they will have adventures only when they see the wings (a nice limitation). On their first adventure they rescue Chinky the pixie from a giant, and for the rest of the adventures Chinky is their guiding Adult, who tells them where they can go and gives them advice (which they do not always heed). The stories are aimed at seven-year-olds and at times are really quite scary, with several instances where the children are trapped by unpleasant people, unable to reach the chair.

Sometimes the lessons are moral, such as the one in which the chair is turned invisible, and they waste the anti-invisibility paint in teasing each other. A bit of the chair will never again be visible (which helps them identify it when it is stolen in an adventure in a later book). In Blyton's *The Enchanted Wood* (1939), Jo, Bessie and Fanny move to the country and find a magical wood in which stands the Faraway Tree. Living in the tree are various magical people including Moonface, Silkie the Fairy and the Saucepan Man. But the real magic is that at the top of the tree is a cloud and above the cloud is a series of lands which move around a hole through the cloud. Each land appeals to the desires of children, such as the Land of Take What you Want, or a land that rocks underfoot, or the Land of Birthdays to which only children having a birthday party can go. As Rudd concludes, 'it is only by viewing the books as staging desire through fantasy that they seem to cohere'.[18]

Compared to the nineteenth-century texts, the trajectory of children in all of these stories is outwards: the inward-facing tales of the nineteenth century, which trapped children in home or garden, are mostly gone. Now, home is a place to leave and the great outdoors a locus for adventure, although the lands in *The Enchanted Wood* feel about as free and wild as a theme park (it is perhaps not coincidental that this is the heyday of the boarding school adventure story for both boys and girls). One of the best demonstrations of this is *Canadian Magic* by Mary F. Moore (1946). Moore's novel is both a very traditional story of plucky schoolgirl bravery and an unusual fantasy in the tradition of *Puck of Pook's Hill*. Priscilla's parents are dead and her brother takes off to Canada. She goes to live with a great-aunt but hopes to emigrate also. Priscilla's great-aunt, who is a medium, introduces her to the spirit of Chief Great Shining Path who turns out to be an avatar of Will o' the Wisp. Will takes on various personas from Canada's past, teaching Priscilla enough to win a writing competition, and to persuade someone to take her to Canada as a companion to his daughter. Although the entire novel is set in England (often in a garden), it yearns outwards.

The animal tales of this period are so close to toy tales that we have chosen not to separate the two. With three exceptions – Hugh Lofting's *The Story of Doctor Dolittle* (1920), Beatrix Potter's *The Fairy Caravan* (1929) and BB's *The Little Grey Men* (1942) – the animals featured are barely animal. *Doctor Dolittle* is, in many ways, closer to a science fiction tale since the good doctor learns to speak the different languages of animals by perfectly natural means; that it is often included as fantasy lies in its status as a fanciful picaresque. *The Fairy Caravan* is an extended

Beatrix Potter story in which animals talk to each other, wear clothes and are anthropomorphized to a degree (although they retain some of their species characteristics: Mary Ellen, a cat brought in to nurse, has an 'unnecessarily purry manner. If people only looked at her she purred, and scrubbed her head against them'). Its fantastical setting is primarily restricted to its opening in which the guinea pigs of Marmalade Town club together to buy a hair growth potion (with which they hope to emulate the Abyssinian Caveys), and then try it on Mr Tuppence, a rather mangy guinea pig. Its success forces him to run away to join the caravan of the title. BB's *The Little Grey Men* is heavily influenced by the Panthesis we also see in the work of Arthur Machen and Kenneth Grahame (see Chapter 5), but this very beautiful tale of three gnomes working their way up the river to find a fourth, is essentially a nature book. The encounters with wildlife – the assistance of Otter for example – are part of an exploration and enjoyment of the wild and are anthropomorphic only to the degree necessary to promote an encounter between animals and miniature persons.

More typical is John Masefield's *The Midnight Folk* (1927), a dream-like adventure in which Kay consorts with both talking animals and toys as he seeks the treasure which can save his house. The book's setting is neither quite a dream, nor a fully separate secondary world. Kay is never surprised that his toys and animals can talk, nor that the magic begins to leak from the night into the day, as he discovers that his governess is one of a coven of witches. The story itself is rambling, with Kay wandering through the woods, spying on and observing others. On one occasion, for no apparent reason, Kay meets Arthur, Lancelot and Guinevere. His relations with these characters and with the animals (cats and fox) are all essentially similar. They lead him into adventure and serve his needs – as at the end his old toys and protectors, banished by his governess, return to him the treasure his ancestor lost.

This notion of animals and toys as both at the service of humans is played lightly in A. A. Milne's *Winnie-the-Pooh* (1926). The tale is embedded within a narrative technique of secondary-world fantasy and the mode liberates the toys from the demands of children and makes them more animal-like than many of the animals in these tales. The same could have been true for the adventure story *Happy Magic* (1934) by Mrs F. Crombie, but her tale of a Golliwog toy places the toy, Gorly, and his associates the cat Ginger and the Captain of the boat in the same fantastical world, able to communicate and co-operate with each other in protecting the Girl from the dastardly plans of the Rat.[19] Ursula Moray

Williams's *Adventures of the Little Wooden Horse* (1938) is perhaps the most extreme of the 'service books' with its tale of a wooden horse begging its maker to stay home, and then eventually setting out in the world to earn money for its master. The horse tries out various roles, all of which it at first succeeds in because of its diligence, but eventually fails at through misfortune, forcing the horse back to its old home in a narrative arc more reminiscent of earlier, nineteenth-century fantasies. The horse is humble and unctuous, with no true sense of self but only of service. Later, in Williams's *Gobbolino, the Witch's Cat* (1942), service is again at the heart of the story, with the little tabby cat anxiously seeking a home where he can serve *despite* his magic.

In contrast, Mumfie is a toy of spirit. Katharine Tozer's *Here Comes Mumfie* (1937) is a hugely confident toy fantasy that ranges through the traditions of toy story, elemental adventure, quest narrative and an encounter with Father Christmas. Tommy is given Mumfie, a talking baby elephant toy, in his Christmas stocking. (All the adults can hear him and accept that he is alive.) Mumfie wants to find his friend the scarecrow, and his search takes him into an underground world of talking postboxes, frightening policemen, wizards, an enchantress who wants all the toys back under her control, and eventually the scarecrow. Mumfie recruits Tommy and his neighbour Selina, and defeats the enchantress, after which they find themselves in a land of ice cream and balloons. It is fascinating to see Mumfie as an analogue of a small child, leaving behind the small child of the story and eventually creating a quest that is actually for toys.

Barbara Euphan Todd's anarchic tale of a Scarecrow and an Aunt Sally in *Worzel Gummidge* (begun in 1936 but continuing into the 1960s and eventually being turned into a highly successful television programme) does not fit in easily anywhere. The main plot device of the book is Worzel's failure to scare the crows because he is too busy courting. These are mishap adventures, and the role of the children – to cover up for Worzel – keeps to the role reversal that frequently in this period came to position children as the responsible ones in such adventures.

The idea that toys and animals are only there to amuse humans, whether directly in the plot or indirectly by being the subject of the story, is challenged by T. H. White in the highly unusual *Mistress Masham's Repose* (1946). Although the story has an old-fashioned feel – Maria is an orphan living in the dilapidated family mansion with her cruel governess and watched over by her unpleasant vicar guardian – there are mentions of farming machinery and small hints throughout that it is actually a contemporary fiction, confirmed with a reference to a list of kings and a brief mention of blackout curtains (though with no mention of a war). The politics of the text, however, are firmly post-war, and chime well with Geoffrey Trease's call for a post-imperial fiction for children. One day, Maria discovers the Lilliputians on the island where Mistress Masham's Repose – a summer house – is built. She kidnaps a Lilliputian woman and child and takes them to show her professor. He works out where they came from, but gives Maria a lesson on the evils of colonialism and imperialism – in childish terms. She takes them back and makes peace, but at nine years old Maria cannot resist trying to turn them into dolls. When this almost kills one of them, Maria gets the message and reforms her behaviour. They become friends and allies and, when the adults discover the Lilliputians, the latter repay Maria for her silence by rescuing her from her guardians. The adventure is about this rescue.

All of these stories contain the trajectory of escape from containment that was starting to shape children's fantasy. When aimed at the relatively young there were limitations. However, older children had greater freedom. At this period most working-class children were working by the age of twelve, and many middle-class children were only a very few years from work; and, as we will discuss in Chapter 5, the Second World War was changing ideas of how much freedom children and teens should have. As people started to write consciously for an older age group – perhaps eight- to twelve-year-olds although it is always difficult to tell – ways to facilitate freedom came to the fore.

Tales of flying carpets such as Edith Nesbit's *The Phoenix and the Carpet* (1904) were already becoming somewhat dated by the inter-war period and were relatively rare, but there were some. The best examples of the form are Mary Norton's *The Magic Bedknob* (1943) and *Bonfires and Broomsticks* (1945), collected together as *Bedknob and Broomstick* in 1957 (and bowdlerized by Disney). In *The Magic Bedknob* Carey, Charles and Paul are sent to the country to live with their elderly aunt for the summer. One morning they find the very prim Miss Price in the woods, clothes torn and in some distress. Paul observes that she has fallen off her broomstick. Miss Price, it seems, is taking a correspondence course in witchcraft. Paul has seen her several times but has been waiting for her to get good at flying before he mentions his discovery. Miss Price bribes the children to keep quiet with a piece of magic. This turns out to be a bedknob (something that can be twisted). Only Paul can use it, but the bed will take them anywhere in the world or in the past. The rules of Norton's fantasy are remarkably like those of Nesbit: all magic goes wrong, and they end up soaked, almost eaten and generally exhausted.

In the sequel, *Bonfires and Broomsticks*, the children accompany Miss Price to the year 1666, where they meet a somewhat confused necromancer, Emelius Jones, and bring him back to the present for a week. Sometime later, Miss Price decides it would be nice to visit Emelius, and they go back only to discover he has been arrested after the Great Fire and sentenced to burn as a witch. She leaves the children with the bed and sets out to rescue him, but they, of course, follow to the burning where they help the broomstick-flying Miss Price free Emelius. After they return to the present, Miss Price announces she is selling her house and donating the money to the Red Cross in order to replace her value to the nation as a capable woman. She and Emelius then return to the seventeenth century together.

Norton's books are perhaps the last of the travel narratives in which adults are a central part of the adventure. In Hilda Lewis's *The Ship that Flew* (1939), clearly influenced by Nesbit, the children are perfectly capable of working out how to use their magic carpet, in this case a miniature ship which once belonged to Odin, safely and adventurously. Peter, sent to the dentist, finds a small shop where an old man with a patch over his eye sells him the small boat he sees in the window for three shillings (all he has and a bit more, because tuppence of that is his father's change). Then, when he gets stranded on the sands walking home, he wishes to be home and the ship expands and flies him back. Peter, his two sisters and a brother then commence adventuring, first, to a rather ordinary bazaar where they are rescued by the local prince, but have to ditch him when he tries to steal the ship. Several adventures later, they go back to 1073, meet a child named Matilda, and try to deal with their own knowledge of William and the Normans (which is generally negative) and their own sense of themselves as English (when everyone assumes Peter is Norman). The follow-up, when they bring Matilda to the present, is even more interesting as she both loves the twentieth century and resents the ease that everyone around her experiences. The novel concludes when Matilda finds a way to contribute to the bazaar to raise money to preserve the church her father commissioned. Eventually the children grow older, and the other three begin to believe that Peter is just telling them wonderful stories, even when they have just been on an adventure themselves. Peter realizes it is time to fulfil his promise to Odin to return the boat, since the children no longer believe.

This book stands out for the simple assurance with which Lewis handles both the presence of the fantastic and the roles given to children. *The Ship that Flew* releases the children from the presence of adults, and although they will eventually forget their adventures, each builds his or her experience into the adults they become. Their time travels are engagements with the past and an understanding of the past, rather than simple observation, and the introduction of a child from the past (Matilda) into their own village gives Lewis the opportunity to explore historical relativism in a way that becomes familiar in post-war historical writing. There is a clear Nesbit influence in the very mundane way in which encounters with time are handled.

Similarly assured is Alison Uttley's *A Traveller through Time* (1939), a very effective and very different time-slip fantasy. Penelope, sent to the farm where her family has lived for generations as the servants of the local great house, finds herself an active observer in the downfall of the Babington family as they become involved with attempts to rescue Mary, Queen of Scots. Although as an observer Penelope has to be told things in order to convey the story, she is emotionally very much part of it. The time travel is handled particularly effectively, with a dreaminess that yet never resolves into dream. But Penelope, like Mary Norton's characters, is essentially an observer.

### *The Hobbit*

The stand-out text of the period is J. R. R. Tolkien's *The Hobbit* (1937). C. S. Lewis nailed what makes this book superb in his anonymous review for *The Times Literary Supplement*: it 'admits us to a world of its own – a world that seems to have been going on before we stumbled into it'.[20] There is no entry point, there is no leaving point. It is, quite simply, unlike anything else written for children in this period. Furthermore, in expecting children to read a text steeped in Nordic culture and mythology, Tolkien treats his child readers with respect: unlike the toy stories and garden stories we have seen, there is no assumption that children should have guarded reading. The role of Bilbo and the dwarves, clearly the counterpart of the child protagonists in more traditional fantasy, is developed quite differently: after reading the children's stories discussed above, which form the context within which Tolkien composed, it is a terrible shock to have Gandalf, partway through the adventure, declare that he will go no further. Some of the apparent unevenness of *The Hobbit* which both current and contemporary critics have observed is technique inherited or selected from Tolkien's medieval sources; for, in the manner of a hero tale, much of the action is told as if offstage, so that action is often something that *has happened* rather than *is* happening. Tolkien's use of this technique shows respect for his child audience.

The flourishing of children's fantasy in the 1930s was wholly in tune with the trend in children's literature across genres; Geoffrey Trease noted in a lecture given to the Welsh College of Librarianship in Aberystwyth, in 1971, that this was the period of Arthur Ransome and Noel Streatfeild, of Eve Garnett and Edward Ardizzone. It was also the period in which the National Book Council 'issued the first selected list of recommended children's books ever produced in this country':[21] *Four to Fourteen* (1938), edited by the Toronto children's librarian, Kathleen Lines.

There is little to hold this period of fantasy for children together except perhaps a willingness to experiment, and as yet no real emergence of common forms. One consequence of this is a frequent feeling of hesitation within the texts, a withholding of full belief in the fantastic. For the modern reader it is a shock when John Masefield's *The Box of Delights* (1935) ends with Kay waking up. Travers does not render adventures with Mary Poppins dream-like, but the adventures exist within a paradigm of denial: *this did not happen*. In Hilda Lewis's *The Ship that Flew*, age takes away memory and adventure is for the metaphorical playground. It is also noticeable how few children in these texts are fully active agents. Unlike the children of the nineteenth century, they are allowed to leave the garden, but they still travel almost nowhere by themselves, instead being led away (and astray) by adults in the form of foxes, witches or gods (Lewis) and wizards (Tolkien). The inter-war period was still a time of nannies and domestic arrangements that enclosed children, but already there were changes that left many children *free range*.

This is also the period in which three ingredients are melded: fairy, animist folk tales and hero tales. You can see all these elements in *The Hobbit*: the goblins are very clearly George MacDonald's goblins; the dwarves and men are part of an old hero/folk tale tradition; the elves hover somewhere between the two, and can be seen elsewhere in Stella Gibbons's *The Untidy Gnome* (1935). The narrative of Bilbo is almost a classic 'Jack and the Giant Killer' story, with Bilbo as a naïf in a world of bigger and cleverer people; its arc is the treasure hunt which Geoffrey Trease identified as one of the key tales of children's fiction and which lacks the import of the quest. We must resist judging the period by what came next, but by the time of Trease's survey of children's literature in 1948 we can feel a convergence of material in common, a use of myths and legends, and expectations of magical animals beginning to emerge.

## CHAPTER 5

# *The changing landscape of post-war fantasy*

In the years between 1950 and 1990, the landscape of children's fantasy in the UK and the Commonwealth changed in both literal and metaphorical ways. The physically constrained fantasies of the previous fifty years fell away as children explored other lands; the depiction of childhood changed; and children gained access to a far greater moral space within the fantastic. As children's fictional playgrounds expanded, so too did their sense of self. The awareness of being a child *in the world* rather than a child at home became an important element of post-war fantasy, and children's adventures became less localized, instead becoming rooted in an awareness of landscape, whether that was in the country, in the city, in the present or across time.

The period was so prolific, and so important to the development of children's fantasy, that we have chosen to split it into three sections. This chapter is concerned with the influence of the war, and the intervention of C. S. Lewis in the shape of children's fantasy. Chapter 6 will explore the growing influence of folklore in the development of urban fantasy. Of the two chapters, Chapter 5 is overwhelmingly concerned with the development of a new British tradition, while Chapter 6 explores the development of new urban folklores and fantasies across the Commonwealth. Chapter 7 returns to many of the authors considered in Chapters 5 and 6, exploring the ways in which they shifted the rhetoric and import of fantasy for children, the effect of this on the development of fantasy for teens, and the closing of the gap between fantasy for children and fantasy for adults.

## The quest story

The thirty years after the war would prove to be a golden age of children's fantasy, fixing some of the dominant forms of the genre long before they became common in fantasy for adults. In this period, with so little fantasy published in the adult market (the influential American Ballantine Adult Fantasy line did not begin until 1969), and with the gradual disappearance of the family reading market which had been the main outlet for much adventure fiction, both fantastical and mimetic, children's fantasy drove innovation. The 1960s and 1970s were good times for short story writers, whose collections were supported in part through purchase by public and school libraries. Short story collections are rarely money-makers, but the libraries stocked hard-back volumes which introduced many readers to new authors willing to emulate de la Mare and Nesbit in playing with the fairy tale as form. Barbara Sleigh, Nicholas Grey and Joan Aiken all offered fairy tale collections for young readers. Aiken's collections, *More Than You Bargained For* (1955), *A Necklace of Raindrops* (1968), *Smoke from Cromwell's Time and Other Stories* (1970) and *A Harp of Fishbones* (1972), were particularly innovative. Each featured new fairy tales, some classic in style, and some, like the Armitage family stories, set in modern suburbia and dealing with the place of curses and magic in everyday life. 'The Rose of Puddle Fratrum', for example, tells of a ballet cursed until it is danced by one-legged dancers, a problem resolved by hiring one-legged robots. The influence of Nesbit is obvious, but in Aiken's hands whimsy becomes something darker and more melancholic.

The period between 1950 and 1985 was also the heyday of television programming for children on the BBC. The popularity of many of the books noted here, and their long-term place in British memory, is due in part to their adaptation as television series, or to being read aloud on the television programme *Jackanory* (which ran weekly from 1969 to 1996). In addition, fantasy from Australia, New Zealand and Canada began to be exchanged across the Commonwealth countries. While British fantasy continued to dominate, the trade was no longer all one way.

Perhaps the most noticeable change in children's fantasy after the war was the dramatic increase in the import of the adventures. From small adventures at the bottom of the garden or struggles with cruel governesses, we move towards adventures in which entire families, empires and even worlds are at stake. No period that we have outlined here is self-contained. There are books in the 1940s and 1950s that clearly share some of the markers of earlier children's fantasy: child-sized adventures confined to house or garden, such as Lucy M. Boston's *The Children of Green Knowe* (1954) and Philippa Pearce's *Tom's Midnight Garden* (1958); and adventures of the ridiculous, as in Michael Bond's *A Bear Called Paddington* (1958). Despite their traditional structures, even these books reflect some of the anxiety of the war and post-war years: Boston's work offers a sense of belonging to the displaced child, Pearce's a way to make new connections in strange places, while Paddington Bear is the quintessential refugee child. But they are essentially domestic fantasies of a kind familiar to the reader from the first half of the twentieth century. In most children's fantasy after the war there is a distinct shift. Adventures have greater import and are less fundamentally oriented to childish concerns; there is a general upgrading of threat.

It has become a habit for those who work in modern Young Adult fiction to complain that the fiction of the 1950s and 1960s did not represent teenage concerns and was, in its magnificent adventures, unrealistic.[1] This argument completely overlooks the childhood and teenage concerns experienced by many in the 1940s and the way these were co-opted into children's fiction and, most particularly, into fantasy.

Prior to the Second World War many working-class and middle-class children in Britain began working between fourteen and seventeen years of age, but they were still fundamentally treated as children, subject to parents and employers, and trusted only with child-sized roles. In the first two years of the First World War many recruiting sergeants (and even parents) had turned a blind eye to fifteen- and sixteen-year-olds signing up, but by 1917 the rule of no under-nineteens serving as privates overseas and no under-eighteens as officers (the officer class was considered combat ready by virtue of birth and breeding) was being enforced. Although the navy continued to take boys younger than that, there was an increasing awareness that no matter what their enthusiasm, the boy's body was not the man's body and while able to fight (often with an enthusiasm driven by naivety), boys lacked stamina.

Adolescence as a social construct lasted from fourteen until marriage in the early twenties and was constrained by certain limitations. Most young people expected to live with their families until they were well established in their working lives and, for the poorer classes, often into the first year of marriage. For those from upper middle-class and upper-class families in the UK, childhood was effectively extended into the very late teens, with school and structured socializing in ways familiar today. Many children's books reflect the important role of the parent and guardian by positioning their characters outside that structure and showing how risky this was for the child's well-being.

The Second World War breached all of this, changing expectations for children, and raising the expectations of children themselves. Many children arrived in Britain as refugees in the period leading up to the war; 10,000 were brought from Germany and Czechoslovakia by the Kindertransport campaign in the last nine months before hostilities commenced. British children were evacuated overseas or to northern towns or to the countryside. While Australian and Canadian children did not experience this directly, children in the Commonwealth were aware of the experiences in Britain, Europe and Asia, thanks to arriving refugees and the campaigns of the strongest cross-Commonwealth organizations, the Scouts and Guides. Crucially, they were aware of how much children and adolescents were doing, as messengers, munitions workers, first aiders and, in places such as Poland and France, as active members of the resistance. A subsequent enormous raising of the stakes in fiction was congruent with children's expectations of themselves, as ingrained in the propaganda and the reality of the war years, and it also reflects a greater sense among children that what happened in the wider world was relevant to them: no longer could British children remain behind the lines of empire.

The work of many of the authors included in this chapter was marked by the war.[2] We can see the ways in which children's roles in the world and in fantasy move from *nice* to *vital* in a range of representations. The work of the Canadian Catherine Anthony Clark, the first well-known Canadian author of children's fantasy, demonstrates an older world in which the levels of threat are still essentially aligned with pre-war expectations. Clark was a first-generation immigrant from Scotland, and her fantasies are all, to one extent or another, explorations of the landscape and the mythos of her adopted land. In *The Golden Pine Cone* (1950), Ben and Lucy go through a portal with their dog, who turns out to be an exiled spirit. In helping him they become entangled in a classic treasure hunt or fairy tale narrative (in which each magical object allows them to trade up for the next) which we can recognize from the inter-war period. The children in *The Golden Pine Cone* have none of the effortless superiority to the people they meet that was to become such a feature of portal fantasies in the wake of *The Lion, the Witch and the Wardrobe*, the book's exact contemporary. The children meet an Indian Princess with no heart (for Clark, Indians were completely generic), her Great Chief lover and an Ice Witch. Throughout these adventures the relationship of the children to those they meet is as children to adults. The adults help the children along – and at times it feels like an adventure especially laid on for their amusement – but they are always the adults, and the children's purpose is to help their dog, not to change the world. Although the scope and geographical scale of these stories is large, and the Canadian landscape a major feature of the texts, the adventures are intimate and the concerns child-sized. Sheila Egoff, in *The New Republic of Childhood*, is rather dismissive of Clark precisely because her work lacks the import which Egoff and many other critics had come to assume was the norm for children's fantasy, but what Egoff has done is to construct this norm from those who were children in Britain during the war. Clark, as a Canadian, was sheltered from this and her work is grounded in pre-war expectations.[3]

In contrast, in the UK from the 1940s onwards, we begin to see the influence of the war seeping through, increasing the import of a child's actions, and changing the relationship of the child to fantasyland inhabitants. Thus, in Elizabeth Goudge's *The Little White Horse* (1946) it is not enough for Maria to have a magical adventure; that adventure must have huge import for her family. Maria proves to be the one who can revive the Moon magic and in doing so heal the rift between two families: a subtle book in many ways, with its combination of caricature and feyness, *The Little White Horse* caters to children's desire to intervene in the lives of adults and fix things. Marcus Crouch describes it as an 'allegory of the war between good and evil' but if that is the case, it appears to imply that good can win through persuasion and intermarriage.[4] The novel works better perhaps if one ignores Maria's desire for a grand resolution and concentrates instead on the domestic romance of her governess.

Pauline Clarke's *The Pekinese Princess* (1948) is doll-play with Pekinese dogs: when the Emperor's daughter is stolen by monkeys, the General's son Amber Face leads a party to find her, meeting dragons on the way. Although the characters are adults they are very much play adults, but the adventure involves young people intervening in the fates of nations. Even Barbara Sleigh's *Carbonel* (1955) shows the change that is taking place: it gives the children the freedom not just of the town but of the rooftops, and they rescue not just a cat, but a King of Cats. Written in the Nesbit tradition, a mode that proved most suitable for the new demands for social realism, Rosemary acquires a cat from a transaction with a witch, and along with it the witch's broom that enables her to understand the cat.

In each of these books, the roles of children/child analogues are not merely significant but crucial, and have a deep effect on the adults around them in ways that are utterly absent from the expectations of inter-war fiction (with perhaps the exception of Hampden Gordon's work, or Tolkien's *The Hobbit*; but even then, the children/child analogues are secondary characters in other people's stories). The change that took place in these books was epitomized and encoded in 1950, by C. S. Lewis, in a set of books that came to define what children's fantasy *was* even while many other forms continued to exist alongside it.

## Narnia and the salvation of the world

The stakes of the Narnia books are far higher than in any preceding fantasy, even *The Hobbit*. The four children of Narnia experience far greater responsibility than do Nesbit's children or those of Hilda Lewis in *The Ship that Flew* (1939). *The Lion, the Witch and the Wardrobe* (1950) allows children to save a world. In all but one of C. S. Lewis's Narnia books (*The Voyage of the Dawn Treader*, 1952, is the exception) the children participate in crucial turning points in Narnian history: in *Prince Caspian* (1951) they are reminiscent of the British supporting the beleaguered Free French; in *The Silver Chair* (1953) they are on a search-and-retrieve mission behind enemy lines; in *The Horse and His Boy* (1954) they are the plucky spies/couriers/fifth columnists who carry the vital message to their leaders; while in the Carnegie Award-winning *The Last Battle* (1956) they support a desperate last stand. In *The Magician's Nephew* (1955) there is a world to be created; in *The Lion, the Witch and the Wardrobe* a world to be saved; and in *Prince Caspian* and *The Horse and His Boy* invaders to be repulsed.

As well as material stakes there are also spiritual stakes, often combined: Edmund's role as a Judas figure is much discussed by critics, who do not always notice that he can also be recognized by children from the war stories they heard and the warnings they received as a *collaborator*. *The Silver Chair* is a fantastical retelling of *The Pilgrim's Progress*, complete with things that must be remembered and people to lead one astray. *The Last Battle* offers the ultimate test to everyone in Narnia – *Is your belief true?* – and offers salvation even to the heathen (a more radical and tolerant move then than it appears now).

*The Lion, the Witch and the Wardrobe* can be understood as an intervention on the developmental path of children's fantasy: Lewis changed the mood and direction in ways that have endured, although other forms were to emerge in the 1970s. Under his influence, the local, secular fantasy took a back seat, yielding to an understanding that much children's fantasy would be otherworldly, either physically or spiritually. Kath Filmer has argued that in the 1960s and 1970s, while religion per se may have remained in the background, the struggle with scepticism and religious plurality which pervades the work of writers such as Garner, Cooper and Madeleine L'Engle is its spiritual descendant.

Writers of the 1960s and 1970s seem to have been almost as concerned with the mechanisms of belief as with the stories that could be extracted from belief. We can see this in Alan Garner's *The Owl Service* and Susan Cooper's *The Dark is Rising* where what is believed in is part of a process in which belief is created through symbols and active metaphors and an engagement with the immanence of the fantastic tradition, something which both Manlove and Filmer have discerned. A sense of religious immanence consequently becomes a given in the form, even when, as in Garner's *Stone Book Quartet*, that immanence is presented as awe in the face of evolution, or in *The Dark is Rising* Will suggests to the vicar that there is not only something before Christianity, but no such thing as before or after, or in *Watership Down* immanence is expressed in the dreams of an epileptic rabbit.

The increasing temporal and spiritual import of adventure took place in unlikely settings and very different types of fantasy. In Dodie Smith's delightful *The Hundred and One Dalmatians* (1956) the dogs rescue not only their own puppies, but probably the entire Dalmatian puppy output of Great Britain. In the sequel, the science-fictional *The Starlight Barking* (1967), the dogs, after spending a day with their people in an unbreakable sleep, find themselves in negotiations with Sirius the Dog Star to save them. The level of expectation is very different from, for example, *The Wind in the Willows* where the trajectory of the novel is the retreat from the outside world (Mole to his burrow, Toad to his home village). French Canadian Paul Berton's *The Secret World of Og* (1961) hints at the changes in import to even the family adventure. This is at first glance an Edith Nesbit-influenced family fantasy in which the characters of the five girls and two boys are central to the story, and very entertaining, but when the children and their dog descend to the underworld of Og to find the things that have gone missing, the Ogs are focused on behaving as much like good Canadian children as possible, and this shifts the position of the children from the explorative tourism of the pre-war fantasy to the assumed cultural superiority and influence of the post-war period. The nation's own language, Og, consisting of just one word, is being discarded in favour of English; they take their vocabulary from comic books and their roles from the other influences they have gathered, although, like the Hoojibahs we met earlier (Chapter 4), the Ogs are aware that they are playing with second-hand cultural material. They are intending to create a melded culture, not merely an imitation of human culture (having discovered rabbit, they eat mushrooms with rabbit sauce and have no intention of eating rabbit with mushroom sauce); they are not, like the Hoojibahs *or like the children*, content with a culture of their own, and their need for new culture gives the children primacy. Berton, however, is clearly aware of the issue and helps children become aware of this too, when he confronts Penny with the different perspectives of the Ogs: the Ogs don't want to be human, they want to be themselves. Penny, not understanding this, asks them 'Why you don't just come up and live like the rest of us?'

> The Chief gave her a queer look.
> 'You don't really mean that,' he said finally.
> 'Of course I mean it.'
> 'You wouldn't like us up there at all,' said the little man. 'We're green, you know. We're different.'
> 'Well, for Heaven's sakes,' Penny said, exasperated. 'We've got all colours up above too. We haven't anybody green but we have them white and brown and yellow and black. So there.'
> 'And how are these people treated?' the little green man said.
> 'Well,' said Penny uneasily, 'it all depends, I guess.'
> 'That's why we stay down here,' the little man said.
> Penny didn't at all like the trend of this talk. But she did see the green man's point.[5]

The children of fantasy prior to 1950 *were children*. Those afterwards were, as Susan Cooper named Will Stanton, *Old Ones*, simultaneously children and carriers of adult responsibilities who looked beyond themselves; and this has continued to the present day. One of the most interesting series to emerge in the 1960s reflects precisely this sense of children looking beyond their own worlds. Animal fantasies of the inter-war years were little distinguishable from toy fantasies. They were projections of the children who played with them, and the animals were as limited as children. Margery Sharp's *The Rescuers* (1959) was among the earliest animal fantasies to allow children to project themselves into the fantastical world in adult roles, in a way that would become familiar with Brian Jacques's *Redwall* series (from 1986). In *The Rescuers* the mice, working-class Bernard and aristocratic Miss Bianca, set about changing a prisoner's aid society that writes encouraging letters (Amnesty International was founded two years later, in 1961) to one that actively rescues prisoners (the much more direct work of the American Friends Service Committee in the years after the war). Miss Bianca is small, delicate and lives in a gilded cage. Like many a Girl Guide before her, she discovers that joining an organization offers a route into the wider world.

That wider world was also a great deal more threatening. The critic Elizabeth R. Baer noted, 'It may not be too farfetched to claim that the candor in post-Holocaust children's literature about evil is owing to the dramatic change in consciousness we have all undergone since World War II.'[6] Books like Robert Cormier's *I Am the Cheese* certainly present us with a nameless, faceless evil that destroys the main character's family life. The same might be said for Susan Cooper's *The Dark Is Rising* series, ostensibly so different from the Cormier book and from Holocaust literature, yet arguably just as committed to the discussion of the nature of evil. This is a series we will discuss a little later in this chapter.

The manifestation of evil could still be metaphorical. C. S. Lewis's White Witch is an ur-evil, underpinning all the evils of the world, but she and her followers are also easy to identify with the Nazi hordes and their allies, while her predecessor Jadis in the later *The Magician's Nephew* may be the serpent in the garden. In addition, for C. S. Lewis winter is the enemy: this may be because in 1947 Britain had experienced a frighteningly cold and snowy winter. Although Britain rarely has blanket snows, the hardship of winter in post-war Britain made a strong enough impact that it cropped up in the work of several post-war writers, including *The Lion, the Witch and the Wardrobe* of course, Penelope Farmer's *Emma in Winter* (1966) and Susan Cooper's *The Dark is Rising* (1973), although Cooper herself cites the Massachusetts snows of her adult life. In all of these books winter snow is both threatening and magical. In contrast, although winter appears in Clark's *The Golden Pine Cone*, her ice witch lacks a sense of ultimate evil.[7] Canada, used to heavy winters and further away from the Nazi menace, did not yet need to use its fantasy to contain the threat, and would not until well into the fantasy revival of the 1990s.

## The nature of evil

Even at the other extreme, in a domestic fantasy such as Roald Dahl's macabre yet whimsical *James and the Giant Peach* (1961), the reaction against the oppression of unfeeling relatives is hugely magnified. James's Aunts are far from the petty crooks of John Masefield's *The Midnight Folk*: they are Grotesques, and their subsequent adventures are too threatening to be truly whimsical (the sharks circling the peach, for example, would have been doubly chilling to those adults who remembered the shark attack on the survivors of the torpedoed *USS Indianapolis* in 1945). James's Aunts demonstrate Baer's observation of the increasing acceptance in children's fiction that there was absolute evil in the world and that children had a responsibility to face it down.[8] Roald Dahl was one of a number of successful children's writers of the 1960s and 1970s who took on the challenge of dealing with absolute evil. Indisputably the biggest name in children's fantasy in this period, Dahl was also one of the darkest and himself something of an ambiguous trickster figure. Peter Hunt describes his books as 'energetic, vulgar, violent, and often blackly farcical' and adds: 'Dahl appears to be wholly on the side of anarchy.'[9] Many of his best works, such as *Charlie and the Chocolate Factory* (1964), *Fantastic Mr Fox* (1970), *The BFG* (1982) or *Matilda* (1988), keep real-world problems – hunger, keeping your family safe from violence, or the threat posed by one's own family or the educational system – front and centre. The escapism in these books is rendered more powerful because *there is something dangerous to escape from*. Although a writer of fantasy, in many ways Dahl is easier to associate with the mainstream trends of social realism because his work addresses the personal issues of children to a degree extremely uncommon in the fantasy of this period.

> Roald Dahl (1916–90) lost both his sister and his father at an early age. Something of a practical joker, he was not a particularly good student and was often in trouble during his school days. A fighter pilot and ace during the Second World War, he at one point survived a crash landing in the Sahara Desert, breaking his skull and temporarily going blind. The events of his early life often made their way into his books, if somewhat indirectly, and no doubt played a part in the books' often angry nature. Dahl, who also wrote for adults, hosted two television programmes, the American *Way Out* (1961) and the British *Tales of the Unexpected* (1979–88), both of which featured presentations of his fiction.

Where he differs is that his heroes, James or Charlie, are both passive and have their passivity rewarded, a much more Victorian model for child protagonists. One problem for the modern critic when dealing with Dahl is that his values are often those of an older period: while the child characters sometimes have a great deal of agency (when they choose to use it) and are independent and isolated in a way common to modern children's fiction, his adult female characters tend to be either saints or sinners with little in between, and his books encourage levels of mockery of others that, while common in the playground, make many adult readers uneasy. Dahl's most famous work, *Charlie and the Chocolate Factory*, is marked not just by violence of a sort that makes adults uncomfortable, but also by racism. Jane Yolen writes:

> When the editor (I was an Ass't Editor) took Dahl out to lunch and questioned the chocolate-color of their skins and the implicit racism in the books, he replied "Racism is an American problem." But a few years after the book was published, and racism became (or at least was seen) as a British problem and more and more critics were pointing the finger at *Charlie* from both sides of the pond, Dahl changed the O-L skin color and place of birth.[10]

This, however, has done little to rescue the book from the charge. Almost as controversial is Dahl's *The Witches* (1983), in part because of its violence – in what amounts to a genocide against evil, the young hero and his grandmother go on a crusade to poison all the witches in the world – and in part because of the author's decision not to change his child hero back to human form, but to leave him as a mouse permanently, the boy apparently being perfectly satisfied with the limited lifespan and abilities of a rodent.

Dahl modelled absolute evil for his child readers. Lewis, while doing the same, seems to have been more interested in why humans ally themselves with evil. In the earliest work of Lewis, Cooper and Garner the division between good and evil may be stark and instantly identifiable, but the central issue is the willingness of human beings to serve that evil, as in the cases of Edmund in *The Lion, the Witch and the Wardrobe* and the Walker in *The Dark is Rising*.

In Susan Cooper's *The Dark is Rising* sequence, the children are pitted against the ultimate dark forces that attract human beings, but Cooper is always careful to deal in *choice*. No one is forced to side with the dark; those who do always have their own reasons. Over and over again in these books we are told that true evil needs human beings to facilitate it: perhaps one of the most intense lessons of the Second World War. Alan Garner's later works, the Carnegie Prize-winning *The Owl Service* (1967) and *Red Shift* (1973), intensify this sense as in each of the books an ancient evil works its way through generations, until someone realizes they can argue with the outcome, that disaster is not inevitable. *The Owl Service* is based on one of the stories in the great Welsh collection of tales, the Mabinogion: the tragedy of Lleu Llaw Gyffes and Blodeuwedd, the woman made of flowers. Two modern boys, one local and one not, become rivals over the attention of a young woman. When Alison finds plates in the attic and begins first to trace their figure-ground pattern of flowers/owls, and then to make paper owls, the story of Blodeuwedd, wife to one man, lover of another, begins to play out once more. One strength of this book is that Garner uses the cultural solution embedded in the original to undercut the murderous rage that is its traditional conclusion.[11] In *Red Shift*, the violent rages and mysticism of one man shape the actions of a Roman legion gone wrong, and the lives of two other men in the future. A difference between the two books is that in *The Owl Service* it is a matter of making a different choice, of choosing not to turn on one's brother; in *Red Shift*, it is the acceptance of a gift that proves crucial. In neither book, however, is anyone depicted as being *evil* as such. Even in Richard Adams's animal fantasy *Watership Down* (1972) we sense evil as a *thing*, lurking and infecting those who choose to collaborate.

What that means in turn is that each of these authors emphasizes the importance of human agency in holding back evil. *The Dark is Rising* sequence concludes, in *Silver on the Tree* (1977), with the resonant voice of Merriman, a Merlin figure, declaring: 'For Drake is no longer in his hammock, children, nor is Arthur somewhere sleeping, and you may not lie idly expecting the second coming of anybody now, because the world is yours, and it is up to you.'[12] Lloyd Alexander's *Prydain* sequence similarly ends – memorably and heartbreakingly – with Taran, the assistant pig-keeper, refusing the chance to leave Prydain for the Summer Country and immortality, prepared even to give up his childhood sweetheart, in order to take on the responsibility of a war-ravaged land. For all that these texts are fantasy, they are *not* tales of escapism, but are structured to encourage the post-war generations to accept a collective responsibility for their world. Cooper makes it even more blatant; after the lines quoted above, Merriman adds, 'Now especially since man has the strength to destroy his own world, it is the responsibility of man to keep it alive, in all its beauty and marvellous joy.'[13]

The endings of the *Prydain* and *Dark is Rising* sequences point to another change. Along with this increase in import in the fantasy, and the increasing emphasis on *choice*, came a decline in the popularity of the 'companionate fantasy'. In the early twentieth century and the inter-war period it is noticeable how few children get to have adventures on their own: the Nesbit children have the Psammead, Kay Harker is accompanied by his cat, the Brown children go everywhere with Mary Poppins. Someone, an adult figure or guide, is always present. Now, however, young heroes are likely to find themselves alone, ultimately expected to accomplish their tasks with a minimum of help from friends or mentors.

## Destiny

Each of the post-war quest fantasies we have discussed *begins* with the companionate form: the Pevensies first follow Mr Tumnus into Narnia, then meet Mr and Mrs Beaver, and later Aslan; in Garner's *The Weirdstone of Brisingamen* Susan and Colin meet Cadellin Silverbrow; in Cooper's books the Drew children and Will Stanton are both accompanied by Merriman. But in each and every one of these fantasies (as at the end of Tolkien's quest fantasy for adults, *The Lord of the Rings*) there is a lecture about the need to leave magic behind and to part from the companion or guide. The abandonment of magic in these texts (and the implication that this is a route to adulthood) is much discussed by critics, but the waving goodbye to the companion, something that *does not* happen in the post-1970s, is far less remarked on, yet it is a clear part of the trajectory. The beavers just disappear from the story. Merriman, Cadellin Silverbrow and other magical companions all say goodbye. Even Aslan withdraws his visible presence from the children with the injunction to stand on their own two feet. One of the clearest depictions of this trajectory comes in the *Prydain* books.

The first of these, *The Book of Three* (1964), resembles Alan Garner's *The Weirdstone of Brisingamen* (1960) in bringing a child, Taran, into the affairs of wizards and great men, but by the final book, *The High King* (1968), the fate of Prydain rests on Taran's shoulders. In what was to become a cliché of quest fantasy, Taran is a foundling, the ultimate separated child. But perhaps more interesting, he is also a meritocrat who finds his education where he may, who refuses the easy option of adoption into a royal house, and creates a narrative of *possibility* in which destiny is contingent. Alexander makes visible a shift we see even in that most conservative of writers, C. S. Lewis: the Pevensies may be destined for their roles, but Jill and Eustace – even if products of a private education – earn their place in Narnia through their skills, and Lewis's Cabbie and his wife, who become the King and Queen of Archenland, are more beneficiaries of 'right time, right place' than any hint of destiny.

Even that ultimate of destinarian fantasies, *The Dark is Rising*, which has at its centre Will Stanton, the last of the Old Ones, and Bran Davies, the son of King Arthur (transported to and brought up in the modern world), undercuts its destinarianism at the end. In the choices Bran Davies makes – to grow up as the son of a shepherd in an age of grammar school opportunities, rather than return to inherit his father's kingdom – he is in effect rejecting heredity for meritocracy, giving preference to the

humble products of humanity over the aristocracy of legend. It also sig-
nals the end for some time of the role of the magical guide, as children
increasingly strike out into the world on their own.

Still, despite these gestures towards free will, destinarianism wins out
in the end. In the novels of the 1930s and 1940s, adventures were stumbled upon and children's involvement in adventure was contingent upon
their own characters. *The Lion, the Witch and the Wardrobe*, however, not
only gives children a destiny but requires it for the plot: Edmund *must*
betray Aslan or the High Magic cannot be played out (and it is fascinating that Lewis was willing to give the role of Judas to a child). In the
work of Garner, Alexander and Cooper, even as they wrote stories that
sought to place more ordinary children at the centre of adventures, the
workings of destiny stripped them of their full agency. British fantasy
writer Joy Chant's *Red Moon and Black Mountain* (1970) is another
good example of this: one of the full Other World stories of the period,
it plunges three children into another world where they are quickly
separated. The eldest, Oliver, arrives some time before the others and is
subsumed into the life of the tribe that adopts him as their Young Tiger:
because he was born outside the world, he can defeat a tyrant. As Oliver
says, 'We were only brought because we were – right for the tasks ... we
were the right ages, the right kind, the right time, or something.'[14]

Such destiny was becoming ubiquitous in children's fantasy, in ghost
stories, in the quests, and in the adventures, reaching its zenith in the
1990s in the Harry Potter stories and in Philip Pullman's *His Dark
Materials*, in both of which children are destined by their parentage to
lead revolts against earthly or heavenly tyrants. The one major exception
is Diana Wynne Jones, one of the up-and-coming writers of the period,
who saw a problem with this. Although we can argue that Christopher
(and later Eric) Chant's fate is to become the Chrestomanci (in *The Lives
of Christopher Chant*, 1988, and *Charmed Life*, 1977 respectively), this is a
fate dictated by their specific talents, and although these talents are rare,
it is not completely impossible that there is more than one nine-lived
enchanter available. As Jones's work developed, her uneasiness about
destinarianism became clearer. In the second book of the Dalemark
Quartet, *Drowned Ammet* (1977), Mitt discovers that the constant insist-
ence by others that he has a destiny has served to drown anything resem-
bling critical thinking: trapping others in a destiny, Jones would have
us realize, is very far from appropriate. In *Hexwood* (1993), a very long-
planned revolution is played out in a virtual reality game; the boy Hume

discovers he was once Merlin, who bred an entire people to fight his battles for him, and has it brought home to him exactly how immoral that is.

It is hard to establish what lay behind this creeping destinarianism, which as we will see in Chapter 6 became particularly strong in the medievalist fantasies. One argument that has been made is that as children experienced less destiny in their home lives – their careers no longer decided by parental occupation or even chosen by parents – they preferred books that gave them a sense of order and fate to compensate for the unpredictability of their reality. Another possible influence was the postcolonial rhetoric of the dying British Empire. By the 1950s the British Empire was clearly being wound up. India had gone in 1947; in 1956 the British lost the Suez Canal, and in the same decade Sudan, the Gold Coast and Malaya. Most African colonies gained their independence in the 1960s. One of the ways the British created a counter-narrative to this trajectory was to construct a rhetoric, still common in British foreign policy speeches, and which can be found through a simple internet search, of a country 'punching above its weight'. In almost every one of the portal and quest fantasies of the period this describes the position of the children: their presence in any given adventure adds significantly more weight than might be expected. Rhiannon Lassiter's much later Rights of Passage sequence, *Borderland* (2003), *Outland* (2004) and *Shadowland* (2005), functions as a deliberate critique of this pattern.

There is no clear date or world-changing event to end this period: scholars think of it as a golden age of children's fantasy, but it is hard to summarize. The scope of children's fantasy widened, and children increasingly roamed the world outside their front garden, taking British/colonial values through portals, and boundaries became more fluid: 'A housing estate can at any moment become a forest, the present-day can slip not just to another time in history but to *any* or *all* time in *both history and myth*, and the kindly fisherman might turn out to be Sir Lancelot.'[15] Time itself became a route to knowledge and to power as the mythos of the land became the stuff of fantasy. The quest fantasies entered the realm of children's literature, but even though the stakes rose, they initially felt more like adventure fiction than the climactic battles of good and evil that were a feature of the adult form in the 1970s. This changed only gradually. The influence of social realism was felt in the urban fantasies, and whimsy continued in the work of Roald Dahl though, again, it became increasingly menacing. The sense that children could be independent thinkers was clearly growing. Almost all the stories discussed here not only show children acting alone, but increasingly position children as interrogators of their world. It is noticeable how much more writers expected children to *know* as the stuff of fantasy expanded to encompass far more than traditional fairy tale material, and this is the concern of the next chapter.

## CHAPTER 6

# *Folklore, fantasy and indigenous fantasy*

In Chapter 4 we argued that in the inter-war period myth, folk tale and fairy tale were mostly kept separate from fantasy: even in Patricia Lynch's *The Turf-Cutter's Donkey* (1934) which used all three, the result was three distinct sections with their own flavours. In the post-war period fantasy writers began to plunder the legendary archaeology of Britain. A new paganism, which we can see threaded through the fantasy writing of the 1970s, focused on a range of things: although Celtic lore was to recede into the background (taken up far more by US and Canadian writers who often continued to struggle with what Baum believed was a lack of indigenous material), English traditions were brought into focus. *Englishness* became, for the first time, a distinct trope in UK fantasy, and at the same time indigenous traditions were brought into the new fantasy of Canada, Australia and New Zealand.

Peter Bramwell has observed that despite the retellings from Lancelyn Green and others, the figure of Pan, and the classical tradition more generally, declined in children's literature in the post-war period. Pan seems to have retained only a small place in children's fiction up to the 1970s, reduced to appearing as a magical statue in *Panchit's Secret* by Vivienne Wayman (1975). Only later, as we shall see, did a revived interest in classicism reposition Pan in his homeland.[1]

In the place of Pan arose an animism with its roots in a variety of factors, among them the emphasis on nature and the natural in the youth movements of Scouts and Guides, the rise of rambling as a leisure activity in Britain, and the deepening historical sensibility towards and encouragement of *Englishness* that we see in children's historical novels. Rosemary Sutcliff, one of the best children's historical writers of the period, allows both Tansy of the non-fantastical *The Armourer's House* (1951) and Jenny of *The Roundabout Horse* (1986) to be influenced by the magic of Midsummer's Eve. In *The Queen Elizabeth Story* (1952) Perdita is able to see the Pharisees because she was born on Midsummer's Eve. The time of the year also structures magic in a number of other books – in Penelope Farmer's *The Summer Birds* (1962), where summer is the time of flight, in Cooper's *The Dark is Rising* sequence, in which the dark comes during winter – but in part these are also the seasons when children (particularly boarding-school children) were at home to have adventures. It was not until the end of the twentieth century that the Green movement truly brought the notion of the natural seasons into the realm of magic.

Peter Bramwell points to a rise in two myths in particular: the Green Man, a nature figure of ambiguous origin, often seen as a foliage-covered face on traditional architecture, and Herne the Hunter, a terrifying figure ostensibly derived from the Welsh god Cernunnos, who leads the Wild Hunt. The Green Man stories, Bramwell suggests, were a sympathetic response to the decline of classicism. The Green Man appeared as a trope as early as 1939, when Lady Raglan suggested in an article in *Folklore* that the heads found in churches were a fertility symbol. Lady Raglan was part of a tradition running from the 1890s into the 1960s that reconstructed folk tales, songs and traditions, with varying levels of authenticity, but the idea of the Green Man being tied to the lost woodlands of England (an idea now questioned even by the geological and archaeological evidence) proved popular. In 1966 Kevin Crossley-Holland wrote *The Green Children*, which retold the story, found in William of Newburgh's and Ralph Coggeshall's twelfth-century accounts, of the green children discovered in Woolpit in Suffolk. Judith Stinton told the story again in *Tom's Tale* (1983). In both, the boy dies and the girl lives, to be assimilated into the local culture. In these variants the trope is barely fantasy, but it is part of the environment of the fantastic. John Gordon's *The Giant Under the Snow* (1968) makes the Green Man metaphorical, a carved giant, like the one at Cerne Abbas in Dorset, whose buckle is the focus for ancient magic, which, as Peter Bramwell points out, is a classic Returned King motif, more Christian than pagan.

There is a sense, however, that writers have not figured out how to use the Green Man/Woman motif; it remains a metaphor, as in C. Butler's *Timon's Tide* (1998) and Kevin Crossley-Holland's *The Seeing Stone* (2000), in both of which it is the *image* of the Green Man that resonates. More evocative is the female form, the Greenwitch of Susan Cooper's book of the same name, who is a holder of secrets and a carrier of confession. Variations on the Green Woman can be found in Lewis's green lady in *The Silver Chair* (1953), who is a witch and kidnapper; the green lady of Helen Cresswell's *Stonestruck* (1995), who wants to trap children in childhood; or *The Green Lady and the King of Shadows* by Moyra Caldecott (1989), in which she is an embodiment of the Persephone myth. It is noticeable, however, that with the exception of the Greenwitch they are not rooted in *place*. Nor are they powers of the land, unlike the Green Man or Herne the Hunter.

Herne had appeared in John Masefield's *The Box of Delights* as a kind of Merlin figure to Kay, repeating the outsider motif we saw in T. H. White's *The Sword in the Stone*. He appeared again – if unnamed – in Penelope Lively's *The Wild Hunt of Hagworthy* (1971) in which a local vicar renews an old tradition with deeper consequences, and more directly in Susan Cooper's *The Dark is Rising*, Jane Yolen's *The Wild Hunt* (1975) and Diana Wynne Jones's *Dogsbody* (1975). *Dogsbody* is particularly interesting here, because its stories are structured around a classical figure, Sirius the Dogstar, portrayed as living in the sky with the kind of home life the Greeks might have given him, literally *brought to Earth* in a number of ways: forced to live out his life as a dog, brought to talk to the Earth herself, and forced to work with the creatures of the Earth. Sirius's run with the Wild Hunt of Herne the Hunter (and with the red and white hounds of Annwn from the Mabinogion) gives him the experience of being both hunted and hunter. The classical world becomes subordinate to the hitherto inferior indigenous world, reflecting the decisive shift to relocate fantasy in the bones of the land, its unchanging geological and deep cultural history. The fundamental characteristic of Herne the Hunter is that he is uncontrolled and unappeasable, like the *wild magic* of Narnia. The rules and systems that have become such a feature of the modern fantastic are swept away, making Herne a symbol of social disorder, much as was Robin Hood, a legendary character whose story is usually told without fantastic content.

## The freedom of the land

The interest in folklore and its incorporation into children's fantasy literature involved a major shift in the landscape of children's fantasy. Gone were the contained house and garden (or even country estate) fictions of the inter-war years. With the growing interest in the physical and mythological archaeology of Britain came a willingness – seen in other branches of children's fiction – to allow middle-class children the freedom of the land. That this was the high point of the British walking movement, as displayed by growing membership in the Ramblers' Association, was not coincidental. Much of the argument of the 1920s through the 1970s was that the wild countryside was fundamentally magical, its magic part of the archaeology of the landscape, and it belonged to all.

The writers of urban and indigenous fantasy were aided by a number of retellers who deliberately targeted their work at children, thus ensuring that children who read fantasy would already be familiar with the stories and motifs that underlay the fantasy tale. Three notable British retellers were Roger Lancelyn Green, Ruth Manning-Sanders and Katharine Briggs.

Green collected tales of Asgard, Egyptian gods and Greek heroes (*Myths of the Norsemen*, 1962, and *The Tale of Troy*, 1958) in the volumes put out by Hamish Hamilton, among which were also *The Book of Princes* by Christopher Sinclair-Stevenson (1964) and *The Book of Princesses* by Sally Patrick Johnson (1963). Katharine Briggs retold the stories of the Lincolnshire Fens and turned the hob into a classic creature of British fantasy (see *A Dictionary of British Folktales in the English Language*, 1971, and many children's titles).

Ruth Manning-Sanders retold folklore of the British Isles in such works as *A Book of Giants* (1962) and from all over the world in the classic *A Book of Charms and Changelings* (1972). One of the things that made Manning-Sanders's series so distinctive was its reliance on the trickster in many of the stories: the passivity of many fairy tale heroes and heroines was replaced by active and awkward teens, a trope taken up by Barbara Sleigh, among others, in her collection *Winged Magic* (1979), where traditional tales are redrawn from a range of sources – Norse, Greek and English – familiar from the collections of the pre-war writers. At novel length, Leon Garfield's Carnegie Medal-winning *The God beneath the Sea* (1972) helped keep alive the Greek legends.

One of the earliest manifestations of the growing role of folklore in children's fantasy occurred in an unexpected place, not really within the remit of this work, Oliver Postgate and Peter Firmin's very humble paper figure animation of *Noggin the Nog* for the BBC (1959–65), with its resonant opening lines:

> In the lands of the North, where the Black Rocks stand guard against the cold sea, in the dark night that is very long the Men of the Northlands sit by their great log fires and they tell a tale …
> And those tales they tell are the stories of a kind and wise king and his people; they are the Sagas of Noggin the Nog. Welcome to Northlands, a tribute to Noggin, King of the Nogs and the People of the Northlands.

Firmin based Noggin the Nog on the Isle of Lewis chess set. These faux Norse tales were revived with a new television series in 1979 and also resulted in a number of book titles, now available as *The Sagas of Noggin the Nog* (2001), and did much to popularize Norse myth.

Yet, although the folk tale was to form much of the stuff of fantasy over the next thirty years, it is notable that writers were looking closer to home. In the 1950s and 1960s there had been a distinct shift in the field: the landscape of *the fantastical* moved from *elsewhere* (Greece, Ireland, Norway, China) to right here, to the landscape and history of Britain and other Commonwealth countries. This was a dramatic ideological shift: in the nineteenth and early twentieth centuries folklore was what less civilized people had in place of culture. It could be collected and admired, but by very definition 'we' did not have it. Of course this claim was utter nonsense and, to a large degree, had been undermined by the folksong and folk dance collectors of the 1920s and earlier, and as the children who had read the work of the collectors *and* the fantasy writers themselves turned to writing, folklore and mythological material began to be the stuff of fantasy. Brownies, the humble hobgoblins of northern England and Scotland, were already common figures in British popular culture, their mythlore having been freely adapted by the junior branch of the Girl Guides (Brownie packs had toadstools), so that Katharine Briggs's *Hobberdy Dick* (1962) both resonated with common knowledge and attempted – as others would again with popular folklore – to return it to its roots in a brownie and his house.

In Australia and New Zealand, the work of Patricia Wrightson and Margaret Mahy reflected growing desire for a home-grown fantasy. Wrightson develops a common folklore for the white (European) children of Australia in *The Nargun and the Stars* (1973), which pits the machinery of Europe against the indigenous creatures of Australia, combining European folk traditions concerning iron with the local material. One issue about the use of local material, however, is that 'local' is not the same as 'inherited'. Patricia Wrightson has been criticized for using indigenous Australian folklore and characters in novels like *The Nargun and the Stars*, and in the 1990s such criticism was to become a constant in the discussion of the use of folklore and local tradition by writers to whom this material was seen not to belong.

Historical and fantasy fictions for children in this period were playing with similar material: Englishness/Britishness, and the construction of a previously rejected indigenous, and often localist, identity was a growing theme in English fantasy. Time-slip novels of the 1960s frequently expressed this with quite intimate connections. In Antonia Barber's *The Amazing Mr Blunden* (first published as *The Ghosts*, 1969), a family is asked to act as caretakers for a ruined mansion. The solicitor, Mr Blunden, asks Lucy and Jamie, the two children, if they are afraid of ghosts – he has a mission for them. In what may be the best time-slip novel since Uttley's earlier *A Traveller through Time*, Jamie and Lucy find themselves meeting the ghosts of two children in the gardens, and setting out to slip through time with the aid of a rather noxious potion, in the hope of changing the past and saving Sara and Georgie from their fate. They do of course succeed, and in what will later become a cliché, find they are rewarded by having their own lineage tweaked: they are descended from Sara and the house belongs to them. More crucially, however, *they* belong to the house: the image of the uncared-for ruins is removed.

This sense of belonging to a place plays out differently in *Charlotte Sometimes* (1969) by Penelope Farmer. Charlotte's time-slip into the past is resolutely linked to her very specific locality – the bed she sleeps in, the school she attends: when Charlotte finds herself in Clare's place, it is quite literally in place, emphasizing the human heritage of a boarding school. In Penelope Lively's *The Ghost of Thomas Kempe* (1973) the ghost is rooted in a sense of an English village as both a living thing and an old thing: it is not considered incredible that an alchemist/sorcerer should once have inhabited a house now belonging to a modern family, nor that he should find a way to reinterpret his grievances in the modern world. In Diana Wynne Jones's *Archer's Goon* (1984), an otherwise very modern or even postmodern fantasy, localism, heritage and unexpected family connections turn out to be key to unravelling the plot, although as this is a Jones novel and therefore unpredictable, the conclusion promises a breaking of local bonds. Helen Cresswell, in both *The Secret World of Polly Flint* (1982) and *Moondial* (1987), sees the making of bonds to new localities as key to the *entry into magic*: Polly begins to see the 'time gypsies' in the new area to which she has moved; Minty connects to the great house where her godmother used to live through her ability to hear the ghosts in the landscape and to slip through time in the physical landscape, propelled by the power of a sun/moondial.

Such emphasis on belonging of course is not without its problems. Although British fantasy stayed mostly monocultural for far longer than it should have given the nation's changing demographics, Diana Wynne Jones in *Wilkins' Tooth* (1973) and Susan Cooper at the beginning of *Silver on the Tree* (1977) both sought to question what belonging meant. Wilkins claims his Britishness ironically through the loss of his mother's culture and acculturation to British norms (including a knowledge of European fairy tales); various figures in *Silver on the Tree* emphasize the mongrel nature of the British, but inadvertently suggest that *only* through hybridity can one's descendants belong, an option not open to all immigrant groups.

Alongside intimate connections, British fantasy demonstrated an increasing awareness of the archaeology of Britain, the age of its culture, particularly its pre-Roman culture, and a physical awareness of *localism* that C. Butler discusses in *Four British Fantasists*. Alan Garner has looked ever closer and deeper into the landscape, with his non-fantastic *Stone Book Quartet* awakening the reader to the magic that was in the land, his *Red Shift* relying on an awareness of the long history of the land, and his *Thursbitch* (2003) being told in part in a Cheshire dialect. In Garner's work, from very early on, to be foreign to a landscape is to be in danger. You can also see this localist fascination in William Mayne's *Earthfasts* (1967) and its sequels – a rare fantasy outing from a mostly mainstream author. Nellie Jack John emerges from under a castle after two hundred years but is recognized by the hill folk who are descended from much the same families. Marcus Crouch writes of Mayne's Swaledale setting that, 'In such a landscape there is no incongruity in a story which brings together a Neolithic stone circle, an eighteenth-century drummer boy, and the kind of boggart who, given the right circumstances, is likely to pop up in any century.'[2] We can push this further: for Mayne and Garner, the writing and the landscape are intensely intertwined; the landscape creates the folk tale and both create the people who will inhabit the tale.

## The Matter of Britain

A second aspect to this interest in Englishness/Britishness was expressed in often conjoined fascinations with the legend of Arthur and the notion of hybridity. Both crop up in T. H. White's *The Once and Future King* (1958), in Susan Cooper's *The Dark is Rising* sequence (where Welsh, Saxon and English traditions all mix, to be joined by Asians in *Silver on the Tree*), in William Mayne's *Earthfasts* and in the Arthurian historical novels of Rosemary Sutcliff. All appear to be connected directly to the move to reposition Britain as a 'mongrel nation', an idea which in the early twentieth century had been used to undercut class conflict. John Stephens and Robyn McCallum argued that 'in the postwar years there was a nationalist motive for retelling the Arthur story from a more historical base, as it now becomes an account of the struggle to sustain sovereignty and civilization in the face of invasion from Europe'.[3] Its popularity in the post-war period may have come from the Left, to bolster the idea that it was the British melting pot that won the war (similar rhetoric could be seen applied to the extremely successful Team GB during the 2012 Olympics) and from the Right which sought to defend a 'pure hybridity' in which certain ingredients would taint the recipe. In both these contexts Arthur became a figure of unity, fending off foreign threats. Perhaps the strongest link between Arthur, the land and magical identity is found in Diana Wynne Jones's *The Merlin Conspiracy* (2003). In the Island of Blest, a parallel world, the King still rides his domains in order to preserve the magic and integrity of the land, and is served by the Merlin, an appointed wizard. When the magic becomes sick, the land must be magically lifted and repositioned because land *is* magic.

The rise of the Matter of Britain as an element in children's fantasy also draws attention to the degree to which Welsh folklore became a staple of the genre. Alan Garner's early works, *The Weirdstone of Brisingamen* (1960) and *The Moon of Gomrath* (1963), borrowed freely from the Mabinogion, as did Lloyd Alexander's *Prydain* sequence and Susan Cooper's *The Dark is Rising* sequence. It is probably not a coincidence that in the 1960s, when there was a conscious attempt to revive the Welsh language, it was Welsh myth which was most popular as source material, not only in fantasy, but in the outpouring of Arthurian historical fiction for both children and adults. Rising Welsh pride and nationalism, and the growing awareness of Welsh language and culture, helped make indigenous Welsh material more available to outsiders, continuing a pattern of appropriation of the myths of the Other that we saw in Irish folk tales in the inter-war period (and which is paralleled in the 1970s by the appropriation of Native American mythologies in US and Canadian fantasies). Not until Penelope Lively's *The Wild Hunt of Hagworthy* (1971) do we really see English folk traditions deployed in quite the same way, although historical author Rosemary Sutcliff's presentation of Arthur appropriated him for a British history that was in part about English continuity.

Yet, there was one significant counter-narrative to the sense of Britain unified by folklore. The first three novels of Joan Aiken's *Wolves* sequence – *The Wolves of Willoughby Chase* (1962), *Black Hearts in Battersea* (1965) and *Nightbirds on Nantucket* (1966) – introduce us to a world where something very different happened in 1714. Instead of George I ascending the throne despite over fifty Roman Catholic heirs with stronger claims, the throne has reverted to the Stuarts (religion not given in these books) and James III is on the throne. The books draw attention to a period in history that was extremely turbulent but that is portrayed to the English as inevitable. As alternative histories most of these books contain no magic per se but as the series develops they begin to *slip* into the stream of the fantastic. There is also magic in Aiken's *The Stolen Lake* (1981), for instance, when Dido Twite, on her way home from her adventures in *Nightbirds on Nantucket* (1966), becomes involved with immortal Ginevra, once Arthur's consort and now the Queen of New Cumbria.

## Fantastic nation-building in the Commonwealth

In Canada, a different kind of fantasy became engaged with nation-building. Canada is an immigrant culture, with a far greater sense of itself as such than is perhaps true of the United States. There was an active migration policy from Europe well into the second half of the twentieth century, and *becoming Canadian* was clearly a process that began from the moment of arrival and was intrinsic to *being* a Canadian. Many of the writers discussed as Canadian began life as immigrants but identified themselves as Canadian writers. Furthermore, encoded into much Canadian fantasy until well into the 1980s is a sense that fiction for children (and perhaps also for adults) is fiction *for* nation-building. One consequence is that before the 1980s only a tiny number of time-slip stories involve any visit to Britain. Instead, in this period such tales were mostly about creating a sense of identity with the Canadian past.

Janet Lunn, the first Canadian writer to really have a career writing fantasy, wrote books that were all very much grounded in contemporary or historical Canada rather than a mythic Canada, but used hauntings and time-slips that set a trend in the genre positioning of Canadian children's fantasy: in *Double Spell* (1968), about twins haunted by the deaths of twins in their family, *The Root Cellar* (1981), in which a young girl finds herself in 1860s Canada, and *Shadow in Hawthorn Bay* (1986), about a young woman emigrating to Canada to find her lost love, the magic works primarily to facilitate these stories.

The mechanisms of time-slip, or the fantastical elements, are not themselves the source of wonder. K. V. Johansen, a very fine contemporary Canadian fantasy writer in her own right, has noted that 'Looking beyond Canada, one sees that not all time-travel stories for young people need to be about learning history or coming to appreciate a family in a new light' but it is clear that among Canadian writers, time-slip stories are far more strongly identified with historical fiction than with the fantastic.[4] This unfortunate tendency, to regard magic as merely a utilitarian component in the story and to make very little use of it, does not harm Lunn's work, but it is very noticeable as a trope in many of the time-slip and hauntings texts of the second half of the twentieth century.

The Québécois revival of the 1970s moved across the country during the 1970s and 1980s in the form of French immersion schools in which English-speakers could become bilingual and, along with language acquisition, become bicultural. The effect of this biculturalism was particularly significant in the Maritime Provinces where groups of Acadians who had survived, or returned after, the British-instigated mass deportations of the 1750s and 1760s had endured as minority communities. The new order changed the way this was understood and Acadian history emerged as a significant contribution to the mosaic. Time-slips became the obvious way to explore this theme, in part because such narratives offer a fake verisimilitude, a way of presenting history as witness. One of the earliest tales in this tradition is a picture book, *The Magic Rug of Grand-Pré* by Réjean Aucoin and Jean-Claude Tremblay (translated into English in 1989) in which two children travel back in time and to magical lands to find the twelve missing threads of a tapestry abandoned during the deportation.

The narratives of cohabitation and co-existence observed in earlier fantasies re-emerged in the time-slip stories. Alongside the desire to rescue the Acadian story was a desire to emphasize the collaboration that existed between the Acadians and the native population, the Mi'kmaq and the Maliseet. In these narratives, a shared victimhood – as both groups became caught in the machinations of the French and British Empires – becomes a narrative of tolerance. In the 1990s Elaine Breault Hammond offered a series of time-slip novels, in the first of which Marc and Maggie are sent back to Acadia to experience life there and to help the deportees pack and ensure they travel in their family groups (something that was not ensured by the British soldiers). Lois Donovan's *Winds of L'Acadie* (2007) is a much more detailed book, which focuses both on the past and on the nature of history. Both of these texts are well researched but it is noticeable that each offers a reward to the time travellers in the form of a genetic connection to the French deportation, to create, as Johansen argues, 'an illusion of identification'.[5] Furthermore, they are tourist books: for all that the time travellers are engaged in the daily life of farm work, they feel as if they are pretending. When, in the Acadian writer Hélène Boudreau's *Acadian Star* (2008), Meg Gallant is sent back to her Tante Pearl, her connection is real and immediate: she must prevent her family from being split up in the deportation if she is to undo a family curse, and part of her experience is precisely about turning a narrative legacy expressed in communal re-enactment into something that is felt more intimately.

Antipodean fantasy began to develop a stronger identity in the early 1980s. The international success of New Zealander Margaret Mahy supported a growing sense among Australians and New Zealanders that they were not only a British outpost. Mahy brought her own unique brand of myth into Young Adult fantasy, mixing Western lore with Maori traditions, often coupled with just a touch of surrealism. In *The Haunting* (1982) she introduces young Barney Palmer, who discovers that he is being haunted by the ghost of his recently deceased great-uncle Cole, whom he has never met. Barney is terrified until he and his sister Tabitha ask help from his remaining great-uncles and discover that each generation of their family produces one individual with supernatural abilities, and he is it. *The Changeover: A Supernatural Romance* (1984) portrays part-Maori Laura Chant, a modern New Zealand girl who is given to odd premonitions which she never knows quite how to handle. Then on her way home from school one day, she and her little brother Jacko meet the bizarre and ominous Carmody Braque who stamps Jacko's hand with an ink stamp of Braque's own face, making the poor boy ill and allowing the monstrous Braque to possess him. In a variation of the Goblin King plot, Laura sets out to save her brother, whose life-force is being vampirized by the preternaturally ancient Braque. Aided by a local family of witches, she must make a 'changeover', the dangerous and extended rebirthing process necessary to become a witch.

> [Laura] began crawling on knees largely made of cotton-wool and rubber, but unlike cotton-wool and rubber able to bleed. At first the rocks shrank back from the wand but as she went on, they closed in, tighter and tighter, so that she had to squeeze through cracks no bigger than that under a door which grudgingly gave way to the wand and let her slide through … It grew so tight she began to despair, for though the wand like a rod divining spaces in solid rock, showed her a path, she was not sure she could follow it. Like Alice she did not think she would ever be small enough to reach the beautiful garden.[6]

In Mahy's work we also see that clear reference back to earlier fantasy, and to a community of fantasy readers, that would become so evident in the 1980s, an assumption that fantasy readers had mostly read the same texts and that as a result, the fantastic did not have to be explained.

Margaret Mahy (1936–2012), after Katherine Mansfield and Ngaio Marsh, may well be New Zealand's best-known writer. She is a winner of the Hans Christian Andersen Award and one of only seven children's writers to have won the Carnegie twice, for *The Haunting* and *The Changeover*. She is also a two-time winner of the Children's Literature Association's Phoenix Award. Mahy published her first story at the age of seven. She worked as a librarian until, after a flurry of successful picture books, she became a full-time writer in 1980. She was revered in New Zealand, and two different awards for outstanding children's literature in that country are named for her.

Time-slip narratives had a role to play here also, as in Helen Frances's *The Devil's Stone* (1983), in which the Australian twins Emma and Leigh discover that their family's claim to the land is a challenge to the land itself. Unlike the Canadian time-slip stories, this novel has a far greater sense of the contestation of the past and of the present, as does Joanna Orwin's *The Guardian of the Land* (1985) in which David Brownlie and Rua Jackson (one European, one Maori) engage in both archaeology and time-travel to retrieve a Maori artefact that was lost in the nineteenth century: clearly linked to the Nesbit tradition, it fits well with C. Butler's arguments about time-slip and archaeology both generating a sense of ownership over the land.

For British fantasy writers, love of land and the role of indigeneity were relatively uncomplicated – many of the real battles over the rights of access had taken place in the 1930s – and although we can see the growing resentment felt by the Welsh mirrored in Alan Garner's and Susan Cooper's work, no Welsh writers in this period challenged the English for ownership of their beliefs, land and mythology. In Canada and Australia, however, this was not the case. Rod McGillis queries the habit of children's literature of introducing 'young readers to a range of cultural experiences in the hope that knowing about other cultures will lead to tolerance' without necessarily considering the balance of power in what is 'known' or who is doing the tolerating.[7] One of the texts he identified as problematic is Welwyn Wilton Katz's *False Face* (1987) which, as he points out, has aroused a range of responses, only some of which include that word 'tolerance'. The problems begin, as McGillis suggests, because in this fantasy, 'the artifacts of one culture serve the ends of the author' from another culture; the white child is presented as ordinary, the Other child as hybrid and as both a literal and metaphorical bridge between cultures. She is protagonist, he is purpose.[8] Furthermore, as McGillis demonstrates, Katz (who otherwise wrote predominantly Celtic fantasies) took serious liberties with Iroquois face mask traditions, repurposing something that is essentially fluid to serve the binaries that underlie traditional Western theologies and magics, and furthermore endowing the masks with a finders-keepers ethos that is thoroughly colonialist.[9]

In *False Face* Laney finds a small mask in a bog and her introduction of the mask to the urban environment disrupts her world. Katz uses the magic to allow Laney to resolve her feelings towards her mother, to discuss the ethics of antiquities hunting, and to explore the position of Tom, Laney's friend, whose mother is white and whose father is from the local reserve. But while the book does assert that material ownership lies with the Mohawk, Clare Bradford points out that ownership of knowledge and interpretation rests mostly with the Europeans. Tom is presented as estranged from his tribal knowledge, and perhaps more seriously, is presented as moving *forward* to white civilization rather than *backward* to Mohawk culture, and Mohawk culture itself can only exist as history rather than as an element of the contemporary world.[10]

Equally controversial was Cam Hubert's *Dreamspeaker* (1978). In this Canadian fantasy a badly brutalized boy runs away from his foster home after wrecking the place. He falls in with an elderly Notka man and his mute adopted son, and is rehabilitated by absorption into their ritual beliefs (the older man is never named, the son is He Who Would Sing). The boy is found by the police and a judge refuses him permission to live with the two men, because of the crime he committed in the care home. The boy hangs himself, and in a final ritual He Who Would Sing commits suicide and joins the boy in a very real afterlife. The realism of the suicide scene moves the book from metaphor into religious fantasy (in the sense of the Christian fantasy written by believers in the nineteenth century). *Dreamspeaker* is one of the first of the fantasy texts to move away from the generic Indian, in the sense that the characters are given a specific tribal identity with specific tribal traditions, but the book has been controversial because the author is not a member of a First Nations tribe and there have been accusations of cultural appropriation which, while less heated than those in the USA or Australia, are every bit as urgent. As Bradford argues, one of the difficulties with 'Settler society children's literature, by non-indigenous authors' is that 'white authors continue to claim specialist knowledge of and access to indigenous cultures' in a deeply asymmetric power relationship.[11]

The countries whose fantasy has been most affected by this issue are Australia and New Zealand. Not all colonialism looks the same after all. The American belief in 'manifest destiny' is different from Australia's belief in *terra nullius* or New Zealand's policy of conquer and domesticate, and different yet again from Canada's belief that its indigenous peoples have been treated fairly, an idea which is now being repeatedly challenged by First Nations people. Until the 1990s, the use of indigenous practices and beliefs by non-indigenous writers was considered both liberal and enlightened. Patricia Wrightson, Australia's best-known children's fantasy writer for many years, made her name with *The Ice is Coming* (1977), the first of her Wirrun trilogy, which can loosely be thought of as a quest fantasy which takes place in the Dreamtime and in the outback, and with urban fantasies that will be discussed later. Bradford points out that Wrightson's own account of her research acknowledges not the people about whom she was writing but the anthropologists and (non-Aboriginal) folklorists who made them objects for study.[12] Wrightson continued working with Aboriginal material into the 1980s.

Such novels all, however liberal and well meaning, encoded Aboriginal or Maori culture as something Other, and most significantly, as something that could be packaged and sold. By the end of the 1990s this belief was under challenge by Aboriginal writers and campaigners. Perhaps the most recent of these appropriative novels is Gary Crew and Michael O'Hara's *The Blue Feather* (1997), a magic realist novel in which two scientists and a boy search for a legendary bird that can carry a man away. It is very fey, and very oriented to landscape, and tries to create an Australian fantastic, but it is notable because it does *not* refer directly to the indigenous peoples of Australia. They have been effectively erased from the book's Australian landscape. As we shall see in later chapters, one consequence of the pushback against this appropriation is that most Australian writers have either turned to European settings or to urban Australia for their inspiration.

### Coming out of the woodwork

One way in which folklore was revisited was the growing presence of the wainscot fantasy. The wainscot fantasy, where the fantastic occurs under our floors, behind our skirting boards (hence wainscots) or in the margins of our lives, had been popular in the inter-war period. T. H. White had used the Lilliputians, and BB had invented the Little Grey Men. These characters made lives for themselves, knowing that the world belonged to those larger than them. In the 1950s these small, marginal figures became a popular thread in fantasy when Mary Norton conjured up the Carnegie Medal-winning *The Borrowers* (1952) and four subsequent volumes. Their inspiration may have been the successful translations of Tove Jansson's *Comet in Moominland* (trans. 1946) and *Finn Family Moomintroll* (trans. 1950). These rather gentle books explore the lives of a small colony of trolls and their friends of varied species and, although they introduce children to things in life that are scary, they also assert that such things can be overcome. In Australian author S. A. Wakefield's *Bottersnikes and Gumbles* (1967), Bottersnikes are rather stupid and very lazy lizard creatures, who spend their lives trying to force the smart but very giggly Gumbles to work for them. In Britain, Elisabeth Beresford's *The Wombles* (1968) introduced a quiet set of stories about very large furry creatures inhabiting Wimbledon common (they were reduced in size for the later TV series), helpfully tidying up after humans and making use of things left behind. Read metaphorically, all of these stories might be understood as a reaction to the more intense quest fantasies that emerged after the war years. All of these are stories about hiding from the outside world, of sheltering children from menace. The Wombles, with their 'make do and mend' ethos, co-opted in the 1970s by the nascent ecology movement, are as much heirs to the bombsites of Britain – still extant in the 1970s – as are the children they entertained.

Yet the wainscot books can also be linked to the traditions that were emerging in the quest fantasies which developed in the same period. A US book published first in the UK, Carol Kendall's *The Minnipins* (1959; US, *The Gammage Cup*, 1959), tells of an isolated group of Minnipins forced to confront both invaders and the stifling conformity of their culture. Although Patricia Wrightson's work is not often read this way in Australia, where it is often seen more as in the trickster tradition, we can include it here, not least because there has long been an overlap between tricksters and the wainscot tradition (see the many accounts of brownies and house elves). In Wrightson's *An Older Kind of Magic* (1972), a group of children attempt to save a park; the wainscot creatures also trying to save it, the Nyol, Net-Net, Pot-Korook and Bitarr, stay beneath the earth, fairy folk who act in secret and are seen out of the corner of your eyes. *The Nargun and the Stars* is rural and set on a sheep station but the same theme, of hidden spirits of the land, acting to save the landscape, is visible. A similar use of wainscot fantasy to embed ecological messages can be found in Jackie French's later *The Boy Who Had Wings* (1993) which, however, is rather troubling in its political complacency. Mary is introduced by her father to the Grunkwunks who live in caves and are threatened by mining. She is asked to take Grrreee to school with her, passing him off as her part Eskimo cousin but not until he has shaved, hidden his wings and generally 'passed'. The book ends happily, but the continual refrain that *no one is discriminated against* and the presentation of Grrreee as a representation of the environment is disturbing.

The Wombles, the Borrowers and the Net-Net were relatively comfortable in their niches, still part of their own landscape, embedded in much the same way as Hobberdy Dick, quintessentially English or Australian. Their green radicalism disguises an Englander/Australian attitude that was in part about retaining the last moments of national homogeneity as it had been constructed by politicians in the 1950s, but never actually existed. Thus it was a shock to the children's literature establishment when Michael de Larrabeiti published *The Borribles* (1976). It is unclear whether in the writing this was intended as a children's book, but it is clearly *engaged* with children's literature. The Borribles are feral children who, once Borribled, grow long pointed ears, retain their apparent youth for a very long time, and hang out in the interstices of the urban environment, always at war with the Rumbles of Rumbledon: huge, furry creatures with snouts who live in burrows and call themselves (because they cannot pronounce their 'rrrs'), the Wumbles of Wumbledon. The book has the slightest of plots: young Borribles must go on an adventure to earn their names, and eight of them, plus one historian, are sent to kill the chief Rumbles. They travel there, have cursory and violent adventures, assassinate the leaders and four of them escape. The book is a satire on the embedded class and pastoral assumptions of Elisabeth Beresford's *Wombles* but, like Jan Needle's later *Wild Wood* (1981), cannot have been consciously aimed at children, for it is simply too violent. These are not the lost children of *Peter Pan* but the untamed thugs of the street. *The Borribles* was one of the first entries in a new Young Adult tradition, a precursor to a writer such as Melvyn Burgess but without the moral narratives often overlooked in Burgess's work. In *The Borribles* there is no redemption, no salvaging of the feral: the feral win. In 1981, in the face of riots across the UK, the publishers withdrew the third volume, and it was not published until Pan Macmillan produced an omnibus edition in 2003.

## CHAPTER 7

# Middle Earth, medievalism and mythopoeic fantasy

As we discussed in Chapter 5, the influence of C. S. Lewis changed the shape of British children's fantasy, pushing it towards portals, myth-magic and destinarianism, and perhaps most important, towards what Marek Oziewicz has argued is the dominance of the mythopoeic; that is, the making of myths. As children's and teen fantasy developed in the 1960s, this element came sufficiently to the fore that it began to dominate the public perception of what fantasy was. In his book *One Earth, One People* (2008), Oziewicz writes of almost all the authors we will be discussing in this chapter that they have 'strong convictions about fantasy as fulfilling vital human needs, as concerned with human values, and spiritual yearnings, and as grounded in archetypal patterns and poetic mode[s] of expression'.[1] They also have an intense sense of seriousness, suggesting that the fantasy matters in a way that was absent from pre-1950s fantasy.[2]

This sense of scaling up, of fantasy as containing *universals*, became in the 1960s and 1970s one of the dominant ways of critiquing the genre: it is no longer enough for the fantastic to disrupt the lives of children, for them to learn to negotiate the world around them; it is no longer enough for fantasy to *intrude*. Fantasy after fantasy has world-shattering consequences. The effect of this change can, perhaps, be best seen in the difference between the first three Enid Blytonesque Harry Potter books, and the following four, which moved us from the amusement of Hogwarts into the cataclysmic consequences of Lord Voldemort's war.

The changes that took place in fantasy in this period are several: first, the decisive move towards full secondary worlds totally separate from our own, like Middle Earth (although some, like Narnia, remain accessible through a portal); second, the increasing integration of myth and legend drawn by the British from their native traditions and those of Scandinavia, and by Americans, Canadians and Australians from much the same pool, until well into the 1990s; and third, the increasing role of the quest structure. This last narrative trajectory caught on substantially in the United States long before it became a strong trope in British and Commonwealth literature.[3]

An additional change, that emerged not in the literature but in the readers, was the clear development of a teen market. Until the 1980s, children's fantasy as a publishing category was a relatively clear-cut thing, quite separate from adult fantasy, however many teens read it, but it is in this period that the concept of 'appeals to teens' became a reality, focused around many of the mythopoeic and medievalist fantasies discussed here. As these readers began to converge and to be identified, the concept of the Young Adult market in fantasy, which we will discuss more fully in Chapters 8 and 9, began to cohere. Where it differed decisively in this period from the already established Young Adult market is precisely in this concern for the mythopoeic. Whereas relevance in the mimetic market was concerned with matters close to teenagers' lives, relevance in this new market responded to teen concerns about the state of the world.

### *The Lord of the Rings* and secondary-world fantasy

Although it was never intended for children, J. R. R. Tolkien's *The Lord of the Rings* is overwhelmingly the most significant publication to affect the development of children's and teen's fantasy in the 1960s; so significant that in Attebery's fine *Strategies of Fantasy* he thinks nothing of accepting his survey pool's assertion that it is the core of what fantasy is. Attebery's pool was, of course, made up predominantly of his contemporaries, however, all of whom were relatively young readers when *The Lord of the Rings* came out. His and their assertion is less a comment on the centrality of *The Lord of the Rings* than it is on the book's impact on the American market, for it was in the USA that the direction of fantasy was substantially altered by the influence of Tolkien's work. At a time when British, Irish, Canadian and Australian fantasy began to turn inwards to local traditions, American fantasy mostly ignored the legacy of Baum and turned back to Europe. However, the classic 'Tolkienization' of the genre (the ongoing production of three-volume, or more-than-a-dozen-volume, travel fantasies) was never as strong in children's fiction as it was to be in the adult genre.[4]

*The Lord of the Rings* was first published in Great Britain in 1954 and 1955, and then in the United States in an unauthorized Ace paperback and an authorized Ballantine paperback in 1965. Like *The Lion, the Witch and the Wardrobe*, it upped the stakes in fantasy, not just for the protagonists but for the world as a whole. *The Lord of the Rings* reinforced the idea that fantasies should reach out to heal the world rather than merely solve a personal problem, that they should assert the importance of idealism and great deeds. In addition, *The Lord of the Rings* introduced several key tropes that cropped up repeatedly in later fiction: a medievalist world of varying periods; prophecies (seen also in Narnia); the cataclysmic world-changing quest (as opposed to the less charged treasure hunts of the inter-war years); and the lost heir (previously the domain of swashbuckling Ruritanian historical romances such as Anthony Hope's *The Prisoner of Zenda*, 1894). The high stakes of such tales have often led to their being labelled High or Heroic Fantasy.

Tolkien's massive novel takes place in the quasi-medieval world of its predecessor, *The Hobbit*, a world totally disconnected from our own. It has its own deep history, as recounted in its extensive appendices and in a later companion volume, *The Silmarillion* (1977). The world of *The Lord of the Rings* is peopled by a variety of humanoid races – humans, elves, dwarves, hobbits, orcs, wizards – each of which has its own innate tendencies, traditions and magics, and many of which detest each other en masse. There are also a number of non-humanoid sentient races, including wolves, spiders, bears, eagles and, most importantly, dragons, at least in *The Hobbit*. Tolkien's tale, as most readers of this current volume will know, relates the story of the War of the Ring, for control of the entire world, between the demonic Sauron and his minions, and the free peoples of Middle Earth; more specifically it tells the story of the hobbit Frodo Baggins, a quintessential English yeoman type who, aided by his faithful servant Sam, saves the day for everyone by destroying the One Ring by throwing it into the fires of Mount Doom.

*The Lord of the Rings* was a bestseller, and in plot, structure and rhetoric it influenced an entire generation of authors and critics, although it would be twenty years before this became evident. In addition, although this is not directly relevant to this book, the success of *The Lord of the Rings* encouraged the US publisher Ballantine to launch a series of adult or 'literary' fantasies, bringing writers such as William Morris, James Branch Cabell, Hope Mirrlees, Evangeline Walton and George MacDonald back into print. The significance of this for our purposes is twofold: the publication of *The Lord of the Rings*, and of the Ballantine classics, demonstrated that there was a coherent book market for fantasy; and even though Ballantine rapidly moved to new authors, it also told American readers and authors that *this* was what fantasy looked like – European, medievalist and with high stakes.

Two very clear examples of this influence are Peter Beagle's *The Last Unicorn* (1968) and Terry Brooks's *The Sword of Shannara* (1977), the latter even more influential on what was to come and a deliberate, almost slavish attempt to create a Tolkienian fantasy (although a close reading suggests it is actually post-apocalyptic science fiction). Although it was not until the 1980s that children's fantasy would see a large number of Terry Brooks-style quests, the influence of Tolkien – the resituating of much fantasy in the medieval and in the mythopoeic – drowned much of the indigenous, whimsical and this-world fantasy tradition of E. B. White, James Thurber and Natalie Babbitt. In addition it led to an upsurge in the sheer numbers of fantasies on the market, and as this and succeeding chapters enter the 1980s, it will be necessary to concentrate increasingly on a mere sampling of the most significant new children's fantasy.

The first of the new 'Tolkienistas' in Britain was Alan Garner, although he has disclaimed Tolkien's influence and he quickly moved in other directions. In *The Weirdstone of Brisingamen* (1960) and *The Moon of Gomrath* (1963) the mythopoeic is displaced to a secondary world but it clearly fits Oziewicz's conceptualization of 'an imaginative experience in which metaphysical concepts are objective realities and the protagonists' responses to those realities reflect on their lives'.[5] In *Elidor* (1965), when the children bring objects back through the portal the adventure bleeds between worlds (in a way which Lewis rarely and Tolkien never allowed), and Garner permitted the fantastic to gain in metaphysical weight. *The Owl Service* (1967), although superficially conforming to the older tradition of British intrusion fantasy, is grounded in this desire for mythopoesis: the force that intrudes on our world is *myth itself* as the tale of Lleu Llaw Gyffes and his bride made of flowers begins to reshape the world of three teenagers, not so that it can affect their lives, but so their lives can affect the myth.

The intrusion of children and teens into the mythopoesis is the strongest of the trajectories we will see over the next thirty years. We can see it also in the development of the work of Susan Cooper. The early books of the *Dark is Rising* sequence, particularly *Over Sea, Under Stone*, published in 1965, just before the publication of *The Lord of the Rings* in the USA, are old-style fantastical treasure hunts. By 1973, however, in *The Dark is Rising* Will's treasure hunt acquires a myth structure, *Greenwitch* (1974) is rooted in local folklore as is *The Grey King* (1975), and while Will's symbols, the Greenwitch herself, and the harp on the mountain repel only local dangers, these dangers are significant. In *The Grey King*, the penultimate book in the series, which is very much influenced by Welsh myth,[6] the power of mythopoesis and the quest fantasy come into their own. In this book we have the sense continually that there is more to the harp that is sought than meets the eye. The boy Bran connects past and present, reality and legend (using an understanding of Arthur created by T. H. White, Mary Stewart and Rosemary Sutcliff). In *Silver on the Tree* (1977) Bran is the link between the mundane children Barney, Simon and Jane, and the otherworldly Will. Furthermore, while the first three adventures are clearly guided by Merriman/Merlin, in the last two Will and Bran themselves become the guides.

In the USA the first of the new mythopoeists was Lloyd Alexander, discussed first in Chapter 5 because he is so hard to separate from the British tradition. *The Chronicles of Prydain*, it seems probable, was influenced directly by Alexander's reading of the Mabinogion and of Robert Graves's *The White Goddess*, so that this is one of the few Celtic fantasies which is not Arthurian.[7] As Donna White recounts, the original plan was for a rather more faithful recounting of three tales from the Mabinogion (the same three Robert Graves had taken from Lady Charlotte Guest's 1849 translation), but the creation of two child characters, Taran and Eilonwy, derailed the plan in highly creative ways.

*The Chronicles of Prydain*, which begins with *The Book of Three* (1964), traces the rise of Taran, from Assistant Pig-Keeper of Hen Wen, the Oracular Pig, to become – at the end of a climactic fight clearly influenced by *The Lord of the Rings* – High King of Prydain (in the Newbery Award-winning *The High King*, 1968). As with Cooper's series, we see a gradual increase in the import of the work from the treasure hunt structure of the earliest books, through to the world-shattering outcomes of the conclusion.

The Prydain books are set in a generic early medieval period, and although there are elements of high fantasy, in that Taran comes to consort with kings, this is not *court* fantasy (that is, fantasy set at the king's court and centring on the nobility), which is indeed notably absent from children's fantasy (it begins to emerge in the adult world in the work of Terry Brooks and Katherine Kurtz). The most interesting and subtle of the books is *Taran Wanderer* – which was inserted into the series after the climactic volume, *The High King*, had already been delivered, by Alexander's editor Ann Durrell – in which Taran, in search of his parentage, undertakes successive apprenticeships as an artisan. The book is crucial to the Americanness of the series, for it insists not on heritage but on a combination of hard work, talent and luck as the fundamentals of manhood. Taran may eventually be gifted his kingship but there is a feeling of *election* (in an older, sacred sense) when it is awarded, for, like Dalben, the prophet and wizard of the series, we can trace Taran's route not through destiny, but through a series of 'what ifs'. However, this does draw attention by contrast to one of the key shifts in the rise of 'Tolkienism': where Frodo gives away power (a motif repeated in the plot of *The Black Cauldron*), in the end Taran is rewarded for his rejection of reward (a place on the ship going to the Summer Country) *with* power, although it is framed as responsibility.

The most important writer, in terms of her impact on the field in this period, to be influenced visibly by Tolkien was probably Ursula K. Le Guin (the influences on Diana Wynne Jones are less immediately obvious and her impact emerged twenty years after she began writing). With the exception of the Earthsea books (and despite having written a variety of picture books and several other children's novels), Le Guin is not usually thought of as a writer for children, nor is she known predominantly for fantasy, but when she undertook to write a fantasy series for young people, it was Tolkien to whom she responded, reactively rather than in emulation. Le Guin said: 'I am grateful that I was in my twenties when I first read Tolkien and had gone far enough towards finding my own voice and way as a writer that I could learn from him (endlessly) without being overwhelmed, over-influenced by him.'[8] Le Guin's work demonstrates a clear understanding of Tolkien's fear of power and shows once again the surge in his influence. Both Ged in *A Wizard of Earthsea* (1968) and Tenar in *The Tombs of Atuan* (1970) conclude their stories by rejecting power, understanding that it can destroy the world. By the final book in the initial trilogy, *The Farthest Shore* (1972), once more the significance of Ged's adventures has increased to the cataclysmic, although in a twist not taken up by other authors, Ged himself (and by implication humanity itself) is a far greater threat than any intruding dark lord.

Ursula K. Le Guin's *A Wizard of Earthsea* is a full immersive fantasy like Tolkien's, though with a twist. Noting perhaps that such stories almost always come with maps of the fantasy world, but that the maps always fade around the edges to some sort of *terra incognita* when either the author's ingenuity or space on the page runs out, Le Guin intentionally made Earthsea into a pocket universe. There's nothing beyond the edge of her map except the Land of the Dead, a practice that influenced other fantasy writers like P. C. Hodgell in *God Stalk* (1982) and sequels. Another variation Le Guin introduced to high fantasy was the brown protagonist. Ged and most other characters of *A Wizard of Earthsea* are clearly described as something other than Caucasian, a dilemma for publishers intent on selling the books primarily to a white audience, which led to a series of covers for the Earthsea books that showed the protagonist either at a distance, with his face turned partly away from the reader, or as a tanned Caucasian. Years later, when Le Guin's publisher brought out an advance reading copy of her novel *Powers* (2007) with a white face on the cover, despite the fact that the protagonist was explicitly written as a person of colour, Le Guin, who by that time had more control over her work than most writers, objected strenuously until the picture was, after several revisions, replaced by the black character actually seen on the first edition of the novel.

Le Guin's rejection and reworking of Tolkien is in part rooted in a rejection of Christianity and we can see this in parallels, resonances and shifts in values. Like Frodo in *The Lord of the Rings*, Le Guin's protagonists learn to define themselves and discover who they really are in part by making connections with other people. Unlike in Tolkien, however, the impulse to act is not celebrated, but regarded with unease: Sandra Lindow argues that in Le Guin's fiction those characters who 'act on impulse ... end up causing much more suffering to themselves and others than if they had stayed home and taken up goat farming'.[9] Yet Le Guin's protagonists are also fundamentally a part of the world in a way that becomes a strong element of the Tolkien tradition: Tolkien's landscapes indicate the health of the land, and he emphasizes a strong connection between King and (literally) country (see for example Robin McKinley's *Chalice*, 2008, as the ultimate working out of this idea). Le Guin intensifies this relationship to the point that the wisdom of 'not doing' replaces even the most heroic (and unpretentious) doing, for Ged's actions reverberate at both the natural and the supernatural level. Thus Ged, like Frodo, gives up his magic to live humbly in retirement, refusing all attempts to honour him or entice him to further service. Although a limited form of heroism is possible, the best activity in the Earthsea books, when activity is pursued at all, is handled after discussion and through communal action and this, as with Tolkien, leads to a fantasy that is concerned with the relationships between people: what is the proper relationship between the individual and the Other, whether that Other be another person or another part of oneself? Kath Filmer points to the dogmatism of the God King, the title of the Priestess, the 'Eaten One', in *Tehanu*, and its reversal of the Eucharist.[10] Attebery's argument that 'Light and shadow, names, balance, communication cross barriers: these are ever present themes in Le Guin's fiction' could be as true for *The Lord of the Rings* and can be understood as one of the driving impulses behind Tolkienian fantasy.[11]

John Stephens and Robyn McCallum have argued that 'One of the obvious attractions of the Middle Ages is its otherness ... Although such societies may be depicted as racked by political conflict ... they are nevertheless societies to which clear principles of order, justice and morality can be attributed, usually as principles reinstated by events of the text.'[12] However, one difficulty for the authors who wrote under the influence of Tolkien, in a field in which at least half of their readers were female (despite popular assumptions), was the absence of women in his world, and the suggestion – still accepted by many today despite plenty of historical evidence of significant medieval women to the contrary – that it is not possible to give significant roles to a woman in a medievalist fantasy. A few heroic and powerful female characters could be found in Tolkien, of course (Galadriel, Arwen and Éowyn), but Le Guin, looking back on her career, acknowledged that when she wrote the first three Earthsea books, she was still working with traditional, pre-feminist ideas of heroism, power and agency. Ged, though brown, was still a man and was conditioned to regard women with suspicion and women's magic as inherently dubious. Only some of this is corrected in *The Tombs of Atuan*. In this book Tenar has power, but no agency until she rescues Ged at the end and resigns her magic. Women could not be wizards in Earthsea. In *Tehanu* (1990), the fourth volume of the series (and the first aimed at an adult readership), which came out after Le Guin had been through the feminist consciousness-raising process of the late 1970s, she revisited a traditional Earthsea saying 'Weak as woman's magic, wicked as woman's magic'[13] and thoroughly undermined it by reframing the entire structure of mythopoeic heroism which Tolkien had bequeathed us into a different sense of duty, refiguring Frodo's quiet stoicism into domestic duty.

While the medievalist setting of Tolkienian fantasy superficially precluded women from important roles, it offered new possibilities to writers of fantasy for girls because it involved multiple heroes and a recognized role for sidekicks, and because, unlike other forms of fantasy prior to this, it took place almost entirely *outdoors*, the main locus for violent adventure and a place that had been previously regarded as out of bounds for many girls, as we have seen in Chapters 2 and 4. Outdoors was still predominantly where boys played. Only in the gang detective stories had girls accompanied boys on adventures. Fantasy in the style of Tolkien and Lewis likewise allowed girls to be included in gang adventures – C. S. Lewis has to remember to restrict the roles of Lucy and Susan because they are having far too much fun for decorum, but loosens the bonds of propriety on Jill in later books; Lloyd Alexander sends Taran out with the plucky and talkative Princess Eilonwy; and Tolkien himself has a place for Éowyn. Furthermore, as many writers were quick to point out, having few women of power in medieval Europe did not mean there were *no* women of power: Eleanor of Aquitaine, Isabella of Castile, Matilda of Tuscany and, briefly, Joan of Arc all demonstrated their power as female rulers and, sometimes, as warriors. As more and more writers came to the field with degrees in English, history or medieval studies, and as women's studies began to examine the roles of different classes of women, writers began to find effective niches for female protagonists.

## A sudden flowering of heroines

Enter Patricia McKillip and Robin McKinley. McKillip's beautifully written *The Forgotten Beasts of Eld* (1974) tells the story of Sybel, a powerful young wizard who lives in isolation on top of a mountain with a menagerie of powerful magical animals to keep her company. She is innocent and unworldly, wise in wizard's lore but deeply ignorant both of the complex dynastic politics that obsess the warring kingdoms at her mountain's foot and of human sexual politics as well. Sybel is slowly drawn into the political whirlpool around her when she agrees to raise an endangered baby boy, a distant relative of hers who may be the heir of the king. As the years pass, a number of powerful men pay suit to her, each hoping to co-opt her magic for their own use. Sybel, who appears reminiscent of a young Galadriel, seems thoroughly out of her depth despite her power. At one point she is almost raped by an older wizard who has been hired to subjugate her and force her to marry the king. Instead, she marries Coren, the handsome young lord who had initially brought her the child to raise. Coren, brave, and relatively honest, would be the hero of a more traditional tale, but here he is merely love interest and sidekick. It is Sybel who destroys the wizard who has tried to rape her and Sybel herself who eventually brings down the wicked king.

In her next novel, *The Riddle-Master of Hed* (1976), McKillip returned to the use of a male hero, Morgon, the land-ruler of a minor kingdom who has little interest in heroics but finds himself forced to follow a greater destiny. The sequel, *Heir of Sea and Fire* (1977), however, centres on Raederle, the young daughter of a neighbouring lord who was promised to Morgon in marriage in *Riddle-Master*. In *Heir*, Raederle, who may well have been influenced by Alexander's Princess Eilonwy, goes off on her own quest to find Morgon, who has been missing for a year. In doing so, she discovers both her own agency and her own magical powers, becoming one of the most engaging and beloved characters in the children's fantasy of the period. In the final volume of the series, *Harpist in the Wind* (1979), Morgon achieves a sort of godhood, but Raederle maintains her own agency and is an active hero throughout.

In her 1985 Newbery acceptance speech for *The Hero and the Crown* (1985), Robin McKinley wrote that as a child she 'wished desperately for books like *Hero*', books that didn't necessitate being 'untrue to my gender'.[14] In both this book and *The Blue Sword* (1982) McKinley demonstrated the high-stakes, big-armies influence of Tolkien. *The Blue Sword*, with its nineteenth-century setting, will be discussed below, but its prequel *The Hero and the Crown* is set in what is for the characters of *The Blue Sword* the medieval past. Aerin is the younger daughter of the King of Damar, but her dead mother is widely thought to have been a witch who seduced the King, and Aerin, big, red-haired, shy and apparently lacking in *kelar*, the royal magic of Damar, is not very popular in the kingdom: until, that is, she becomes a dragonslayer. Teaching herself how to fight with minimal help, she makes it her job to rid the kingdom of its few small but still dangerous dragons. Then, and not by coincidence, just as her father rides out to deal with a traitor and possible civil war, the great dragon Maur returns to Damar and wreaks havoc. In a ferocious battle scene Aerin slays him, but barely survives. Healed and rendered more than human by the wizard, Luthe, who gives her the fabled blue sword, Aerin then gathers an army of beasts to fight two great battles against monstrous villains. Her father, the king, dies in the final battle and Aerin, now recognized as a great hero by her people, marries Tor, the king's chosen heir.

One of the opportunities that appealed to some women writers, and has continued to appeal, has been the gender disguise adopted by Tolkien's Éowyn that – at a stage in feminism where men's roles were simply more attractive than women's – allowed women to perform *as* men. Perhaps the most successful writer to use this strategy was Tamora Pierce. In *Alanna: The First Adventure* (1983) Alanna, in a world where the daughters of nobility invariably go to convents to be trained to become wives and mothers, wants to be a knight. To accomplish this objective, she disguises herself as a boy and replaces her brother Thom, who has been sent off for military training but would rather become a sorcerer. As Alan, Alanna proves herself the equal of her male counterparts in all aspects of knightly training, although Pierce doesn't ignore the problems involved in doing so with a small, female body. Rife with magic, the subsequent series, which covers a decade in Alanna's life, also provides one of the most realistic portrayals, in all fantasy literature, of what a knight's training might really be like. Equally important, Alanna, although heroic, is also very much a young woman who has to deal with real women's issues such as the prejudiced gender essentialism that surrounds her, being weaker than most of her peers, hiding her menstruation, handling crushes, and eventually sexual intercourse.

Jane Yolen, one of the most versatile writers in the history of children's literature, contributed *Sister Light, Sister Dark* (1988) and *White Jenna* (1989) to this growing subgenre. The much later sequel, *The One-Armed Queen* (1998), was originally marketed to adults, but quickly gained popularity with Yolen's teenaged fans. *White Jenna*'s publisher chose to include a blurb on the cover from Marion Zimmer Bradley, comparing the work to that of both Le Guin and McKillip, suggesting a growing affinity of writers and readers. Set in a typically medieval kingdom, the books tell the story of a white-haired warrior girl, White Jenna, who, in a noteworthy trope for fantasies with strong female characters, is raised isolated from the world of men on a mountainside. Prophesied to be the one who will reunite the shattered kingdom of the Dales and return the King to his throne, Jenna has the magical power to call forth her shadow sister Skada to fight with her, though Skada can only exist by the light of the moon or in the flickering light of a fire. Yolen skilfully divides sections of her tale into different genres. Thus we get paragraphs labelled 'The Myth', told in an elevated voice, and similar sections called 'The Legend' or 'The Song' or 'The History', followed by longer chapters titled 'The Story' written in a more traditional narrative voice. In this Yolen may also have been influenced by one of the least commented-on aspects of Tolkien, the degree to which he moves between the demotic and the courtly voice in *The Lord of the Rings*.

Jane Yolen (1939–), who in 2009 received the World Fantasy Award for Life Achievement, has produced hundreds of picture books, chapter books and children's novels, as well as a number of works for adults. Some of her fantasy is directly relevant to this chapter, and some not, but all of it is worth reading. Among her many fine books not discussed here are *The Pit Dragon Chronicles*, beginning with *Dragon's Blood* (1982), a science fantasy series concerning a boy growing up at a dragon-breeding centre; the Mythopoeic Fantasy Award-winning *Cards of Grief* (1985), an adult science fiction novel set on a planet where grieving is an art form; *The Devil's Arithmetic* (1988), a time-slip story set in a concentration camp during the Second World War; the Mythopoeic Fantasy Award-winning *Briar Rose* (1992), which retells that fairy tale in terms of the Holocaust; *Sword of the Rightful King* (2003), an ALA Best Book-winning tale of King Arthur; and *Pay the Piper: A Rock and Roll Fairy Tale* (2005), one of several novels she has co-authored with her son Adam Stemple. Yolen's adult fiction has won or been nominated for science fiction's Nebula Award on numerous occasions and her anthology *Favorite Folktales from Around the World* (1986) won the World Fantasy Award.

Sherwood Smith, another writer with a long and complex career, contributed *Wren to the Rescue* (1990) to this growing tradition. Like many children's fantasies, this book features a spunky orphan, in this case the titular Wren, who befriends Tess, whom she thinks is another orphan but who turns out to be a princess in hiding from Andreus, the evil king of a neighbouring nation. When Tess is indeed kidnapped, Wren, finding her suggestions ignored by Tess's parents, goes off on her own, enlisting the aid of Tyron, an apprentice magician, and Tess's young uncle Connor, who can speak with animals. In various sequels Andreus makes further attempts upon Tess's person and her kingdom, and the four young people continue to fight him to a draw.

By the 2000s male writers were also looking to infuse their writing with feminism and feminist heroines, not least because the teen market was disproportionately female. An important mythopoeic work that shares with *The Blue Sword* a combination of medievalish and more modern backgrounds is the Australian writer Garth Nix's *The Old Kingdom* series, beginning with *Sabriel* (1995), followed by *Lirael* (2001), *Abhorsen* (2003), the short story collection *Across the Wall* (2005) and *Clariel* (2014). The series, like so much mythopoeic fantasy, concerns various attempts by black magicians and other creatures of evil, particularly the restless dead, to take control of both kingdoms and the heroic efforts of the various title characters to prevent this. Sabriel is a schoolgirl in industrialized

Ancelstierre who finds herself summoned back to the Old Kingdom to rescue her father, a powerful necromancer called the Abhorsen, from Death, which is itself a complex place with its own well-developed geography. Lirael is an orphaned librarian who, seemingly by chance, meets Sabriel's son and helps him defeat another black necromancer, but eventually discovers that she is in fact Sabriel's sister. Nix creates a variety of fascinating magical systems, bell-magic for example, and his beautifully written, complex plots are endlessly interesting. Again, as is the case in so much mythopoeic fantasy, destiny plays an important role and the stakes rise from book to book until, eventually, the fate of both lands is at stake. Nix's novels show the obvious influence of their predecessors, Tolkien of course, and also, particularly, Le Guin's *A Wizard of Earthsea*. Various connections can also be hypothesized to the near-genocidal interactions between Australians of European ancestry and their indigenous countrymen. Guilt may lie not all that far beneath the surface for many Australians, a guilt that could manifest itself in Nix's introduction into his stories of the restless dead who refuse to stay in their graves, not to mention what he calls Free Magic, an ancient, dangerous and wild form of magic, now exceedingly rare, which stands in opposition to the lawful Charter Magic that governs the lives of all of the major characters in the series.

Tolkien's influence was complex: by the 1980s, the quest fantasy and a version of an older heroic fantasy predating Tolkien were merging to create the modern fantasy swashbuckler. One of the most engaging and complex series was the *Redwall* sequence of animal fantasies produced by Brian Jacques, beginning with *Redwall* in 1986 and continuing through twenty-two core books and many spinoffs to 2011. *Redwall* uses anthropomorphized animals, creating for them a medievalist world of heroics and derring-do. In the first book a mouse called Matthias sets out on a quest for a lost sword to enable him to defeat Cluny, the rat threatening the abbey. Although the sword is retrieved, there is a strong implication that it is Matthias's adventures that have enabled him to win the day, and there is more of sword and sorcery than there is of the high fantasy tradition of Tolkien.

Robin Jarvis, a contemporary of Brian Jacques, also used animal substitutes in *The Deptford Mice* (1989) to tell a much darker but still heroic tale of mice who worship the Green Mouse of Spring and set out to defeat the Dark Lord. The first book is relatively realistic in the same sense as Robert C. O'Brien's Newbery Award-winning *Mrs. Frisby and the Rats of NIMH* (1971), in that the characters live and act in a world with no more supernatural content than our own, but in *The Crystal Prison* (1989) and *The Final Reckoning* (1990) the books become darker and far more engaged with spirits and ghosts. A decade later, the Canadian writer Kenneth Oppel offered an even darker take on the romantic animal tale of derring-do with *Silverwing* (1997), *Sunwing* (1999) and *Firewing* (2002). The first two stories are relatively conventional in the *Watership Down* tradition but the third takes us into the underworld and rewrites the world of bats with the aid of a large helping of *Faust*.

### The Matter of Britain, again

For many writers, what Tolkien opened up was not medievalist fantasy, but simply the medieval and in particular the early medieval, and the ability to combine local folklore with the fantastic. As we discussed in Chapter 4, in the 1930s folk tale and fantasy, although clearly related, had not entirely merged. In the works discussed in Chapters 5 and 6, 1950s and 1960s British authors, inspired by Lewis and Tolkien and by the work of historical fiction writers, turned to folklore and increasingly to Arthuriana. English writer Peter Dickinson introduced Merlin into his futuristic *Changes* trilogy (see *The Weathermonger*, 1968). Susan Cooper's *The Dark is Rising* sequence, including the Newbery Award-winning *The Grey King*, while it did not kick off a craze for Arthuriana – that had been well under way since the 1850s and had been solidly incorporated into children's historical fiction by Rosemary Sutcliff and into the mainstream by Mary Stewart – did bring the Matter of Britain into the stuff that was forming the working palette of fantasy.

The popularity of Arthur has been sustained but has veered radically between reinterpretation and adherence to tradition. The American writer Andre Norton's Arthur series, beginning with *Steel Magic* (1978), sent contemporary children through a time-slip to the island of Avalon. American author Elizabeth Wein produced a version of the Arthurian legends, *The Winter Prince* (1993) and its sequels, which is narrated by Medraut the son of Artos as a tale of brotherly jealousy rather than adultery. Jane Yolen, one of the authors more aware of the field and often responding to it, produced *Merlin's Booke* (1986), a collection of stories and poems. In *The Seeing Stone* (2000) and its sequels, the British author Kevin Crossley-Holland produced an award-winning, strongly historical look at the Arthur stories. The UK author Philip Reeve, in the Carnegie Medal-winning *Here Lies Arthur* (2007), also strips Arthur of his magic, and turns Merlin into a con-artist determined to create a myth around which to reunite Britain. By contrast, the American Gerald Morris, in *The Squire's Tale* (1998), began an extended series of Arthurian tales more heavily influenced by Malory and the old romances than anything else. More often than not these stories have tended to centre on Merlin as much as Arthur, as in T. A. Barron's *The Lost Years of Merlin* (1996) and its many sequels or Yolen's brief *The Young Merlin Trilogy* (2004).

The Carnegie Medal was given annually to the finest children's books published in Britain. After 1969 this was expanded to include writers from beyond the UK. Authors of fantasies who have won the Medal include:

- BB (D. J. Watkins-Pitchford, 1942)
- Eric Linklater (1944)
- C. S. Lewis (1945)
- Elizabeth Goudge (1946)
- Walter de la Mare (1947)
- Mary Norton (1952)
- Philippa Pearce (1958)
- Lucy M. Boston (1961)
- Pauline Clarke (1962)
- Alan Garner (1967)
- Rosemary Harris (1968)
- Leon Garfield (1970)
- Richard Adams (1972)
- Penelope Lively (1973)
- Robert Westall (1981)
- Margaret Mahy (1982, 1984)
- Kevin Crossley-Holland (1985)
- Susan Price (1987)
- Philip Pullman (1995)
- David Almond (1998)
- Terry Pratchett (2001)
- Philip Reeve (2008)
- Neil Gaiman (2010)
- Patrick Ness (2011, 2012)

Peter Dickinson, one of the most distinguished British writers of fantasy for children, has also won the Carnegie twice, but, oddly enough, not for works of fantasy.

A particularly disturbing Arthurian fantasy, *The Third Magic* (1988), came from Canadian writer Welwyn Winton Katz. Written in three tracks or plotlines, it is a story about male and female magic, neither of which is particularly nice. Rigan is sent by the Sisters of the Circle to be born in a new world and fight for it to join the Circle. She finds herself up against Merllend of the Line for control over the child Arthur, but bit by bit loses. Arddu is Rigan's unwanted twin, male with the pale colouring of Circle magic users but with no magic. Left behind, he becomes prey to the men who wield the magic of the Line. They use his pattern/dna to find his sister Rigan, but it is not she they pull back but Morgan Lefevre from the 1980s. Morgan is in Tintagel with her father who is a documentary maker. She wonders why people around her pronounce Lefevre as LeFey, and why she sees visions that can be driven away by cold iron. When she finds herself in Nwm with Arddu all they can do is run. Eventually they find a way to Earth and insinuate themselves into the story, replacing both Arthur and Rigan and healing the legend, while holding Earth out of the fight between Line and Circle. Although the Arthur story matters, it doesn't overwhelm the characters – when Morgan thinks they are about to be overwhelmed she is enormously resentful that her sense of herself is being taken over. Although they heal the story of Arthur, this is not the main point of the novel. Looking at this book and Le Guin's original *Earthsea* trilogy, it is fascinating to see the suspicion of women's power embedded in these early medievalist fantasies *by* women writers.

Arthur and Merlin are sufficiently powerful names that they have also been deployed in more nebulous ways, often coming close to science fiction: *Merlin's Candles*, by Canadian L. B. MacDonald, tells of Morgan Le Fay's attempt to kill Merlin in his youth. But Merlin lives backwards (an idea taken from T. H. White) and when she finds the young Merlin he is John Merlin, a science teacher who is mentoring a young black Canadian boy in whom he sees potential. When he uses the Fountain of Youth to counteract one of Morgan's spells, he triggers the process whereby he begins to wake up yesterday. In *The Merlin Conspiracy*, by Diana Wynne Jones (2003), the Merlin is an office, the title of the King's First Minister on the Island of Blest. More recently, the British writer Sarwat Chadda has created in *The Devil's Kiss* (2009) a Dan Brown-inspired tale of a girl who discovers that her father is one of the last members of the order of the Holy Grail, dedicated to fighting demons in the world.

From Arthur specifically, it was a short step to the more generic Celtic fantasy, which has overwhelmingly come from outside the British Isles. The Canadian author O. R. Melling, for example, set a number of fantasies in prehistoric Ireland, and although the writing is often pedestrian, her books have been very popular. In *The Druid's Tune* (1983),

Rosemary and Jim are sent from Canada to stay with their aunt and uncle in Connaught. They meet a druid, slip through time, and go on holiday in the Táin Bó Cúailnge, the national epic of Ireland, in which the tribes fight over cattle, and supposed heroes kill each other (it makes the Trojan War look sophisticated). In *The Singing Stone* (1986), Kay Warrick, an orphan, inherits a mysterious package of books that leads her to travel to Ireland, where she is sent back in time to help a tribe, the Tuatha de Danann, who are under vicious attack. Kay, in a classic fantasy convention, is then sent on a quest to find four magical objects. She succeeds with the help of a Mage figure and in the end turns out to be a daughter of the people she helped, as well as a sorceress and time traveller. In Australia, although Welsh material has not had wide influence, Brian Caswell's *Merryll of the Stones* (1989) intertwined a modern Australian girl of Welsh descent and the Merryll of legends, while in Louise Katz's *Myfanwy's Demon* (1996) Meg is called back in time to Wales by a white witch to help battle the evil forces that enslave the local people. A great number of these Celtic fantasies have involved time travel, but N. M. Browne put a new twist on it in *Warriors of Alvana* (2000) and its sequels when she sent her protagonists back to an alternative Celtic and Roman Britain in which everything was just slightly askew.

## Fairy tale fantasy

One of the strongest romance elements to be incorporated into medieval fantasy can be seen in the use made of the linked ballads of *Thomas the Rhymer* and *Tam Lin*. Both ballads were incorporated into fantasy through the Elizabethan notions of fairies which began to be seen in historical fiction in the 1960s (note *The Armourer's House*, 1951, by Rosemary Sutcliff, and the general growth of *A Midsummer's Night's Dream* as an ur-text for fantasy). Not all of these texts were written for children or teens as such, but as the awareness of a specific late teen market emerged, writers like Ellen Kushner and Pamela Dean were adopted into the new Young Adult field. US author Kushner's *Thomas the Rhymer* (1990) is perhaps the most traditional of these tales. Related from four perspectives (those of an old shepherd, his wife, Thomas and his true love, Elspeth), it retells Thomas's journey with the Queen of Elfland and his disappearance from thirteenth-century Scotland for seven years. More importantly, it tells the story of how a man can be reabsorbed into a community when he has experienced fantastic events about which he cannot lie. In its focus on the relationship between Thomas and a growing girl, it has some of the markers of the later Young Adult form. Kushner's book and Canadian author Janet McNaughton's later *An Earthly Knight* (2004) (which combined *Tam Lin* with another ballad, *Lady Isabel and the Elf Knight*) hewed closest to the original stories (McNaughton has a PhD in folklore) and made the most serious attempt at a medievalist setting.

Among the best of the Tam Lin tales are Pamela Dean's *Tam Lin* (1991) and Diana Wynne Jones's *Fire and Hemlock* (1984). Dean's novel, which has sometimes been classified as an urban fantasy and sometimes as a fairy tale fantasy, concerns Janet Carter, a student at fictional Blackstock College in Minnesota in the 1970s, and devotes as much time to her everyday life, academic struggles and romantic entanglements. The tale is significant for the flawless way in which it maps the life of a studious but brave college girl onto that of the heroine of an ancient ballad.

There is no obvious single place to focus on Diana Wynne Jones in this study – she explored with great success almost every form of fantasy and is thus an oft-recurring name in this book – but *Fire and Hemlock* is probably her masterpiece (if not necessarily everyone's favourite). The novel is a contemporary fantasy that entwines the stories of Tam Lin and Thomas the Rhymer on the grounds that any fairy tale when repeated in life takes a slightly different turn (a little like Garner's *The Owl Service* and *Red Shift*). It rifles through the stock of myth, legend, poetry and children's fantasy to create a complexly layered text, and it is ferociously critical of some of the romantic assumptions of Jones's contemporaries. Unlike Kushner's Elspeth, Jones's Polly resents being isolated from her friends by Tom and effectively groomed to rescue him. In *Fire and Hemlock* Polly strays into the fairy world when she inadvertently gatecrashes a funeral at the old manor house and meets Tom who, she will eventually figure out, is due to die to make way for the next consort of the elf queen. Tom has partially broken free but he needs his freedom to be bought from outside and over the next seven years, with books and letters, he will both court and train Polly. Jones appears to have been influenced by Tolkien to a far greater degree as a critic than as a fiction author (her one Tolkienish fantasy is the excoriating satire *Dark Lord of Derkholm*, 1998) but we can see this influence in *Fire and Hemlock*. It is a multivalent text that uses exactly the musical structures she describes in her 1983 article on Tolkien, 'The Shape of the Narrative in *The Lord of the Rings*'.

C. S. Lewis and Diana Wynne Jones (1934–2011) are the two most extensively discussed authors in this book, a mark not only of Jones's large and varied oeuvre, but also of the high regard in which she is held by both of this volume's authors, one of whom (Mendlesohn) has written an entire book on Jones's work. Of particular note, we believe, is her non-fiction *The Tough Guide to Fantasyland* (1996, rev. edn 2006), which purports to be a travel guide (with a nod to the *Rough Guide* series) to a sort of generic fantasy world and which is written, on the surface, as if all of the places mentioned are every bit as real as, say, Norway or Spain. What Jones is really doing, as she does so brilliantly in many of her novels, is spearing the various clichés of heroic fantasy, pointing out such invariable idiocies of the genre as 'Forest of Doom. This is usually the home of mobile and prehensile Trees. There will be giant SPIDERS too'; or 'Slender Youth. A TOUR Companion who may be either a lost PRINCE or a girl/PRINCESS in disguise. In the latter case it is tactful to pretend you think she is a boy.'[15] The capitalized words, of course, are cross-references for other entries. Novice readers of fantasy may simply not 'get' this book, but veteran readers are likely to find it both funny and uncomfortable.

The wide span of Jones's work draws attention to the degree to which medieval folklore, and an interest in Greek and other myths, had truly become possessions of the fantasy writers by the 1980s, both in medievalist fantasy and in urban fantasy. She herself used the Norse gods in *Eight Days of Luke* (1975), Greek cosmology in *Dogsbody* (1975) and elsewhere, and English folklore in *Power of Three* (1976); in each book we find that we live much closer to the fantastic than we thought and that the gods have not gone away. In Irish writer Pat O'Shea's *The Hounds of the Morrigan* (1985), Irish legend manifests itself in the form of the Morrigan, although the setting and structure owe more to Nesbit. In Welsh writer Catherine Fisher's *The Snow-Walker's Son* (1993) and *Belin's Hill* (1997) Norse and Celtic myth are engagingly explored. More recently, Kate Thompson's *The New Policeman* (2005) is set in a village in Ireland where time from Tir Nan Og, the otherworld of Irish mythology, is leaking into our world. C. Butler's *Death of a Ghost* (2006) is set in a modern mansion but alongside this setting is told the tale of the ghost that haunts it and the prehistoric goddess Sulis who wants to trace her lost lover through time.

Sometimes the past lives alongside us in more literal ways: the Canadian Donn Kushner's *A Book Dragon* (1987) sees a creature from legend live into the present. It begins when Nonesuch is a young dragon in early Norman England. We watch him learn from the follies of his relatives, and we explore the world through his fresh and innocent eyes.

When he falls in love with a medieval church and then a manuscript, we fall in love with him. The book works through to the twentieth century with the dragon choosing to become small enough to fit inside the book and becoming the book's guardian. In this sense the medievalism is encoded quite practically as the medieval of memory. In all of these books the medieval lives alongside us. With the exception of Kushner's tale, there is a sense that the books make fantastical the lived realities of many in Britain and Europe where the palimpsest of ages is embodied in the physical landscape: if the buildings of the ancient and medieval saints and gods and ghosts are amid us, so too are their inhabitants.

One development from the medievalist tradition, and one which also drew on the tradition of folklore, was the 'rewritten fairy tale'. In *Don't Bet on the Prince* (1986) Jack Zipes noted the rise of the subversive, feminist fairy tale, of which Angela Carter was probably the leading exponent. By the 1980s a number of fantasy writers were experimenting with the possibilities of fairy tales in fantasy, incorporating more genuinely medieval settings, mostly late medieval, and like earlier writers such as Farjeon or Uttley, seeking to find the grain of truth in the tale. Writers such as Gail Carson Levine, Donna Jo Napoli, Shannon Hale and Patrice Kindl found in late medievalist fairy tales a rich vein.

Napoli's *Zel* (1996) tells the story of Rapunzel, but with significant variations. In this powerful story it is Zel's mother who will do anything to prevent her daughter from leaving her for a young man. Gail Carson Levine's best-known fairy tale, *Ella Enchanted* (1997), is a gentle but subversive take on Cinderella. Set around the fifteenth century, this Cinderella is not obedient because she is good, but because she has been 'blessed' by a fairy godmother with little understanding of the human condition. Ella spends much of the book resisting the curse as well as she can, and in doing so, learns a great deal about her kingdom. Levine's *The Two Princesses of Bamarre* (2001) has even more of the quest about it as one sister sets out to rescue another and what begins as a treasure hunt transforms into a bid to revive magic in the world.

In a similar vein is the work of Shannon Hale. *The Goose Girl* (2003) is a retelling of the story of the princess who hides out as a goose girl, but it and the sequel *Enna Burning* (2004) leave the original stories behind, using them as a frame to explore stories about power and misuse of magical talents. *Rapunzel's Revenge* (2008) and its sequel *Calamity Jack* (2010) are even further removed from their origin stories as Rapunzel embarks on adventures beyond the walls of captivity. Patrice Kindl's *Goose Chase* (2001) tells the story of a displaced Princess who knows herself only as a goose girl, charged by her mother to take very good care of the rather irritating geese she inherits, and never, ever to eat one of them. When she helps an old lady and is transformed into an astonishing beauty her problems really begin, as she must rescue a prince and turn her flock of geese back into her sisters (she doesn't like some of them any more than she did before).

While most of the folk and fairy tale retellings have been set in mid to late medieval cultures, some have been set in earlier periods, particularly in recent years. Neil Gaiman's *Odd and the Frost Giants* (2008) turns back to Tolkien's use of the Norse myths in its tale of a disabled boy who finds himself coming to the aid of three deposed gods out to retake Asgard from their frost giant enemies. The Canadian writer K. V. Johansen has done the same with her *Torrie and the Dragon* (1997), an early medieval (pre-1000) fantasy with two sequels. In Johansen's Young Adult *Blackdog* (2011) we also have an early-medieval-influenced tale of manifest gods and the devils who hunt them. Katherine Langrish's protagonist Peer Ulfsson lives under the shadow of Troll Fell, a mountain inhabited by trolls, in the Troll Trilogy, beginning with *Troll Fell* (2004). Peer finds himself negotiating with trolls, raising a selkie's child and travelling the seas to Vinland.

One of the most interesting recent books is Janet McNaughton's *Dragon Seer* (2009), a fantasy set in eighth-century Orkney, in which dragon seers are fighting to protect their charges against those who eye them with suspicion in a world in which dragon-ships are warnings of Viking raids. Unusual also is Jonathan Stroud's *Heroes of the Valley* (2009), an otherworld, immersive fantasy. Haille Sveinsson is a young man living in an enclosed valley where a small number of families appear to have become trapped by the existence of malicious and dangerous beings, the Trows. Haille's attempt to sort through legend to find truth is, like much of Stroud's work (which is discussed further in Chapter 8), intensely complex, and the book ends inconclusively and with a rather darker tinge than is usual in fantasy for children and younger teens.

## Diana Wynne Jones

Medievalist settings became, for a very long time, one of the defaults of children's fantasy, but while many of the writers mentioned here thought through their medieval worlds, making things as accurate as possible, some critics felt that there was too much 'cod' medievalism in the world. Almost all of the texts discussed here could easily be disputed as containing too sanitized a view of the Middle Ages: in these books no one starves, social mobility is intrinsic to the text, and it is very common indeed for people to swap places with others of differing social experiences and *for no one to notice*, a trope inherited from fairy tale and entrenched by Mark Twain's *The Prince and the Pauper* (1881).

The change to greater realism of setting was inspired in part, once again, by Diana Wynne Jones, whose career (from 1973 to 2014 – her last book was published posthumously) influenced many writers who began writing in the 1990s. Jones did not generally choose the medieval period for her work, but the exception is the Dalemark quartet. Three of the books, *Cart and Cwidder* (1975), *Drowned Ammet* (1977) and *The Crown of Dalemark* (1993), are set in a late medieval, faintly Scandinavian (but in its divisions, North American) land, while *The Spellcoats* (1979) is set in a fair resemblance of prehistoric or early medieval Norfolk fen country.

The first of the Dalemark quartet, *Cart and Cwidder*, is notable because of its unexpected brutality. Set in a fairly generic medieval landscape, it is shocking that a book for twelve-year-olds begins with the murder of the protagonist's father; we later discover that the incognito prince he befriends has been forced to watch his brother hanged, and escaped himself only because of his age, and that the protagonist's elder brother is also seriously at risk of execution – escaping only because he turns out to be the heir to an earldom, though in this case utterly unwanted by the other earls. *Cart and Cwidder* is a book with three stories, one in which Moril learns to use the magical stringed instrument in the title, the cwidder, and one in which children learn some of the realities of oppressive nations and revolutions. It is, however, also a mythopoeic story in which, in the tradition which we have seen emerge, the protagonists are both bound into the myth and reconfigure it, for Moril and his friend Kialan both long to have lived in the time of their heroes, Osfameron and the Adon. Only at the end do they realize that they have *relived* the story and so contributed their part to the mythopoesis.

In *Cart and Cwidder* Jones asserts that the making of legend is part of the everyday and she reasserts this in every book in the sequence. *The Spellcoats*, set many centuries earlier, is constructed as the translation of two coats which tell of four children's involvement in world-shattering events which shape the politics and the landscape of a kingdom and which *may* render two of the children immortal. In *Drowned Ammet*, Mitt takes part in a holiday ritual to celebrate the gods, only to find himself later riding with them as he escapes from his pursuers.

*Drowned Ammet* is possibly the hardest-hitting of Jones's works, for it parallels the mythopoeic with the brutal realities of oppression and revolution. Mitt is the orphan of a revolutionary hero. He is told this almost every day of his childhood. His mother and his father's friends are anxious that he should grow up and take his father's place and, inspired by the oppressions of the Southern earls and the stories he hears of revolution, he dutifully does so, accepting a mission to assassinate the local earl. Almost from the start, however, Jones sets us in a different direction. Dressed in the costume of a page, Mitt quickly realizes he cannot pass from close up: he is not as tall, not as smooth-skinned, not as *youthful*-looking as the court boys. What he is, and how he has grown up, are written on his body. As the book proceeds Mitt learns that the revolutionaries are far less organized than he had understood, and the earl far more entrenched, that assassination will achieve little, and that he must find allies where he can. Mitt's movement through the world is away from the centres of power towards the gods, but he is cold, hungry and scared for almost the entire book. In that, he is probably closer to the depictions of Frodo and Sam than almost any protagonist of any other Tolkienian children's fantasy.

## Other medievalisms

Another interesting development has been the emergence of other medievalisms, in particular those of Japan and China. This is not uncontested territory: the degree to which modern fantasy has come to rifle the culture of the Other is now considered a serious issue, discussed extensively by authors and critics, although it was evident early in the introduction of Celtic traditions: none of the Welsh-influenced writers of fantasy for children were Welsh, and current Welsh writers such as Kari Sperring have talked online about the degree to which they feel their culture appears to have open access written over it. Today, writers settled in the USA but with origins elsewhere, such as Ashok Banker, Mary Anne Mohanraj and Saladin Ahmad, Native American authors such as Owl Goingback, and writers from many other traditions, have begun protesting the same willingness of white Anglo-American authors to see the fantastic always in the Other, and to regard it as so much exotic stuff to be used as the writer sees fit. So when we discuss fantasy set in other medievalisms or in societies portrayed as medieval or in other ways backward, we need to proceed with caution.

A book which illustrates the issue is Robin McKinley's *The Blue Sword* (1982), written as multiculturalism began to move centre stage and as imperialism was coming under fire, but before discussions of appropriation arose. The magical land of Damar is a country with strong similarities to the Middle East and Afghanistan as portrayed in the fiction of Rudyard Kipling and other late nineteenth- and early twentieth-century imperialist adventure writers. An empire called the Homeland, which is never explicitly identified as late Victorian Great Britain (and could well stand in for any of the great colonial powers of that day), believes itself justified in ruling over the eastern land of Damar because it has for several generations controlled the ports and more fertile coastline of the country. Aside from the local natives who have been Westernized, the Damarians are simply believed to be barbarians, mysterious desert people who interact with their colonizers on only the most limited basis.

Enter Angharad 'Harry' Crewe, an orphan and tomboy, shipped out to Damar from the Homeland to be with her brother, a military officer stationed in the country. Harry is drawn to the desert, in part because she is by nature adventurous, in part, we eventually discover, because she has one-eighth Damarian ancestry and thus carries the ancient magic called *kelar* in her blood. In a plot uncomfortably reminiscent of *The Sheik* by E. M. Hull (1921), she is kidnapped by Corlath, a dashing and driven Damarian leader, who shares this magical power. Forced to adopt desert ways, Harry slips free from her culturally imposed feminine limitations and, having visions of Lady Aerin, the ancient Damarian hero and the protagonist of *The Hero and the Crown* discussed above, develops with relative ease into a great warrior. Damar, we discover, faces an invasion from the North by hideous, orc-like creatures unknown to the Homelanders, ruled by a monstrous demon-wizard and capable of exterminating both the Damarians and their complacent colonizers.

In an essay comparing *The Blue Sword* to Frances Hodgson Burnett's *The Secret Garden* (1911), Mike Cadden makes an important point about both books, and about fantasy literature in general, by foregrounding the concept of the blood quantum. In the novels it is clear that the people of the mysterious East are Other, not just because they have eccentric customs, but because they are inherently (perhaps genetically) different in their abilities. This involves a sort of magical essentialism which is not uncommon in fantasy and is one of the disturbing inheritances from Tolkien, and from the folklore traditions in which he was embedded. In Burnett's day such differences were simply assumed and accepted. One might tame and partially assimilate the Other but never make him entirely British. McKinley, however, is very conscious of what she is doing. As Cadden suggests, 'In both *The Secret Garden* and *The Blue Sword*, home is connected to issues of blood; Harry is one-eighth Damarian and strong blood it must be to so overwhelm the seven-eighths Homelander blood. Any bit of "contagion" will poison the rest, after all' (an attitude well known in American racial relationships).[16] McKinley is confronting one of the key tropes of such fantasy, the innate differences between races, and interrogating it. '*The Blue Sword* seems to be hopeful regarding cultural syncretism; after all, if one could overcome the exaggerated racial divisions in fantasy, it seems to say, then *any* cultural obstacle in our own world is paltry in comparison',[17] but it cannot overcome the underpinnings it has inherited.

Australian writers have been particularly fascinated with China and Japan. Veteran children's novelist Gillian Rubenstein, writing as Lian Hearn (a name borrowed perhaps from one of the first Western fiction writers to work with Japanese material, Lafcadio Hearn), has made use of a fictionalized medieval Japan in the bestselling series *Tales of the Otori*, beginning with *Across the Nightingale Floor* (2002), in which sixteen-year-old Tomasu returns from a journey to find his family murdered. What follows is a byzantine tale of politics, warfare and assassination in which Tomasu is adopted into another family, renamed Takeo, trained to be a warrior, falls in love and seeks revenge. Alison Goodman's *The Two Pearls of Wisdom* (2008; US, *Eon: Dragoneye Reborn*) and sequel, set in a country that might be ancient China, features an elaborate system of god-like dragons, each with a pearl of magical importance, and a teenage girl who cross-dresses and trains to become a great warrior. The novel is particularly interesting for its positive portrayal of people with a wide variety of sexual identities, including a heroic eunuch warrior and a wise if somewhat vain transvestite courtesan.

Paul Collins has worked with medieval China in his story *Dragonlinks* (2008), which also makes use of cross-dressing in order to deploy a female protagonist. Jelindel's family is killed in a political brouhaha and she finds herself on the streets. Disguised as a boy, she becomes involved with and eventually leads a hunt for the missing links on a mail shirt that might be an alien artefact. The setting is only vaguely Asian, and Collins, by bringing a mixture of both European and Asian ethnicities into his content, shifts the dynamic somewhat. Like many of these fantasies, however, *Dragonlinks* suffers from the problem of orientalism: there is no sense of historical change, no sense that he's dealing with a living, breathing culture, only a feeling that this is how it has always been.

In the United States and Canada, and to a lesser extent in the UK, there is now a growing amount of fantastic fiction by immigrant or native-born writers of Asian heritage, which will be discussed in Chapters 8 and 9. Of the medievalist writers, however, the first and most important of these is the prolific Chinese-American writer Laurence Yep, winner of two Newbery Honor Awards for historical fiction, but also the author of a number of fantasies, including his Dragon series, beginning with *Dragon of the Lost Sea* (1982), and his City trilogy, beginning with *City of Fire* (2009). In the former, which is deeply steeped in Chinese mythology, a dragon princess named Shimmer travels disguised as a human being while looking for a way to rescue her lost home, the Inland Sea, after it has been stolen by an evil witch and turned into a pebble. She is aided by a teenaged orphan named Thorn, and the two encounter a variety of characters out of Chinese myth and history, including the Monkey King. The *City* trilogy similarly involves dragons, Chinese mythology and a quest, though it does so within the context of an alternative-universe 1941. Chinese-born American Malinda Lo published *Ash* in 2009, a fantasy that mixes Chinese and Western supernatural themes to construct a rather different take on Cinderella. Its prequel, *Huntress* (2011), is a more traditional but equally assured tale of adventure in an Asian-influenced medieval world. Both books are notable for their front-and-centre romantic treatment of lesbian love, in a quest tradition where romance is often sidelined or treated as structural. For younger readers, veteran picture book author and illustrator Grace Lin wrote and illustrated the delightful Newbery Honor book *Where the Mountain Meets the Moon* (2011), which follows the adventures of Minli on her quest to track down the Old Man in the Moon. In a related tale, *Starry River of the Sky* (2012), a boy named Rendi goes on a quest to find the lost moon.

By the end of the 1980s the market was changing, as we shall see in more detail in the next chapter. The most significant change, already becoming evident in the 1980s, and which will shape the next two chapters, was that fantasy was beginning to reconfigure itself around different age levels. Prior to the mid nineties fantasy had mostly remained outside the juvenile category which had developed in nineties fiction, in the chapter books, and had been adopted by science fiction. As can be seen in this chapter, the books for teens were, as often as not, written for an adult market and appropriated by teenage readers; this included such writers as Robin McKinley and later most of the work of Terry Pratchett, whose subversive take on Tolkienian fantasy in the early books of *Discworld* became a virtual cult. These appropriated books tended towards otherworld fantasy. Books for children – as we saw in Chapter 5 – tended to be set in this world and were heavily influenced by folk tales and a sense of the land. All of this took place in a publishing world unfriendly to children's fantasy and where fantasy was seen as a distinctly minority interest. The publication of Philip Pullman's *Northern Lights* (1995) and J. K. Rowling's *Harry Potter and the Philosopher's Stone* (1997, with a cover that, at first glance, conjures up 1950s school stories, not magic) alerted publishers to both the possibilities of fantasy literature and the different possibilities of children's and Young Adult literature.

## CHAPTER 8

# Harry Potter and children's fantasy since the 1990s

Throughout this book we have seen a slow, progressive extension of the age groups for which children's fantasy was being written. By the 1980s it was clear that there was a developing teen market; as we entered the 1990s the sense that there was a distinction between children's fantasy and fantasy for teens became stronger, with clear markers separating the teen market from the children's market, to the degree that it no longer made sense for publishers and authors to conflate the two age groups and their literature. We need to emphasize, however, that there has never been a time when teens and adults did not continue to read fantasy written for children. As it is not possible to say that the age of a protagonist is an absolute indicator of the target market, in essence the division that emerged was between fiction which recognizes puberty and adolescence, and that which does not. This chapter is concerned entirely with that which does not.

## Social realism in fantasy

In the late 1980s and early 1990s children's fantasy appeared to be in decline, overtaken by the demand for social realism. This change in the market was one of the contributing factors in the growing division between children's and teen or Young Adult fiction. Although books for both groups could include material that was quite threatening (particularly to parents), the influence of social realism made it likely that books for older children would tend to be more grim or violent. Books for children, however, tended towards younger protagonists, lighter endings, cartoon violence and no sex. Books for teens headed in the opposite direction. It became increasingly untenable to market traditional fantasy to older teens. This division between children's and Young Adult fiction can be disputed but it is the one we will use here.

Some children's writers whose careers continued felt it was possible to write both social realism and the fantastic. In the introduction to her 1971 collection *West of Widdershins*, Barbara Sleigh wrote: 'Why should we feel that it [magic] should always be in period dress? Surely, if we look for it, it can be found in the class-room, the public parks, in anyone's back garden, even in supermarkets.'[1] She had already demonstrated how this might be done in her own *Carbonel* (1955), which we discussed in Chapter 5. Rosemary and John explore their town and interact with adults in ways drawn straight from the social realist children's fiction of the period, ways which were to become crucial to the development of children's urban fantasy in the 1990s and 2000s, and which can be seen in *Harry Potter and the Deathly Hallows* (2007), where the freedom the protagonists have to roam the London streets is in marked contrast to their mostly confined adventures in the earlier Harry Potter books.

This drive to social realism shaped the work of a number of writers, in particular placing an emphasis on multiculturalism. Perhaps pre-eminent in making the new rules work for her was Diana Wynne Jones. *Wilkins' Tooth* (1973) was written specifically to reflect the multicultural and urban world of the city. The children of *Wilkins' Tooth* roam their suburb and deal with a local gang and an urban witch in ways that draw on the resources of *being* urban children. The book's fairy tale plot comes with radical trappings: a black boy who is the intellectual leader of the group, and a girl who is the physically bravest of them. In later books such as *The Homeward Bounders* (1981) and *Archer's Goon* (1984), the willingness of the protagonists to explore the city or suburb is both what gets the characters into the adventure and what eventually demonstrates the solution, and the magic is integral to the town, situated in its museums and parks. In many of Jones's books there is a conscious effort, even when dealing with other worlds, to create characters who live lives at least somewhat similar to those of her readers. *Witch Week* (1982), for example, is as much a fantasy *Grange Hill* (a very successful UK television programme about a day school, which ran from 1978–2008) as it is a boarding-school story.

One of the best of the new social realist fantasies was Robert Leeson's *The Third Class Genie* (1975). When Alec finds a beer-can in the dump, his encounter with its genie Abu Salem is an encounter with magical and racial intrusions. The genie can only manage small magics and doesn't understand the modern world – how do you conjure plimsolls when rubber is no more than a plant? Alec has other real-world decisions to deal with, such as whether to side with the white gang he dislikes against the West Indian boy who has taken against him, and how his parents are coping in an overcrowded council house, with the threat of being moved elsewhere being held against them to limit their expectations. As the novel works itself out, Alec realizes he has far more in common with the West Indian boy than with his white classmates, and when the genie is accidentally materialized as an African slave (he is also Muslim but this is handled with less insight), he and Ginger Wallace and Ginger's sister Lucille collaborate to protect him until he can return to the beer-can he regards as home. Like a number of the urban fantasies of this period, its adherence to social realism is such that *The Third Class Genie* reads like a historical novel of pre-Thatcherite Britain.

In the USA the new social realism and the space it opened for multicultural fantasy was reflected first and foremost in the work of the African-American children's writer Virginia Hamilton, who was often a realist writer, winning the Newbery Award for her contemporary novel *M. C. Higgins the Great* (1974), but frequently diverged into folk tales, science fiction and fantasy. Her second novel, *The House of Dies Drear* (1968), concerns an African-American family, the Smalls, who move into an old house that was once a stop on the underground railroad, and its mysterious old caretaker, Mr Pluto, who is rumoured to be the devil. The story eventually resolves into a straight mystery, but sets the stage for Hamilton to explore the supernatural in later tales like her richly dialectical *Sweet Whispers, Brother Rush* (1982). Here, fourteen-year-old Tree finds herself unhappily stuck at home as caretaker for her mentally challenged brother Dabney, while her single mother works. Then Tree meets Brother Rush, a mysterious young man who brings new insight into her family's difficult past and the reasons why her mother is the way she is. Brother Rush, it seems, is a ghost and he knows secrets. This at times deeply disturbing novel mixes its supernatural content with a clear-eyed look at the dark times to be found in the family trees of virtually all African Americans. In the historical fantasy *The Magical Adventures of Pretty Pearl* (1983) a goddess comes down from her mountain in Africa to have adventures in the world but soon discovers the evils of slavery. In *Drylongso* (1994), a tale beautifully illustrated by Jerry Pinkney, a farm family in the 1970s suffering from a terrible drought is aided by the mystical title character.

## Pullman and Rowling

Overall, despite the steady but quiet success of writers such as Jones and the emergence of new writers such as Tamora Pierce (who like Jane Yolen writes a fair number of multicultural tales), much of what was available in the 1980s was reprints and continuations of series and, as we saw in the previous chapter, fantasy for adults (Terry Brooks, Robin McKinley and others) appropriated by teens. In the 1990s all of this changed, and fantasy became, if not the dominant genre in books for children and teens, then one of the most visible. There were three factors: the first and the most easily recognized was the dual success of Philip Pullman's Carnegie Medal-winning *Northern Lights* (1995) and the mega-bestselling *Harry Potter and the Philosopher's Stone* by J. K. Rowling (1997); the second was the internationalization of the book trade through the drop in postal rates and the rise of Amazon; and third, the development of overseas contracts, which changed the nature of the market.

In his history of British publishing, John Feather has written, 'The battleground for competition after World War II was actually not in North America itself, or in Britain, but in the rest of the world. The end of the Market Rights Agreement in 1976 … was unequivocally welcomed by American publishers who, according to contemporary analysts, began to compete successfully in former British colonies and in the Commonwealth.'[2] In practice this meant that Australian and Canadian publishers began to look to the large US market for publishing deals and that American books became increasingly available in the UK (particularly during the period that Borders traded in Britain, from 1998–2009). In the fantasy world, peer-to-peer book swaps gradually gave way to an assumption that one could buy overseas books online, and once a range of social media had emerged, fans (often adults) had a ready way to track new and exciting titles.

In addition, the rise of internet selling, while causing many issues for booksellers, actively supported the stocking of niche titles that, while selling poorly regionally, might well pick up a substantial following if available in the new international mass market. Both the Australian and Irish book industries, which had been maturing in the 1980s, began in the 1990s to send far more children's and teen fantasy into the market. The Canadian book publishers were increasingly co-publishing with US rather than UK houses (which had themselves been bought out by multinational companies), and by 2010 it is fair to say that although many books were not printed worldwide, any determined reader could discover and acquire books from across the English-speaking world. One consequence of the changing market is that *Harry Potter and the Philosopher's Stone* (US, *Harry Potter and the Sorcerer's Stone*) may be the last British children's book to have received the cross-cultural editing for unfamiliar terms or grammatical expressions that was once common.

Although the initial success of Philip Pullman's *Northern Lights* (1995; US, *The Golden Compass*) seemed to strengthen the children's market, a discussion of this book, and the entire *His Dark Materials* trilogy, is better aligned with developments for teens, due to the sophistication and very bitter tone of much of the narrative. *Harry Potter and the Philosopher's Stone*, however, spoke directly and immediately to the hearts and minds of millions of children around the world. It also turned into a world-wide publishing phenomenon, making far more money for its publishers (Bloomsbury in the UK, Scholastic in the USA) than anyone had dreamed possible. It was, of course, followed by six increasingly popular sequels, a number of bestselling spin-off volumes, an enormously successful film series, video games, an entire theme park in Florida and countless websites and merchandise, creating profits that have made J. K. Rowling the first self-made billionaire author and one of the richest women in Great Britain.

In the United States the pre-publication orders for *Harry Potter and the Sorcerer's Stone* were so great that *The New York Times* (followed by other publishing icons around the world) was prompted to create a separate children's bestseller list just to keep adult bestsellers from the embarrassment of being outdone by a children's book. To date the series has sold more than 450 million copies, second only in series sales to Georges Simenon's seventy-five volume series of adult detective novels featuring Inspector Maigret. Many of Rowling's sales were to adult readers, of course, and she thus set the stage for other crossover successes such as Stephenie Meyer's *Twilight* books (2005–8), Suzanne Collins's *The Hunger Games* trilogy (2008–10) and Veronica Roth's *Divergent* series (2011–13).

> We do not know if Bloomsbury, the original British publisher of *Harry Potter and the Philosopher's Stone*, actually initiated the practice, but later editions of the book were issued with two different covers, one specifically designed to attract child readers and the other, perhaps, to save adult readers from embarrassment while carrying the book on the commuter train. The former contained a cartoonish illustration of Harry looking quizzically at a rather jolly and retro railway engine labelled Hogwarts Express, and the other featured a black and white photograph – oddly enough taken in West Virginia – of a much larger, mid-twentieth-century railway engine.

The plot of *Harry Potter and the Philosopher's Stone* is too well known to bear repeating here in any detail, beyond the bare-bones facts that it concerns an abused orphan boy, Harry, who discovers that he is in fact a wizard, heir to two martyred magic users, and destined not just to attend a wizards' school but to become a great hero in the fight against the evil Lord Voldemort. Going beyond all of the hype that surrounds the entire Harry Potter phenomenon, it is important to recognize that, despite the fact that, as every critic of children's literature will tell you, the story has its shortcomings, it is also a genuinely good book. Still, there are many genuinely good children's fantasy novels, especially including those in the time-honoured wizards' school tradition, and innumerable articles have been written that attempt to pin down the reasons why Potter, rather than say a novel by Jane Yolen, or Ursula K. Le Guin, or Diana Wynne Jones, or Lloyd Alexander, or Susan Cooper, attained the status it did.

We would argue that the success of the Harry Potter books lies in a number of different factors. The series features a particularly winning hero, a number of well-realized, endearing secondary characters and an unusually well-developed magic system. It also combines a rich textual surface, replete with clever ideas and language play (a rarely noticed equivalent may be Piers Anthony's *Xanth* novels, beginning with *A Spell for Chameleon*, 1977), with traditional but vaguely liberal values that are not too challenging to the young (or adult) reader's intellect. Rowling is for the underdog and the middle class, but against the snooty rich and materialistic social climbers. She champions goodness, hard work and acceptance of the Other, and is against racism and prejudice of all sorts. She is in favour of strong girls and non-white characters, but, even in the case of Hermione Granger, only in so far as they are highly competent sidekicks. Readers accept her ideas and feel good about themselves for doing so, whereas better writers, like Le Guin, Jones or Yolen, do more to force readers to think about the complexity of both the world and their place in it. Rowling's biggest influence may well have been Enid Blyton, for the continual discovery of new magic objects revives the pleasure found in *The Magic Faraway Tree* (discussed in Chapter 4). Furthermore, for all the superficial multiculturalism of the series and the pleasure young readers can take in Hermione's role, overall the familial and relationship politics of the books are pretty much mired in the 1950s, complete with non-working wives and early marriage.

The Harry Potter books are also, in terms of both plot and vocabulary, highly accessible to people who rarely read fiction, whereas many of the authors named in this book, even those writing for a younger audience, appeal primarily to experienced and devoted readers of the genre. Rowling's genius may have been the ability to capture both of these markets.

## A fantasy revival

One of the first things that happened in the wake of the Rowling boom was that a number of earlier wizard or witch school stories were brought back into print. Diane Duane, Diana Wynne Jones, Sherwood Smith, Caroline Stevermer and Jane Yolen all had titles republished. Duane's *Young Wizards* series, beginning with *So You Want to Be a Wizard* (1983), was very much what the title describes and very popular. The republication of Smith's *Wren to the Rescue* (1990) and sequels in 2004, along with the continuing popularity of *Crown Duel* (originally published in two parts in 1997/1998) established her career as a significant fantasist. Yolen's humorous *Wizard's Hall* (1991) featured a tremendously incompetent magic student in an academic setting remarkably similar to that of the Harry Potter books. Caroline Stevermer was able to publish a sequel to her *A College of Magics* (1994), *A Scholar of Magics* (2004), which was loosely based on her own college experiences. Diana Wynne Jones's *Witch Week* (1982), her *Chrestomanci* stories, including the Guardian Children's Fiction Prize-winning *Charmed Life* (1977), *The Magicians of Caprona* (1980) and *The Lives of Christopher Chant* (1988), along with most of her back catalogue, were reprinted and repackaged (her publisher, Collins, opted for the sticker slogan *Hotter than Potter*), and she was able to extend the series, and stand-alone titles, into the 2000s. Jill Murphy's *The Worst Witch* series had begun in 1974, set in Miss Cackle's Academy for Witches, where Mildred Hubble got into many of the same scrapes as the juniors and middles of Angela Brazil's and Elinor M. Brent-Dyer's boarding-school stories, but with added magic. This series too was to have a new lease of life with new titles: *The Worst Witch All at Sea* (1993), *The Worst Witch Saves the Day* (2005) and *The Worst Witch to the Rescue* (2007). Eva Ibbotson saw *Which Witch* (1979) revived, which may have been some consolation for the fate of *The Secret of Platform 13* (1994), in which an orphan consigned by his step-family to live under the stairs departs, Harry Potter-like, for a fantasyland from a hidden platform at King's Cross,[3] and which gained little traction. Among this revival, however, were the new writers who pointed to a second golden age of children's fantasy and who looked to many different sources.

The first element of the revival we need to consider was a revival of, or nostalgia for, older forms. The Harry Potter books captured the imagination not with something new, but with that very old form, the school story (see Jeffrey Richards, *Happiest Days: The Public Schools in English Fiction* for the basic formula, and an argument for the form's longevity).

Although the USA lacks the tradition of the boarding-school story, schools more generally had become particularly popular settings on television throughout the English-speaking world: *Glenview High* (1977–8) in Australia, *Degrassi High* (1987) in Canada and *Beverly Hills 90210* (1990–2000) in the USA. Schools offer completely closed environments which the outside world does not permeate and where even the teachers are distant, leaving teens with great autonomy and plenty of space to interact with each other. One asset is that they allow a clear focus not just on children but on a peer group: for example, there are relatively few younger and older children (besides the Weasleys) who attract more than cursory attention in the Harry Potter novels.

Nostalgia is also to be found in G. P. Taylor's *Shadowmancer* (2002), one of two big hits to come from initially self-published authors. Taylor had been involved in rock bands when young, dabbled in the occult, and then converted to Christianity and become a vicar in the Church of England. *Shadowmancer* tells of the arrival of an Ethiopian boy named Raphah in Whitby to search for the Keruvim, powerful amulets, one of which has ended up in the hands of the evil sorcerer Reverend Obadiah Demurrai. The books are intended as Christian allegory, which causes some difficulty for those attempting to read them as fantasy, for in these books anything performed by Raphah is from God, and therefore not magic; whereas magic is from the Devil and is an indication of evil. This is further complicated by an ultra-conservative, nineteenth-century system of morality which appears to rate playing cards as innately more sinful than beating one's child. These two elements may explain why this British author has been hugely successful in the Christian book market in the USA.

The other nostalgic writer, although this nostalgia was much more genre-oriented, was the author of the other self-published hit, Christopher Paolini. Home-schooled in Montana, Paolini, while still in his teens, self-published and self-marketed *Eragon* (2002), which was then picked up by Alfred Knopf. The story tells of a young boy who finds a stone which hatches into a dragon. He is then sought by an evil King who wants the dragon. *Eragon* proved fascinating because it answered the question, What would children want from literature if they could write their own and be their own publishing gateway? The answer turned out to be more of the same: Amazon reviews for this book, if sorted by stars, reveal a clear age divide in the response.

The Harry Potter books also revived Lewis's destinarianism, and that element can be seen in many of the texts discussed in this chapter. The archaic railway carriages of the books can be read as a metaphor for the position of the whole and for a tendency to look backward rather than forward for identity. Thus Chinese-American novelist Laurence Yep (discussed briefly in Chapter 6 as a writer of historical fantasy) offered *The Imp that Ate My Homework* (1998), about a boy who simply wants to be American but must come to terms with his grandfather's magical legacy; and *The Tiger's Apprentice* (2003), in which Yep tells the exciting tale of a modern Chinese-American boy who discovers his destiny as a warrior in a hidden world out of Chinese myth. Like Virginia Hamilton, Yep is frequently concerned with conflict between the present and the past, with a child's desire to be simply an American as opposed to a hyphenated-American whose historical roots frequently impinge on his life.

The role of destiny generally, which had declined in the 1970s and 1980s, returned to dominate the most successful texts of the early 2000s. After Harry Potter, the two most important are perhaps Garth Nix's *Keys to the Kingdom* sequence (2003–10) and Rick Riordan's *Percy Jackson and the Olympians* books (2005–9). Garth Nix was the first writer of children's fantasy from Australia to really make an impact in the US and UK markets, first with the *Old Kingdom* trilogy (1995–2014), to be discussed in the next chapter, and then with the story of Arthur Penhalligon, asthmatic, twelve years old and rightful heir of the House, the centre of the Universe. In each book, which is named for the day on which it takes place, Arthur encounters one of the Trustees now in charge of the fractured House and, guided by the Will, a supernatural legal document, sets out to reunite the House. Riordan's *Percy Jackson* series began with *The Lightning Thief* (2005) in which Percy Jackson, a twelve-year-old boy with dyslexia and Attention Deficit Hyperactivity Disorder, discovers after he is attacked by a Fury (one of his teachers) and a minotaur who kidnaps his sister, that he is a demigod, although no one knows who his father might be. At the end of various adventures in which he works out who stole Zeus's lightning rod, he returns to school, only for it all to begin again the following year. As with the Harry Potter novels, the series deepens in import as it proceeds.

It is a puzzle why the concept of destiny should have proved so attractive to the current generation who have had far greater freedom of choice – despite slowing social mobility – than did their grandparents, but it might well be precisely that wider world, with its attendant uncertainty, which led to a certain level of comfort in knowing what one's *place* will be, even when, as in the Jackson books, the future which comes with that place is potentially very threatening. The comfort of destiny clearly had a market, for it became one of the distinguishing markers of both many of the children's books discussed here and the Young Adult paranormal novel that we will discuss in Chapter 9.

## In the wake of the Potter boom

Rowling's books rapidly spawned emulators, of which one of the best is Jenny Nimmo's *Charlie Bone* series. In *Midnight for Charlie Bone* (2002) Charlie discovers he can hear sounds in photographs and is packed off to a rather strange school by his aunts where he proceeds to have adventures over an eight-book series. As with the Harry Potter series, Charlie Bone's adventures begin with specific, school-based difficulties and escalate. By *Charlie Bone and the Red Knight* (2009), the fate of the school and the city are in Charlie's hands.

Also fascinating is the degree to which, in the early 2000s, many successful books have spawned not so much emulators as subversive responses; for example, almost immediately after the success of *Eragon*, Cressida Cowell published the first of the very funny *How to Train Your Dragon* series. *How to Train Your Dragon* (2003) follows Hiccup as he captures his own dragon as a rite of passage and discovers that the training manual is empty. Hiccup's training of his own dragon by eccentric methods leads to the successful defeat of a foreign dragon.

After Tolkien, if anyone had suggested to children's literature fans that Victorian fairies would be revived in children's fantasy, it is quite probable they would have been laughed out of the library. Yet, although Rowling's work was not directly fairy-related, her reintroduction of gnomes, elves and other fairy creatures stimulated subversion in that direction as well. First off the blocks was Eoin Colfer, an Irish writer, with *Artemis Fowl* (2001). Fowl, a brilliant teenage criminal mastermind, kidnaps a fairy and holds her to ransom. In later books he creates an organized crime ring, but eventually ends up helping the fairy in a number of ways. The books were hugely successful: written on the rhetorical borders of science fiction, fantasy and crime novels, they created a new way of bringing fairy into the modern world and demonstrated the possibilities of Victorian/Enid Blytonesque fairy characters. In 2003 *Rainbow Magic*, a brand owned by HIT Entertainment, launched a series of books about Kirsty Tate and Rachel Walker and their fairy friends, ghostwritten and packaged under the name Daisy Meadows. These books were immensely successful, and returned as the most borrowed children's books in the UK lending figures for 2010 and 2011. Herbie Brennan's *Fairie Wars* combines action adventure, clan wars and major quests.

Only a little more traditional was Tony DiTerlizzi and Holly Black's *Spiderwick Chronicles* (beginning with *The Field Guide*, 2003), in which twins find a field guide to fairies and other supernatural creatures in an old house and rapidly find themselves dealing with brownies, and then (in *The Seeing Stone*, 2003) goblins.

Other takes on old fairy tales have also developed. Caro King's *Seven Sorcerers* (2009) used the tale of the kidnapped baby brother and the journey to the Elven King to take the heroine into a sinister alternative world, although in the sequel *Shadow Spell* (2010) the stakes are upped to involve saving the world. Michael Buckley's *The Fairy Tale Detectives* (2005) sends Sabrina and Daphne Grimm to live with their grandmother, who reveals that their ancestors' books were really case files and they too have a future as fairy tale detectives. In Steve Augarde's *The Various* (2005), during a stay with her uncle because her mother is too busy working as a musician, Midge finds a small winged horse trapped and injured, and discovers hidden tribes of little people/fairy folk in the wood beyond her garden. The plot revolves around Midge's role in saving the land on which the tribes live, and reads not unlike Diana Wynne Jones's *Power of Three* (1976) in that it reintroduces the idea that the oppressed need a human to save them.

The new fairy tales also incorporated wainscot fantasies of the kind we saw in Chapter 6. Terence Griggs, a Canadian writer of whimsical fantasies, offered *Cat's Eye Corner* (2000) and *The Silver Door* (2004), portal fantasies in which a boy's exploration of his grandmother's house uncovers strange places and unusual peoples living in the interstices of the world. Griggs's work recalls the indoor fantasies of the late nineteenth century but the humour is studded with metatextual irony. Olivier's step-step-step-grandma sends him on a scavenger hunt during which he acquires various companions, including a woodwose (a wild man of the woods), a pen that writes/talks and several cats who don't but who communicate through the pen and are not pets, but poets. The hunt is in part for the Inklings who keep editing words (hence the poets). There are references to Narnia (as well as the Inklings, there is a barn bigger on the inside than the out and completely dark, and the pen is clearly Lewis's Professor Kirke). When Olivier gets home he asks his step-step-step-grandmother if no time has passed and she says actually, several days have passed and they have been making excuses to his parents. Any doubt about the reality of a tale in which many of his companions turn out to be from the local school is ended when the pen continues to talk to him.

As Eoin Colfer and Herbie Brennan demonstrated, not all fairies are nice and not all fairy folk are fun to be with. Terry Pratchett had enormous success with the Wee Free Men. Pratchett's very first book, *The Carpet People* (1971), had already explored the possibilities of a colony of very small people living in the interstices of the world, but it hadn't sold that well. In 1989 he tried again with *Truckers*, the first in the *Bromeliad* trilogy, a classic wainscot fantasy. The nomes of *Truckers* begin the book living in a quarry, barely managing to survive. They know their colony is collapsing and they send Masklin in a truck out of the quarry to find aid. Masklin ends up in Arnold Bros. Department Store where he quickly falls in with the store's own nomes, organized into clans according to which part of the store they occupy. Masklin discovers that the store is to close and the nomes flee to the quarry, and from there, in subsequent books, proceed to work out a path to the stars and their original home. Once we accept that the nomes are aliens, then it is logical to ally the book to science fiction rather than fantasy, but the Bromeliad sequence is a fantasy of perspective and the most fantastical moments are when the nomes come into contact with an impermeable and inexplicable human world.

The success of Pratchett's *Bromeliad* sequence was carried over to the Tiffany Aching sub-sequence within *Discworld*. Here, in *The Wee Free Men* (2003), *A Hat Full of Sky* (2004), *Wintersmith* (2006) and *I Shall Wear Midnight* (2010), the hard-working and terribly respectable nomes were transformed into the boozing, fighting and swearing Nac Mac Feegle, aka the Pictsies, aka the Wee Free Men. Set alongside the at first very young Tiffany Aching, a dairy maid and shepherd on the Downlands of Discworld, they draw attention to the degree to which the more Borrible side of the wainscot fantasy had won out as fantasy writers were beginning to rethink who or what was a suitable fictional companion for a child reader.

Witches and wizards also enjoyed a revival. Jill Murphy and Eva Ibbotson were both reprinted, and Irish writer Michael Scott had a hit with the Nicholas Flamel books. The first book in the series, *The Alchemyst* (2007), sees twins Josh and Sophie discover that their friendly bookstore owner is actually Nicholas Flamel, the fourteenth-century French alchemist. Quickly they are drawn into a battle with Dr John Dee, the Elizabethan magician. More recently Erika McGann, also Irish, has published *The Demon Notebook* (2012), about a group of failed young witches who accidentally stumble on power and conjure something diabolical into their notebook. McGann, Scott and many other Irish writers published with O'Brien Press, which has been very significant in the breakout of Irish writers into the US and UK markets in the past decade.

Intended for an older audience is Sally Green's dark and violent *Half Bad* (2014) and sequels, set in an alternative-universe contemporary England where black and white witches are secretly at war with each other, but without either side having any clear moral superiority. American authors contributing to this wizard and witch subgenre include Sarah Prineas who published *The Magic Thief* (2008), the first of a series, which concerns Conn, a boy who becomes a wizard's apprentice by the simple act of attempting to pick the wizard's pocket and not dying on the spot. Kate DiCamillo's *The Magician's Elephant* (2009) tells the story of Peter, an orphan (many of the children in these stories are orphans), whose search for his lost sister is aided by the magical pachyderm of the title. William Alexander's National Book Award-winning *Goblin Secrets* (2012) and its sequel *Ghoulish Song* (2013) take place in the magical city of Zombay, where Rownie, the youngest boy in the Fagin-like witch Graba's household, runs away to join a theatrical troupe run by goblins and learns more about masks and the magical politics of his city than he cares to know. Yet another orphaned wizard's apprentice is found in Anne Ursu's tale of what in fact makes us human, *The Real Boy* (2013). There are many other wizard and witch books in circulation, demonstrating the degree to which Rowling was able to revive them as protagonists and figures of interest in fantasy.

Philip Reeve, already established as a fantasy author by his Carnegie Medal-winning *Here Lies Arthur* (2007) and *No Such Thing as Dragons* (2010), both counter-fantastical narratives, similarly had fun with *Goblins!* (2012) and *Goblins vs Dwarves* (2013). In these tales Skarper, an unusually intelligent goblin, finds himself at loggerheads with his brethren, who only want to fight all day, and instead goes on a quest for the origin of all things in the Dark Tower. Like a lot of modern quest fantasy, it mocks the form, assuming that children can back-construct the clichés from which the humour is derived. Tobias Druitt's *Corydon* series (beginning with *Corydon and the Island of Monsters*, 2005), which plays rather more with Greek myth than with fantasy per se, may also be considered a subversion, as Corydon sides with the monsters rather than those who want to tackle them. Children have proved very able to take on these new, ironic fantasies.

Finally, an old character – Peter Pan – also experienced a revival. In 2004 the rights-holder to Barrie's *Peter Pan* authorized a sequel by the noted writer Geraldine McCaughrean, *Peter Pan in Scarlet*. American humourist

Dave Barry and suspense novelist Ridley Pearson produced a number of homages, of which the first two are *Peter and the Starcatchers* (2004) and *Peter and the Shadow Thieves* (2006), in which Peter is transformed into an orphan boy having adventures on the ship Never Land, with his trusted companion Tinker Bell, searching for strange treasure and meeting fascinating villains. Karen Wallace's *Wendy* (2003), on the other hand, tells a story from the dark side of Victorian England, stripping the original tale of its fantasy but retaining a sense of the marvellous.

The fantasies that emerged in the 1990s and 2000s expected a reader to be far more immersed in the marvellous than had been their parents and grandparents. Arthur C. Clarke famously said that 'any sufficiently advanced technology is indistinguishable from magic'.[4] Clarke was assuming that such technology was always and forever in the far future, but in the late twentieth century, as we moved from an age of mechanical engineering to one of electrical engineering, from a world of gears to a world of circuit boards, the realms of magic and of technology merged, fostering a new perspective on magic: where, prior to the 1990s, the fantastical is almost always presented as surprising, there is a slow but steady shift to an assumption that the protagonists of children's fantasy are aware of the fantastic. This manifests itself in a variety of ways.

One exponent of the expert and knowing child character was Terry Pratchett. Pratchett's *Discworld* had already proven popular with teens, its ironic poke at Tolkien even working well with those who had read neither *The Lord of the Rings* nor the flood of 1970s and 1980s emulators who rushed out what the critic John Clute has derisively termed Extruded Fantasy Product (also mocked by Diana Wynne Jones in *The Tough Guide to Fantasyland*). In his *Johnny* series and also in the Tiffany Aching books Pratchett created wise and knowing children who exploit the world around them. Both Johnny and Tiffany live, it might be said, crosswise to the world. Johnny is a rather unusual character for adventure novels: diffident, with a philosophy of live and let live, and with – like all Pratchett's protagonists – a deep ethical core. The first book in the series and the last, *Only You Can Save Mankind* (1992) and *Johnny and the Bomb* (1996), can be regarded as science fiction – the aliens in a computer game surrender; four children travel back in time – but *Johnny and the Dead* (1993), in which Johnny finds he can speak with the ghosts in a threatened graveyard, is unequivocally fantasy. Johnny battles not evil powers but bureaucracy and does so in a way that is essentially mundane: he speaks up for the ghosts. Whereas in Diana Wynne Jones's *Archer's Goon* (1984) bureaucracy was the agent of magic, and in Patricia Wrightson's *An Older*

*Kind of Magic* (1972) the magic comes to the aid of those seeking to undo the work of bureaucracy, in *Johnny and the Dead* Johnny learns to make the system work for the magical/supernatural, and unusually, it is the dead, rather than Johnny, who forget at the end. Each of Tiffany's stories could be summarized as teaching a very smart child how to learn from the world, learn from people smarter than herself and treat with respect those who are less smart. In *Wintersmith*, which begins to push Tiffany into her teenage years, there is also a lesson on how not to confuse intellectual prowess with emotional maturity.

Terry Pratchett (1948–2015) was one of the most popular and acclaimed comic writers in the English-speaking world. Although best known for the *Discworld* series for adults and the children's novels discussed in this chapter, he wrote two superb fantasies for teens, *Nation* (2008), a tale set on an alternative-universe South Seas island immediately after virtually the entire population of the area has been wiped out by a tidal wave, and *Dodger* (2012), an alternative-universe variation on Dickens's *Oliver Twist*. Although both tales feature the author's trademark humour, they are a good deal more sombre than most of his earlier work. Both received Printz Honor Awards. Pratchett also received the Carnegie Award for *The Amazing Maurice and his Educated Rodents* (2001), his first *Discworld* novel for children, and his *I Shall Wear Midnight* (2010), the last of the Tiffany Aching novels, won the Andre Norton Award. In 2009 he was knighted for his 'services to literature'.

The idea of the child in command of the bones of the mundane world is central to the work of a number of what we might call ironic fantasy writers. Derek Landy's *Skulduggery Pleasant* (2007) is part of the new trend of detective fantasies for children: in this book and its sequels a dead sorcerer recruits Stephanie to help him save the world from evil. Although Stephanie is a little surprised to meet a sorcerer who is nothing but a skeleton, she adapts very easily to a world of myth and mayhem, as does the hero of Darren Shan's *Cirque du Freak* (2000) who compromises a vampire and finds himself converted. In the *Vampire Blood* trilogy the hero – also Darren Shan – learns how to live as a vampire and with monsters, and lives in fear of his old best friend who had been refused the transition. The trajectory of the series is into, rather than away from, the monstrous.

Daniel Pinkwater is perhaps the best-known writer of the absurd and whimsical for early teens. His early work centred on a unique sort of science fiction parody in books like *Alan Mendelsohn, the Boy from Mars* (1979) and *The Snarkout Boys and the Avocado of Death* (1982).

More recent are the messy and genuinely silly *The Neddiad* (2007), in which a boy named Nedworth Wentworthstein travelling to Hollywood with his parents in the 1940s meets an Indian shaman named Melvin, receives a sacred stone turtle and ends up attempting to avoid the end of the world; and its indirect sequel *The Yggyssey* (2008), told from the point of view of Neddie's friend Yggdrasil Birnbaum, who must journey to Old New Hackensack, which is on another plane, to find out why ghosts are disappearing across California. The children, like Johnny, use their understanding of the way the real world works to understand the super-natural. Violet and Klaus, the protagonists of Lemony Snicket's absurdist Gothic books *A Series of Unfortunate Events* (beginning with *The Bad Beginning*, 1999), are never less than alert to the world in which they live; they may have much to learn as they travel but they are continuously curious and determined to get below the surface of things in a way that was once uncommon in Gothic fiction.

Perhaps the funniest of the ironic fantasies is the comic-book-like *Captain Underpants* (1997 and an ongoing series) by American author Dav Pilkey. Two fourth-graders, George and Harold, are constantly at war with their head teacher. At various moments in the text the boys begin drawing a comic starring him as superhero Captain Underpants. Although not strictly fantasy, the book makes use of the boys' understanding of the fantasy/superhero genre, as does Rhiannon Lassiter's *Super Zeroes* (2005) in which five children try to deal with their relationships with their superhero and arch-villain parents and incidentally save the day. What has clearly shifted from the 1950s is the way in which the fantastic is accepted by children.

Once standing in wide-eyed wonder, children in these fantasies and other more serious tales are now positioned as much more critically aware. In C. Butler's *The Fetch of Mardy Watt* (2004), Mardy already knows she is being haunted and that she is being haunted by herself. The notions of the doubled self, the id and the doppelganger are all ideas Mardy is already comfortable with and can apply to her situation. The titular hero of Neil Gaiman's *Coraline* (2002) is sceptical of both her parents and the fantastic, and her independence enables her to defeat the creature on the other side of the portal. The darkness of this particular portal fantasy is a serious upgrading of expectations as to what children – conditioned by the genre horror of R. L. Stine, horror movies and the nightly news – can handle. In Gaiman's later *Odd and the Frost Giants* (2008) a conventional companionate fantasy is upgraded simply by giving Odd a greater knowledge of his own world than is usual in this form of fantasy, and while Bod of *The Graveyard Book* (2008) is incredibly naive about the world beyond the graveyard, he is able to use his graveyard skills to negotiate his way through life, and his companions progressively take a back seat as the book proceeds.

Frances Hardinge, in *A Face like Glass* (2013), uses a very Bod-like heroine. Neverfell is an orphan in the underground world of Caverna, adopted by and apprenticed to a cheese-maker who makes cheeses that can create emotions. The people of Caverna cannot express emotions on their faces, instead 'learning' facial expressions from models and masks. In this context Neverfell, whose face works just fine, is ignorant, vulnerable and both promise and threat. The most knowing of the fantasy heroines around today, however, is probably Mosca Mye, protagonist of Hardinge's *Fly by Night* (2005) and *Twilight Robbery* (2011; US, *Fly Trap*). Her story is set in an alternative eighteenth century just recovering from a civil war that is at best in abeyance, where the written word has come under suspicion and control. Mosca, the exiled daughter of a stationer, is a spark in a fireworks factory. As she roams her world with her deadly goose Saracen in train, she asks the wrong (right) questions and collects words and stories relentlessly. Mosca is not precisely at the heart of the story in either *Fly by Night* or *Twilight Robbery* (a slightly more conventional story about a swapped child, set in a city that has divided its citizens into denizens by-day and by-night); what she is, is the catalyst, the one whose entry onto the scene sets change in motion.

This structure clearly fascinates Hardinge because she uses it again in *Gullstruck Island* (2009; US, *The Lost Conspiracy*). In this tale Hathin is not the hero of her own story. She thinks of herself as only a tiny seed swept up by the wind as someone out there conspires to destroy her people and find and kill her sister, the Lady Arilou, the only one of the telepathic Lost who has not been killed during one night's violence. Ironically, it is because Hathin moves through the world, creating a wake of change, that she can destroy the person who is behind it all, who also thinks of himself as all but invisible, like Hathin nothing but a servant creating the conditions for the *right decisions*. These two invisible people are both represented by the figure of the Gripping Bird, for 'whoever wore the Gripping Bird mask could change things just like clapping',[5] and suddenly the knowing reader remembers the line 'clap if you believe in fairies', or if you believe in *change*, and remembers that neither fairies nor change are necessarily *nice*.

The wry, somewhat self-indulgent atmosphere that permeates Ysabeau Wilce's fiction becomes immediately apparent when the reader opens her first novel to its title-page and sees the title and subtitle in their entirety: *Flora Segunda of Crackpot Hall: Being the Magickal Mishaps of a Girl of Spirit, Her Glass-Gazing Sidekick, Two Ominous Butlers (One Blue), a House with Eleven Thousand Rooms, and a Red Dog* (2007). Later books in the series, *Flora's Dare* (2008) and *Flora's Fury* (2012), are similarly subtitled. The books chronicle the life and adventures of the nearly fourteen-year-old Flora Fyrdraaca, first in Crackpot Hall, a great house like something out of Mervyn Peake's *Gormenghast* in which she has lived her whole life, where the thousands of rooms move around more or less at random, and then out in the magical world of Califa (which has some not entirely accidental similarities to California). Flora, who is a little bit chubby, more than a little bit grouchy, and very sure of herself, has been largely abandoned by her mother, the Warlord's Commanding General, and her father, a lugubrious drunk. Getting lost in the decaying Hall one day (she shouldn't have taken the forbidden Elevator), she meets and helps restore the banished magical Butler, rescues the Dainty Pirate from the gallows and goes hunting for a Semiote Verb, to help her regain her strength after her Anima has been vampirized by the Butler. And she does all of this in the week before her coming-out party, after which she is expected to enter military service. Throughout the series, Flora remains her own person and perfectly willing to yell if that's what's needed to get her way.

One of the most impressive series of fantasies to work with knowing or at least aware protagonists is Jonathan Stroud's *Bartimaeus* sequence, beginning with *The Amulet of Samarkand* (2003). Although technically set in an alternative twentieth-century London, it is a London we perceive primarily through reports, as young Nathaniel, apprenticed to an older wizard, rarely leaves the house. This is an intentionally claustrophobic novel, for Nathaniel has been wrenched from his family and given to the magicians' adoption service to be trained. A series of events embitters him towards his (rather mediocre) master and Nathaniel sets out to capture the real magic of magicians in this world, the ability to enslave demons. Enter djinni Bartimaeus. This is where the story and the series take an unusual turn, for although Bartimaeus helps Nathaniel to achieve his aims, in the process Nathaniel becomes aware of both the injustice of enslaving the spirits, and the injustices which the magicianocracy has created in Britain. The sequels follow first the activities of a resistance movement (*The Golem's Eye*, 2004), then the reconstruction of constitutional government (*Ptolemy's Gate*, 2005) and the death of Nathaniel, and finally, in *The Ring of Solomon* (2010) we learn about Bartimaeus's earlier relationships with the biblical King Solomon and the other djinni.

All of these fantasies involve children in completely strange worlds but another subset of fantasy has children involved in a distorted version of a world they know. One such fantasy came from German writer Cornelia Funke, one of the few authors not writing in English whose fiction absolutely demands to be mentioned in this book because of its enormous success and critical acclaim in translation. *Inkheart* (2003) and its two sequels, *Inkspell* (2006) and *Inkdeath* (2008) are both metatextual fantasies in which the boundaries between the real world and the fictional world blur. They tell the story of Mo, a humble bookbinder, who has the magical ability to bring to life the characters from the books he reads out loud. Unfortunately, this talent turns to tragedy when the villainous Capricorn and two of his henchmen escape from the book, called *Inkheart*, that he is reading to his small daughter Meggie, and Mo's wife, Meggie's mother, is accidentally trapped in *Inkheart* at the same time. Years later, Capricorn is trying to destroy all copies of the book in order to make sure that he can never be returned to his original world and hopes to force Mo to help him gain power in our world. Meggie, now twelve years old, has just discovered her father's talent and is beginning to develop similar abilities of her own. Helped by her Aunt Elinor and Dustfinger the fire-eater, Capricorn's former henchman, she hopes to bring her mother back to our world while destroying the villain. Although Meggie, who is a strong and competent child, succeeds in her quest, things become increasingly complex, in this novel and the sequels, when more people are found who share her and her father's talent. The volumes also become increasingly solemn, dealing with difficult questions of life and death. It is perhaps not coincidental to the story that Funke's much-loved husband, a printer by trade, died in 2006.

One branch of fantasy might be termed *locationally cryptic*: it takes a city or location familiar to the child but either imposes upon it a strange supernatural topography or takes us through into a mirror world. Mary Hoffman's *Stravaganza* sequence (starting with *City of Masks*, 2002), for example, is set partly in the Islington of this world, but partly in the fantastical world of Talia, which is based on eighteenth-century Italy, complete with rival city-states. In each book a young teenager who is sick or bullied or otherwise unhappy is transported to Talia where they find adventures and a new life. The *Stravaganza* series is escapist in the full sense in that the books offer their protagonists somewhere clearly better than their current situations.

The best of the locationally cryptic fantasies make use of the archaeological and legendary layers of the world around them, and many of these are set in London. Such urban tales as a rule are overwhelmingly intrusion fantasies – the fantastic breaks into the world and disrupts it. The London fantasies of the past decade, however, have predominantly been portal fantasies even as they retain their London settings. In Charlie Fletcher's *Stoneheart* (2006), China Miéville's *Un Lun Dun* (2007) and Tom Pollock's *The City's Son* (2012) and sequels, each of the protagonists finds a way into an alternative London, but unlike in Neil Gaiman's *Neverwhere* (1996), which has clearly inspired all three, the portal is not complete but liminal: London and ur-London overlap so, as George traverses the City of London in *Stoneheart*, he is dealing with both the 'real' city and the city of spits and taints (active statues) who populate shadow London; Beth in *The City's Son* is paralleled by her best friend Pen who travels in both the city above and the city below and who will carry the scars of her involvement with the mythological London to the end of her days. In both *Un Lun Dun* and *The City's Son*, what happens in ur-London profoundly affects the future of London above. *Un Lun Dun* is a modern Blytonesque fantasy with a talking milk carton and a talking prophecy book that is often wrong, where the Clean Air Act is misprisioned as the Klinneract and presented as a mysterious weapon against the Smog but proves crucial in a battle to repollute London. In *The City's Son*, the city itself has been embodied in gods and goddesses who exist in and as buildings. Reach, the god of urban decay, is embodied in the cranes and other construction equipment that disfigure London's vista, his biggest coup the new building works close to St Paul's. *The City's Son*, aimed at somewhat older readers, is grittier and more brutal: a hero dies, and there is little sense that anything has been won but escape. Even a temporary reprieve for the city seems unlikely.

What holds these stories together as a group is the degree to which the protagonists travel. Urban fantasies are usually focused on quite small areas; it is quest fantasies that, as Diana Wynne Jones has observed, send their protagonists across the map (although she herself uses this practice to structure part of the suburban fantasy *Archer's Goon*, 1984). In *Stoneheart* and *The City's Son* in particular, however, we are led across different parts of London. *Stoneheart*'s George travels a route from the Natural History Museum along the Mall and into the City, ending up in Southwark in search of the heart of London. Beth and Pen in *The City's Son* are East-Enders travelling from Hackney to Bethnal Green and south to Docklands. These are books of landscape and of an embeddedness in a place that full secondary-world quest fantasies strive to achieve and never can. They are novels in which the city actually matters, where the myth structure emerges from the archaeological layers of London's subtly anthropomorphized body. In Jones's *The Merlin Conspiracy* (2003), for example, otherwise not particularly concerned with London, Hammersmith has a river god (possibly in a nod to the river god of Beruna in C. S. Lewis's *Prince Caspian*).

Also noticeable, however, is how multicultural these London fantasies are. Both Miéville and Pollock use Asian protagonists (in Pollock's sequel, *The Glass Republic*, 2013, the Muslim Pen dominates). Zizou Corder's *Lionboy* (2003), which could also be considered science fiction, casts Charlie – son of a black father and white mother and hence representative of the more than 25 per cent of London children of mixed parentage – as the protagonist travelling through a near-future landscape and conversing with cats. Corder, it is worth knowing, is a pseudonym for white author Louisa Young and her mixed-race daughter and co-author Isabel Adomakoh Young. Discussed briefly in Chapter 7, the hero of Sarwat Chadda's modern Crusade novel, *The Devil's Kiss* (which also explores the streets of London), Billi Sangreal, is also clearly not white British. In these books the London landscape is people as well as buildings; the London fantastic is an exercise in fantastical psychogeography. All of these novels depend on child characters and child readers to be expert deconstructors of the mundane and fantastical worlds around them.

Although their stances are multicultural, it is noticeable that, with the exception of Sarwat Chadda and Adomakoh Young, all of these new authors are white, and that all of the non-white characters delivered by white fantasy writers have, at least so far, remained pretty much what author Kayla Ancrum has termed Western Neutral.[6] Deeba in Miéville's *Un Lun Dun* and Pen in Tom Pollock's *The City's Son* and his more adult *The Glass Republic* are oddly stripped of religious and ethnic context. Although Pen wears hijab and in the second book is seen to pray, her Islam does not seem to shape her character. However, this period saw a new upsurge in the number of writers of colour from Britain, America and Canada, bringing with them their own sensibilities. We have already mentioned Zizou Corder, whose Charlie is of mixed-race parentage and who, as Kayla Ancrum has pointed out, is fully aware of the implications of this in the way he is treated by those around him. Jackie Kay, best known as a poet, published *Strawgirl* in 2002, a rather elegiac fantasy about a half Scottish, half Nigerian Ibo girl living in an all-white Scottish farming community, who finds consolation and support for her problems in the form of Strawgirl (a scarecrow).

The British Jamila Gavin, although predominantly an author of historical fiction, has written *Three Indian Princesses* (1987) and *Three Indian*

*Goddesses* (2001), collections of short stories based around Indian legends. Vandana Singh from the USA, although predominantly a writer for adults, has a number of whimsical borderline fantasy stories collected under the titles *Younguncle Comes to Town* (2004) and *Younguncle in the Himalayas* (2005). Rhiannon Lassiter is rarely identified as a writer of colour but she is of mixed-race Indian heritage (her mother is the writer Mary Hoffman, whose work is discussed above) and her heritage is reflected in her choice of protagonists in many of her books, perhaps most importantly in her series of portal fantasies, *Rights of Passage* (beginning with *Borderland*, 2003), which are firmly anti-colonialist and deeply sceptical of the entire 'outsider brings salvation' trope which has infected fantasy from Lewis to Rowling.

Along with Lassiter, perhaps the best-known writers of colour for this age group, however, are Nnedi Okorafor (Nigerian-American) and Hiromi Goto (Japanese-Canadian). Okorafor can be seen as a science fiction writer but *Zarah the Windseeker* (2005), although set on an alien planet, has many of the conventions of fantasy, including magical hair and animal companions. *Long Juju Man* (2009) is a ghost story for younger readers, in which Ngoli's grandfather tells her tales that will help her negotiate a friendship with the ghost who lives in the forest. Like other stories we have discussed in this chapter, the knowingness of the child and her ability to manipulate her knowledge to tackle the fantastic stand out: the book won the Macmillan Writers' Prize for Africa. *Akata Witch* (2011) resembles the London fantasies discussed here in being a portal fantasy set in a mundane world, in that Sunny is an American child of Ibo parents who has returned with them to Nigeria. The problem for Sunny is that she is albino and cannot cope with the sun. Then she discovers she is also a Leopard person who can use Juju, but she, unlike others, is not the child of Leopard people but of Lambs, and she must learn to act as a Leopard to discover the city of Leopards where she must save children from an evil kidnapper.

Hiromi Goto writes predominantly for adults but *The Water of Possibility* (2001) is clearly aimed at children. Twelve-year-old Sayuri is very unhappy when her family moves to rural Alberta but with her small brother she finds a way through the root cellar in a classic portal fantasy that takes her to Middle World, inhabited by Japanese folklore characters. Unusually there is no great quest. Sayuri loses her brother and while searching for him she comes into contact with the kappa who helps her find her way in both the secondary world and in her heart.

From India there is Chitra Banerjee Divakaruni. In *The Conch Bearer* (2003) Anand's father disappears after he takes a building job overseas, and the family sinks into poverty. Anand does his best, but when a beggar tempts him with a magic conch shell he joins him in an effort to protect the conch shell from an evil wizard. Along the way he is helped by, and brings along, a beggar girl – there are hints she may be dangerous, but the author never really exploits this. A treasure hunt rather than a quest, which results in the wizard being destroyed and the conch finding safety in Anand's hands and in a sacred valley, it concludes when Anand discovers he has the power to be trained as a wizard.

Other fine contemporary children's fantasies by minority writers include Joseph Bruchac's *Skeleton Man* (2001), which concerns a little girl who has been kidnapped by a strange being out of Mohawk myth; Bruchac's *The Dark Pond* (2004), which involves a monster that haunts a boarding school; and Linda Sue Park's *Archer's Quest* (2006), a reverse time-slip tale in which a contemporary Korean-American boy must find a way to return an ancient Korean warrior to his own era.

Although we have made little use of this method so far, one way to understand the fantastic is by looking at the way in which it enters the text. Portal fantasies feature doorways into fully built worlds that the protagonists understand only as strangers; intrusion fantasies are those in which the fantastic comes into the world from somewhere else; and immersive fantasies are those set entirely in a fantasy world. British, Canadian and Australian fantasy typically embraced the intrusive fantasy until the 1990s when the portal fantasy took over quite decisively. American fantasy tended towards both intrusive and immersive stories with far fewer portal fantasies – *Oz* may have been *too* influential, occupying the space so fully that few new portal tales thrived. However, there is one form that is rare in both adult and children's fantasy, and that is the liminal fantasy, the tale where one is not entirely sure whether one is in a fantastical text or how the fantastic as understood by the characters is at variance with how it is understood by the reader.

Both Joan Aiken, in her Armitage family sequence (where very strange things happen that the children take for granted), and E. B. White in *Stuart Little* understood these forms, but one problem with liminal fantasy is that its tension can rarely be conjured the same way twice (because it depends on uncertainty, and the second time we know we are in the realms of the fantastic) so that the form remains rare within children's fantasy. In this period perhaps the best-known book to be understood this way is Louis Sachar's *Holes* (1998), where the fantasy lurks as a story told behind the text. Stanley Yelnats comes from an unlucky family, unlucky since his great-great-grandfather reneged on a promise to the witch Madame Zeroni to carry her up a mountain in return for advice on courtship. Now in America, Stanley finds himself framed for the theft of a pair of sneakers belonging to a famous baseball star and sent to a juvenile detention centre in the desert where he and his colleagues dig holes for the warden to find a lost treasure. The magic lies in the reversal of Stanley's fortunes after he carries Hector Zeroni, Madame Zeroni's descendant, up a mountain. The sense of the fantastic, however, lies entirely in the way the tale is told, in particular two elements: the different verses of an old ballad that Stanley and Hector each know (joined verses are frequently an element of prophecy); and the singsong ballad of Kissin' Kate Barlow and her love for the black onion-seller, Sam (which makes use of the tradition of using a ballad to structure a story of the fantastic).

Geraldine McCaughrean, otherwise best known for her retellings of myths and hero legends, in *A Pack of Lies* (1988) produced a metafictional story in which a man talks himself into a job in an old antiques shop and proceeds to tell a range of stories, all of which purport to hold some truth. An even stranger tale is *The Stones are Hatching* (1999) which, although set in England and clearly tied to the tradition of the Loathly Worm and of a dragon lying across the back of England, as well as the Jormungand of Norse mythology, also owes something to the structures we saw in Irish fantasy, in which the world of the fantastic is very close to the real world. Phelim's quest to rally the figures of Maiden, Fool and Horse takes place, like that of Will in *The Dark is Rising*, in our own landscape, but the sense of a world put on hold is far more nebulous.

Steve Cockayne's *The Good People* (2006) hovers on the borders of children's and Young Adult fiction, which is appropriate given that it is in part about the liminal stage of the end of childhood and the beginning of adulthood and what might happen if someone refused to cross. Drawing on the traditions of children's fiction established by Arthur Ransome, Kenneth and his brother Robert spend their days playing a war game with fantastical creatures in Arboria. But the game seems to be much older than the two boys, indeed to have been passed down through generations of game players, and there is a very real difference between how Kenneth and Robert interact with and believe in the game. As the war intrudes on their lives and Robert is drawn into the real world, Kenneth becomes more and more a part of the world he understands best. It is never clear in this fascinating book what is or is not real, nor are we ever really asked to decide.

One related area involves stories of hauntings which often hover on the edge of the genre. One of the most interesting of these is Paul Yee's *The Bone Collector's Son* (2003). Bing escapes his father's job as a bone collector (collecting together the bones of Chinese men and shipping them home for permanent burial) by taking a job as a house-boy.

Bing becomes embroiled in releasing his father from the curse of his own bad luck, and also dealing with the ghost of the white man who haunts the house he had built. The various strands of the story are all about connection – connection to one's homeland and connection to the things one has built – and there is always a slight sense of doubt as to the presence of the ghost.

The most successful liminal fantasies of children's literature, however, may well be those of Daniel Handler, aka Lemony Snicket, whose *A Series of Unfortunate Events* (1999–2006) begins with *The Bad Beginning*. These books start as slightly odd but essentially historical mimetic fictions and gradually take more and more spiralling turns until they conclude as metaphysical fiction. In *A Series of Unfortunate Events* Violet, Klaus and Sunny Baudelaire, who appear to reside in a late Edwardian world (and whose story begins with an almost direct quote from Edith Nesbit's *The Wouldbegoods*) are orphaned when their house is burned to the ground and their parents die in the blaze. They are quickly moved to the first of a number of guardians who appear throughout the series. Count Olaf turns out to have ill designs on all of them and it is only through Violet's engineering skills, Klaus's love of books (an interesting gender switch) and Sunny's ability to gnaw things, that they escape. Olaf follows them in each of the first seven books, attempting to capture or kill them in a series of Gothic melodramas, but as the series unfolds and the children discover more about their parents and their parents' colleagues in the secret organization known only as the VFD, good and evil become very slippery and the children realize they have little idea what the truth is of anything. The books end with the children far wiser, but with no closure.

## Horror and dark fantasy

Fantasy for children has always had a dark side, of course, for without danger there is no triumph and with danger comes a certain amount of fear. Most of the stories discussed above have their scary side, but none of them qualifies as horror fiction. Prior to the 1970s, there was little in the way of a specialist horror market for either children or teens. For children, ghost stories were staple fare for Halloween, sleepovers and camp nights, but this was primarily an oral tradition. Many older children came to horror fiction first through pulp magazines like *Weird Tales* or, in the UK, the *Pan Book of Horror Stories* (thirty volumes from 1959–89). These venues and others introduced teens to the greats of nineteenth- and early twentieth-century horror such as Poe, Machen and Lovecraft.

In addition, they laid the groundwork for a generation of new writers such as Ray Bradbury and Shirley Jackson.

The true children's horror market, when it appeared, did so rapidly and under the critical radar. Looking at two standard histories of books for children, Peter Hunt's fine *Children's Literature: An Illustrated History* (1995) has no entry in its index for either 'horror' or 'ghost' and only one for 'Gothic', while Seth Lerer's more recent *Children's Literature: A Reader's History, from Aesop to Harry Potter* (2008) contains no indexed references to any of these terms. Individual authors of terrifying fiction may be mentioned, but there is no sense of a tradition of such fiction for children, at least within the mainstream critical narrative account of children's literature. This is, of course, because children's horror had traditionally been published as penny dreadfuls, dime novels and, later, ghost and fear comics (such as *Adventures into the Unknown*, 1948–67, and *Tales from the Crypt*, 1950–5), with the result that they were disparaged, disregarded and rarely catalogued, but they *did* exist and it was this tradition, and the oral tradition of the camp-fire story, that R. L. Stine was to build on.

Stine did not invent the complex mix of horror, thriller and Gothic fiction that is now marketed as pre-teen and teen horror – there had been a trickle of such books for years and Christopher Pike, Stine's most significant competitor, published *Slumber Party* in 1985 – but Stine soon came to dominate what Kimberley Reynolds has called the 'commodification of horror' for younger readers.[7] Stine's gift lay in being scary without being too scary, in titillating his readers' expectations without going overboard. The tight focus on the child characters is empowering because they clearly have as much agency as their parents, if not more. The cliff-hanger chapter endings and thrill-house pacing are adrenaline-inducing, but the very basic, ten-year-old-level humour defuses the terror. If things don't always end in complete happiness in one of his *Goosebumps* novels, they rarely end in the darkness and despair so common in adult horror fiction.

Perhaps not surprisingly, R. L. Stine (1943–) got his start as a humourist, editing his college humour magazine and, after graduation, writing dozens of joke books for children under the name Jovial Bob Stine. He also created, edited and wrote much of the content for the teen magazine *Bananas*, part *Mad Magazine* and part media-fandom magazine, for Scholastic between 1975 and 1984. In 1986, however, he published the first Point Horror novel, *Blind Date*, and the rest is history. He also created the far from horrific *Eureka's Castle* for Nickelodeon and was their head writer from 1989 to 1995. For several years in the 1990s he was the best-selling writer in the USA.

Patrick Jones, whose *What's So Scary About R. L. Stine?* (1998) is surely the most detailed analysis ever likely to be written of this author's work, describes Stine's fiction as 'books boys were actually excited about'.[8] In his close study of Stine's work, Jones describes in detail how the author gradually developed his trademark methods: 'confusion about identity, characters asking the same questions readers are asking, the abundance of exclamation marks, the short action-packed paragraphs, the use of humour, and finally the cliff-hanger ending'.[9] Once Stine, a prolific author, got started with *Fear Street* and *Goosebumps*, the novels in the two series, taking into account their slightly different audiences, are all pretty much of a piece, and consideration of one will stand for all.

*One Day at Horrorland* (1994), one of the *Goosebumps* novels (it became a best-selling game CD in 1996 as *Escape from Horrorland*), is an intrusive fantasy that concerns the Morrises, a more or less realistically portrayed family who accidentally end up at the previously unheard-of Horrorland theme park, a variation on that favourite location for American horror, the circus, as in Charles Finney's *The Circus of Doctor Lao* (1935), Ray Bradbury's *Something Wicked this Way Comes* (1962) and Erin Morgenstern's *The Night Circus* (2011). In the theme park, as the front cover of the book tells us, 'Nightmares come to life.' The novel features a classic Stine opening line: 'As we entered the gates to Horrorland, we had no idea that, in less than an hour, we would be lying in our coffins.'[10] The children are front and centre as the book opens, fooling around in the family car, cracking jokes and trying to scare one another even before they've heard of Horrorland.

Stine's work is structured like the old Saturday morning serials: the opening chapter ends with a classic Stine cliff-hanger, as the child narrator looks up through his car's sunroof and '"Oh!" I let out a cry as I saw a hideous monster staring down at me, lowering its enormous head, about to crush the car.'[11] Of course it's just a mechanical monster on a sign, but it scares the entire family. As might be expected in Stine's work, when they enter Horrorland things immediately go wrong. Their car explodes for no obvious reason, stranding them at the amusement park, and the ticket-taker, whom they assume is a man in a monster suit, assures them with one of Stine's trademark double-entendres that 'The other Horrors and I will see that you are properly taken care of.'[12] Predictably, the kids then encounter a series of monsters and scary rides. Their emotions teeter back and forth between sheer terror, humorous relief and a desire to see what's next. Each terrifying experience is forgotten almost as soon as it is done with. Even the parents seem childlike, unable to learn from their mistakes, quickly terrified but just as quickly mollified. Eventually, the family discovers that they've secretly been the subjects of a hidden camera television show, one watched by 'nearly two million monsters all over the world'.[13] They escape the final death trap that has been set for them but then, upon reaching home, are astonished when another monster shows up to offer them free passes to Horrorland for next year. Was the family ever actually in danger or was the whole thing an elaborate prank? The reader will never know for sure.

Stine's first thriller, *Blind Date* (1986), a non-supernatural tale of madness and revenge, initiated the influential Point Horror children's publishing label, which has produced upwards of 170 novels and anthologies, including work by Caroline B. Cooney, Celia Rees, Paul Stewart, Diane Hoh and other soon to be noted writers. Among the enormously prolific Stine's long-running series are the teen-oriented *Fear Street* (52 volumes, 1989–2005), beginning with *The New Girl* (1989), and the less gruesome *Goosebumps* (62 volumes, 1992–7), beginning with *Welcome to the Dead House* (1992) and aimed at pre-teens. Many of the individual novels have sequels and even the extended series have sequels, as for example with *Goosebumps 2000* (25 volumes, 1998–2000) and the game books *Give Yourself Goosebumps* (42 volumes, 1995–2000). The formula Stine developed generated many imitations and particularly supported series fiction, which came to dominate the children's and Young Adult bestseller lists. Children's horror has run on much the same lines since. Other current (sometimes comic) horror series for younger readers include M. D. Payne's *Monster Juice* (first volume *Fear the Barfitron*, 2013) and *You're Invited to a Creepover* by P. J. Night (for example, *The House Next Door*, 2013).

The books for older readers published in the Point Horror series, whether by Stine, Hoh or Cooney, were as a rule significantly grimmer and somewhat grosser than are the *Goosebumps* tales, but they too set careful boundaries. There are no normal deaths in these books and no discussion of normal dying either; death is always unnatural, the result of hideous accident, murder or supernatural encounter. Thus, although terrifying, although often set in what at first appears to be a realistic middle-class environment, even the most violent Point Horror novels tend to have constraints, to have clear indications that they are separated from the actual world of the teen reader and are therefore safe to read. Perhaps not surprisingly, since its recent revival after a hiatus of eight years Point Horror has tried to stay up to date by centring on the internet in novels such as *Wickedpedia* (2013) by Chris Van Etten and *Defriended* (2013) by Ruth Baron.

Alongside straight, generally formulaic horror for children, however, there is also what is often called Dark Fantasy, some clearly for pre-teens, some moving into the Young Adult range, the best of it far more ambitious than anything Point Horror produced. Dark Fantasy has no generic form, and it covers a wide range of the horrific. Among the best recent examples of dark fantasies for children of various ages are Joseph Delaney's grim and deceptively simple *Wardstone Chronicles*, beginning with *The Spook's Apprentice* (2004), which concern a boy apprenticed to an old man charged with protecting a vaguely medieval countryside from witches, ghosts and other forms of evil; Rick Yancey's bloody *The Monstrumologist* (2009) and sequels, which concern another apprentice, this time in the nineteenth-century United States, who must also help his master destroy monsters who may or may not be entirely natural; Andrew Smith's magnificent but very dark *The Marbury Lens* (2010) and sequel, a brutal tale of death and abuse set partly in our world and partly in a nightmarish, post-apocalyptic universe; and Brenna Yovanoff's *The Space Between* (2011), the beautifully written story of Lilith's daughter who, having been born and raised in Hell itself, travels to Earth to save the life of her outcast elder brother. What these stories all share is a sense of abiding fear, and a belief that the fantastic is lurking very close.

Joseph Delaney's *Wardstone Chronicles*, which, it is worth noting, is marketed to a ten-year-old-plus audience, are frankly and unrelentingly terrifying. Rick Yancey's somewhat similar *The Monstrumologist* features extraordinarily bloody scenes such as one in which human remains are found plastered across the walls and ceiling of a church. In another memorable scene (among many), teen readers are treated to the following description of one of Yancey's Anthropophagi at work:

> … his legs jerked; his feet pushed against the weathered planks as he tried to yank himself free, but the drag of her bulk upon his captured arm had wedged him even tighter. He threw back his head, twisting his face from side to side, for the she-beast had released his shredded arm, and now her bloody barbs slashed his face and swiped across the throat he had so considerately exposed.[14]

The endings of these books are very grim. In *The Monstrumologist* the protagonist's reward for success is little more than survival and even that is assured only by his willingness to subject himself to a form of monstrous parasite that artificially prolongs his life. The darkness of Yancey's novel is underlined by its last line: 'Yes, my dear child, monsters are real. I happen to have one hanging in my basement.'[15] Writers like Smith and Yancey go about as far as any authors for children and young adults can in terms of sheer bleakness.

Two of the finest and most original dark fantasies of the past two decades are David Almond's *Skellig* (1998) and Neil Gaiman's previously mentioned *The Graveyard Book* (2008). Almond, whose terrors are more existential than physical, has also written *Kit's Wilderness* (1999), *Heaven Eyes* (2000), *Clay* (2005) and the masterful post-apocalyptic novel *The True Tale of the Monster Billy Dean* (2011), among other books, as well as picture books and a series of remarkable graphic novel collaborations with Dave McKean, such as *Slog's Dad* (2010). It is perhaps not a surprise that McKean also collaborates with Gaiman with some frequency.

David Almond (1951–) was born and raised in and around Newcastle-upon-Tyne and has lived there his whole life, creating novels, plays, graphic novels, short stories and picture books that feature a deeply realized sense of place. Heavily influenced by William Blake, he often writes about finding the miraculous in the everyday, the importance of education and the interconnectedness of life and death, the last topic being where most of the darkness is generated in his books. The need to deal with the mortality of a loved one is central not only to *Skellig* but to *Kit's Wilderness*, *Heaven Eyes*, *My Name is Mina* (2010), *Slog's Dad*, *The True Tale of the Monster Billy Dean*, *The Boy who Swam with Piranhas* (2012) and several other of Almond's books. Among his many awards, he is one of only thirty recipients of the prestigious international Hans Christian Andersen award.

The Carnegie Medal-winning *Skellig* involves a boy from a working-class Newcastle background whose family has recently moved to a new home, a decrepit fixer-upper, and whose newborn baby sister has a serious heart problem. Having been told not to enter the property's half-collapsed outbuilding, Michael of course immediately does so and discovers there a mysterious being, Skellig. 'I thought he was dead. He was sitting with his legs stretched out and his head tipped back against the wall. He was covered in dust and webs like everything else and his face was thin and pale.'[16] Discovering that Skellig is both alive and possessed of wings, Michael almost immediately, and for no very obvious reason, asks the creature to save his sister's life.

Geraldine Brennan argues in *Frightening Fiction* that, 'While his books are not marketed as horror fiction, Almond engages with the fears of both child and adult protagonists and charts their efforts to resolve them.'[17] Michael is obsessed with both his sister's potential death and the mysteries of a possible afterlife. The book abounds with allusions to these things taken from Greek myth (Icarus, Persephone), the poetry of William Blake, the folk iconography of Almond's own English Catholic heritage and evolutionary science, with a number of these references being provided by his friend Mina, a home-schooled freethinker. Skellig, who defines himself as 'Something like you, something like a beast, something like a bird, something like an angel … Something like that',[18] is an intensely liminal figure; Almond never actually defines his nature and those who would insist that he's an angel must also deal with the fact that he's not only (at least at first) a crabby old man, but also a carnivore, equally happy eating Chinese food, mice and small insects.

Almond conducts a careful balancing act, exposing Michael to a variety of religious, mythological and scientific ideas about death, resurrection, faith and miracles, allowing him to think deeply about the various possibilities. The loss of his little sister, it seems likely, would devastate both the boy and his family on a spiritual level. Similarly, Skellig, whether he is a fallen angel or not, is clearly headed towards, perhaps is already in, some sort of spiritual Hell. The care that Michael and Mina give Skellig leads to his decision to become involved in the baby's life-and-death struggle for survival, which is portrayed by Almond as a veritable resurrection for both the baby and the winged man.

Neil Gaiman is one of the fantasy genre's best-known writers; beginning with the *Sandman* comics (1989–96), his reputation has risen steadily, due in part to adult novels such as *Stardust* (1999), *American Gods* (2001) and *The Ocean at the End of the Lane* (2013), but also due to his work for children, such as *Coraline* and the picture book *The Wolves in the Walls* (2003), both of which pushed the boundaries of frightening fiction for children. In 2008 he sealed his reputation as a children's writer with the Newbery- and Carnegie-winning *The Graveyard Book* (2008). *Coraline*, which is inspired by Lucy Clifford's short story 'The New Mother' (1882), is also an Alice story, in which Coraline, annoyed with her busy parents, crawls through a portal and finds herself in a world where a 'mother' offers her protection but, as she eventually realizes, in return for her soul. The replacement of eyes with black buttons is depicted in a way that is truly terrifying. *The Wolves in the Walls*, repeating a trademark Gaiman theme that children are basically very smart and we should listen to them, features Lucy, who knows there are wolves hiding in the house but is not believed until the wolves actually do come out of the walls, take over the house and throw wild parties. The book is Rabelaisian in tone, with everything seeming out of control, but is made even scarier by McKean's paintings and Gaiman's 'chant' of '*When the wolves come out of the walls, it's all over!*'

Intensely charismatic, the British-born Neil Gaiman (1960–) has gained a virtual rock star reputation among fans of his adult novels, children's books, comics, graphic novels and television scripts, a reputation that has only grown since his 2011 marriage to a genuine rock star, Amanda Palmer of the Dresden Dolls. A listing of Gaiman's numerous awards and honours would fill an entire page of this book. Besides the Carnegie and the Newbery for *The Graveyard Book*, the major ones include a World Fantasy Award, fifteen Eisner Awards, four Bram Stoker Awards, two Nebulas, four Hugos, three British Fantasy Awards, a British Science Fiction Award, two Shirley Jackson Awards and most recently a fifth Hugo Award for 'The Doctor's Wife', an episode of the long-running television programme *Doctor Who*. More awards may well follow before this book sees print.

*The Graveyard Book* is modelled loosely on Rudyard Kipling's *The Jungle Book* (1894), though it takes a subtle anti-imperialist stance that is at odds with that earlier author's beliefs. It tells the story of a toddler whose parents and sibling are murdered for reasons unknown by a supernaturally endowed professional killer, 'the man Jack'. The little boy, unaware of the tragedy, escapes the killer by wandering into a nearby graveyard where, to protect him from the murderer, he is hidden by a bevy of eccentric ghosts, aided by Silas, a vampire whose position in the novel is loosely parallel to that of Bagheera the black panther in Kipling's book. Since nobody in the cemetery knows the boy's name and the deceased Mr and Mrs Owens agree to raise him, he is called Nobody (Bod) Owens. Powerfully and unsettlingly illustrated in the UK edition by Chris Riddell and in the US edition by Dave McKean, the book, like much of Gaiman's children's fiction, has occasionally been criticized as being too frightening for its intended age group. However, *The Graveyard Book* has won over both the reading public and the critical establishment. Moreover, it manages to be not only rather bucolic, but at times even sweet. Perhaps not since Kingsley's *The Water-Babies* (1863) has a children's fantasy made death seem so comforting and comfortable, for, as Silas says, echoing Hillary Clinton's *It Takes a Village* (1996) on the importance of extended families, 'It's going to take more than just a couple of good-hearted souls to raise this child. It will … take a graveyard.'[19] Discussing the connection to *The Jungle Book* and Gaiman's belief in the importance of family, Christine Robertson suggests that 'Both Gaiman and Kipling choose womb-like, enclosed spaces – the Owenses' underground tomb and the wolves' "home-cave" – in order to evoke the feelings of warmth, comfort, and security that a child would naturally experience in a happy, loving home.'[20] As in *Skellig*, in Gaiman's tale joy may be found in the darkest places. This darkness, as we shall see, continues to make itself known in fiction for older teens.

CHAPTER 9

# *Romancing the teen*

At the end of the 1980s some of the biggest hitters among teens were texts intended for adults but appropriated by children, such as the work of Stephen King, Anne Rice, David Eddings, V. C. Andrews and Terry Brooks, whose power was such that they sold across the market barriers which have shaped this narrative. However, the teen market itself was changing. By the late 1980s not only were most teens still in school, but middle-class US teens were expecting to spend another four years in college. By the end of the 1990s, there was an increasing chance that another two years would be added on to that. Although we have no figures, it is a fair guess that the more likely a teen was to be a reader, the more chance they would be facing this extended delay of full adulthood. Meanwhile, other aspects of adolescent life were changing. The teens who were the targets of the Young Adult movement in the 1970s lived in what to many contemporary Americans would now seem to be a startlingly liberal world: those teens could legally both drink and smoke. By the 1990s, almost every US state had drinking laws which ensured young adults could not drink legally and smoking was gradually becoming socially unacceptable in middle-class circles. While the UK did not experience this particular social change, by 2014 all UK children had to stay in full-time education until they were eighteen.

### Growing to adulthood

In most of the fantasies written for children prior to the 1960s, young people were hardly ever shown growing to adulthood. Even during the 1970s this was uncommon; Lloyd Alexander's work is a rarity, and while Diana Wynne Jones's children sometimes grew up, as in *Fire and Hemlock* or *The Time of the Ghost* (both of which are actually flashback novels), their stories ended, as in Margaret Mahy's *The Changeover*, on the cusp of adolescence. The new teen market demanded that fantasy novels consider

195

growing up as part of the development of character, and increasingly editors and librarians were arguing that readers should be able to find themselves inside the books they read. To some degree, therefore, every title discussed in this chapter (and many more we cannot include) tackles what has become known as The Problem with Susan, not least because – as the texts cited here will make obvious – the readers and protagonists of teen and Young Adult fantasy were increasingly posited as female.

Phillip Pullman raised the 'Susan problem' in 1998 in a column in *The Guardian*. Concerning C. S. Lewis's character: 'in *The Last Battle*, notoriously, there's the turning away of Susan from the Stable (which stands for salvation) because "She's interested in nothing nowadays except nylons and lipstick and invitations. She always was a jolly sight too keen on being grown-up."'[1] Pullman's interpretation is rather crude, in that a contextual reading makes it clear that the issue is that Susan is interested in nothing else (presumably Lucy and Jill also coveted and would eventually wear nylons) and there is a hint in *The Dawn Treader* that it is Susan's parents and upbringing Lewis is criticizing, in their decision to focus on her looks rather than her brains (Lewis makes attacks on parents in almost every book). However, Pullman did seem to be arguing for a space for the feminine girl in a genre which in the 1960s began to favour the boyish (epitomized perhaps in Tamora Pierce's *Alanna* series). As the school age rose, many 'Susans' were specifically sold a form of literature which consisted of 'invitations, lipstick and nylons', or which turned to the dark side of this, as in the classic problem novels of S. E. Hinton and her emulators. Fantasy (and science fiction), as we saw in Chapter 6, had previously been a refuge from this for those girls and boys who found the world of high school gossip and dating either repellent or overwhelming.

When the teen fantasy boom began in the 2000s, Lipstick and Nylons fantasy found a place in some of the more light-hearted fiction for teens. In Ned Vizzini's *Be More Chill* (2004), for example, what is effectively a magic pill whispers in the boy's ear how to go about charming the girl of his dreams. In Justine Larbalestier's *How to Ditch your Fairy* (2008), Charlie lives in a world where everyone has their own fairy with its own special skill. Her best friend has a Clothing fairy who helps her shop the second-hand stores for bargains. Unfortunately, Charlie's fairy is a Car Parking fairy and Charlie is only fourteen. About the only thing it helps with is making Charlie the essential companion on any shopping trip, much like the designated non-drinker. So Charlie spends the book doing her best to lose her fairy, trade her in and eventually trade up in a world in which the winners are those with Charisma fairies. Mindy Klasky tackles the issue of boys in *Girl's Guide to Witchcraft* (2006), in which Jane Madison seeks to establish a college for witches. It is mildly startling that every witch in this book comes accompanied with two hunks, a warder and a familiar, the latter an animal transformed into a man who is unnervingly submissive. This is a sanitized version of Laurell K. Hamilton's *Anita Blake: Vampire Hunter* series where the submissiveness is more overtly sexual. Here, Klasky keeps things clean and safe. Her work is magical Chick-Lit (here a term not intended to be derogatory), as are *Charmed and Dangerous* (2005) by Candace Havens, Shanna Swendson's *Damsel Under Stress* (2007; tag line 'To-do: Stop the bad guys. Rescue the wizard. Find the perfect outfit for New Year's Eve'), Vicki Lewis Thompson's *Blonde with a Wand* (2009) and many more. This kind of fantasy is precisely about granting the Susans of the world rather more agency over the world of invitations.

A logical extension of the Lipstick and Nylons fantasies was the paranormal romance: once dressed up, after all, the young fantasy reader needs somewhere to go. Early signs of this trend can be found in the popularity of Anne Rice's *Interview with the Vampire* (1976) and sequels. Although *The Vampire Chronicles* were not immediately a major success, *The Vampire Lestat*, published in 1985, created a backwash of popularity and after that new titles appeared approximately every three years. The next milestone was the TV show *Buffy the Vampire Slayer* (first run 1997–2003), but *Buffy* was, and remains, an outlier in teen paranormal stories because it keeps the romance firmly within teen dating patterns: impermanent and always set against problems at school (and the regular appearance of monsters). Although actual teen vampire novels had been appearing for years (see, for example, Annette Curtis Klause's popular *The Silver Kiss*, 1992), the real change came with the publication and enormous popularity of Stephenie Meyer's *Twilight* (2005).

In *Buffy the Vampire Slayer*, writer-director Joss Whedon brought in two essential components of the Young Adult world: the belief that one is special, with special problems; and a related belief that one's intimate relationships are essentially more important than the great quests or battles that are taking place out in the world (some of the most effective episodes are entirely personal). In the work of Whedon, of Rice and of new writers for the adult market such as Laurell K. Hamilton and Charlaine Harris (the Sookie Stackhouse series) we saw a new intimacy that was perfectly compatible with the horror genre: the vampire was still placing his teeth to your throat, but now the delicious thrill was made explicit.

Nowhere was this more obvious than in the runaway bestseller, *Twilight* by Stephenie Meyer.

The *Twilight* series made Stephenie Meyer (1973–) the bestselling author in America in 2008 and 2009, following J. K. Rowling and preceding Suzanne Collins and Veronica Roth as children's or Young Adult writers who demonstrated enormous crossover appeal for adults. Like the work of Rowling, Collins and Roth, her books, although far from perfect, have received more than their fair share of criticism, in part due to the failure of their adult readers to understand that they were in fact reading children's books. One source of such criticism, however, is Meyer's strict Mormon faith and its supposed effect on the moral messages in the book. The author graduated from Brigham Young University with a degree in English, married at twenty-one and has three children. She has never worked outside the home except, briefly, as a receptionist. *Twilight*, amazingly enough, was her very first attempt to write a work of fiction. The town of Forks, Washington, made famous as the setting for *Twilight*, holds a Stephenie Meyer Day on 13 September each year, the date of her character Bella Swan's birthday. *USA Today* named Meyer Author of the Year in 2008. In 2009 the series won the Kids' Choice Award for favourite book.

The Young Adult fiction movement was essentially a US phenomenon as the titles in this chapter will indicate. The concept of Young Adult was one the US fiction market nurtured, and one whose contradictions it sheltered, for while the implication of the label suggests more challenging issues, in some areas of the market what often emerged was fiction that primarily concerned control of the body, and this was particularly true of the paranormal romance. Roberta Seelinger Trites has argued that 'Because adults are quite conscious of sexuality as a source of power, they frequently subject adolescent readers to very consistent ideologies that attempt to regulate teen sexuality by repressing it.'[2]

To understand some of the popularity of *Twilight* and the paranormal romance narrative, it helps to understand the disparity in the USA between actual dating patterns and accepted dating ideologies. In *From Front Porch to Back Seat* (1988) Beth L. Bailey charted the changing patterns of courtship in the USA, from a safety in numbers ideology in the 1930s – in which a boy's job was to ensure his girl got as many dances with other boys as possible, and in which there was a horror for a girl in being stuck with just one boy – to a pattern emerging in the 1940s and 1950s in which, with girls in the majority, there came to be a great anxiety about going steady. Both patterns in their day gave girls status and so were essentially matters for public display.[3] By the 1990s, it was still possible to see both patterns in American culture, sometimes alongside each other, but the going-steady pattern (although the term has disappeared) had gained the moral upper hand (Buffy tends to date one partner; Cordelia, her enemy, posited sometimes as Mean Girl and sometimes as used, tends to accept many dates although this is not constant, as when she goes steady with Xander).

In the going-steady system the relative paucity of desirable men means that the steady relationship is flaunted. Fascinatingly, Meyer uses both strategies: Bella is both going steady with Edward, and courted by Jacob. And so she is, publicly, both in possession and in demand. Bailey, studying primarily media in the 1980s, particularly television and the magazines, noted the pressure on parents to train children (particularly, but not only, girls) to date, displayed in a growing emphasis on child dates, clothing that once again resembled adult clothing, and the big senior dance. Michael Cart notes that by the end of the 1980s 34 million copies of *Sweet Valley High* titles had been printed, which also seemed to perform this function within the context of more or less realistic fiction.[4] The paranormal romance, as it emerged in the wake of Stephenie Meyer's success, seems to be one more element in this construction and control of teen sexuality. Young Adult fiction plays the part that tuberculosis romances played in the late nineteenth century, in which life seems short, doomed and therefore intense. As Cart says, 'Unfortunately, kids do overstate their emotional life; for them the possibility of tragedy exists in everything.'[5] For Bella and her successors, and for their readers, everything must be over the top, everything must be a matter of life and death but, paradoxically, it must also be channelled in expected and therefore safe directions.

The four-volume *Twilight* series largely follows the formula which Janice Radway described in *Reading the Romance* (1984): a lower-class girl meets a higher-status boy, she meets opposition (from his family) but eventually proves herself to him (and them) and he discovers she is irresistible and raises her to join him. This of course omits the paranormal elements, but in understanding the popularity of the novels the role of class (elided in the films), and Bella's role as the dutiful working-class daughter who must distance herself from the tarnish of her mother's behaviour, should not be underestimated.

Bella is a teenager with family problems, displaced to a new community. She falls in love with another high school student, the mysterious and attractive Edward Cullen who, of course, is actually a vampire and much older than he looks. They have something of a back and forth relationship and it isn't always clear who is chasing whom. Edward is badly conflicted: he 'wants' Bella in at least two senses of that word, and yet, having a conscience and not wanting to endanger her, knows he should keep his distance. Firmly in the new paranormal tradition established by Rice and extended by Hamilton, Harris and others, Meyer gradually unveils a complex vampire civilization, filled with rivalries and alliances, in which the heroine has the opportunity to become First Lady if she submits to what is in effect a revised eighteenth-century captivity narrative.

Like Hamilton, Meyer offers a multitude of monsters, including a Native American werewolf culture. Bella, like Hamilton's Anita, is conflicted and readers can angst over which monster – the ancient, if young-seeming vampire Edward, or the genuinely teenage werewolf Jacob Black – should triumph in their battle for Bella Swan's affections. Unlike Hamilton's increasingly erotic *Anita Blake* series, however, *Twilight* sublimates all of the sexual energy into highly charged sexual restraint: where Anita dates and has a number of casual lovers, Bella goes steady. Rivalry, along with the various vampire and werewolf pack hatreds, leads to a variety of intense verbal interactions, highly filmable battle scenes, blood-stirring heroics and, eventually, after the longest possible delay, marriage, intensely romantic sexual intercourse, a highly unsettling pregnancy and birth and Bella's transformation into a powerful vampire in her own right.

Stephenie Meyer's *Twilight* aroused a great deal of criticism. Like much popular literature, it was roundly castigated for its occasional poor writing, stereotypical characters and formulaic plotting, along with its anti-feminist values and its sparkly vampires, which for many purists seemed a subversion too far, but in general Meyer only made explicit what is present in vampire texts from *Dracula* onwards. Not all of the critics have hated her books. For example, *Twilight* was named an ALA Top Ten Book for Young Adults and a *Publishers Weekly* Best Book of the Year, and the final volume, *Breaking Dawn* (2008), won the British Book Award for Children's Book of the Year. The criticism that the books have attracted has, among other things, exposed to public gaze the complex ways in which books for children and teens are understood. The novels have a strong political and religious ideology (Meyer is a Mormon) which has been explored extensively by Anna Silver and by Sarah Schwartzman. Abstinence teaching, the proper roles of men and women and the structure of the family are all central to the novel, and this has incensed many feminist readers. However, English professor Holly Virginia Blackford, in her work with girls, has argued that girls recognize the difference between social reality and social aspiration. Of the attraction of the teen girls in her study to the Gothic, she argues, 'the girls implicitly expect Gothic horror to unsettle cultural boundaries, and formally express the position of girls and women in culture, at risk for becoming victims or monstrous bodies, while striving to be participants and producers of culture'.[6] In this understanding, *Twilight*, for all that it is overwrought, may well reflect the reality of dating patterns for girls in high school and college culture where boys still control access to status.

The success of *Twilight* led to a boom in sexy vampires. In her recent study of Young Adult horror fiction specifically featuring supernatural monsters, *They Suck, They Bite, They Eat, They Kill* (2012), Joni Richards Bodart lists some forty individual series devoted to vampires with almost as many more stand-alone novels. Teen vampire tales that are particularly popular or worthy of recommendation include Rachel Caine's *Morganville Vampires* series, beginning with *Glass Houses* (2006); Melissa de la Cruz's *Blue Bloods* series, beginning with *Blue Bloods* (2006); P. C. Cast and Kristin Cast's *House of Night* series, beginning with *Marked* (2007); Richelle Mead's *Vampire Academy* series, beginning with *Vampire Academy* (2007); Alyson Noël's *Immortals* series, beginning with *Evermore* (2009); and Tate Hallaway's delightfully snarky *Vampire Princess of St. Paul* series, beginning with *Almost to Die For* (2010). Although the surge in paranormal romance was primarily American, from New Zealand we have Karen Healey's *Guardian of the Dead* (2010) and from Australia Keri Arthur's science fiction *Dark Angels* series (2011–14) among other titles, and Tracey O'Hara's *Dark Brethren* series (2009–12).

## Fantasy romance

By the beginning of the twenty-first century, romance was one of the dominant themes in teen fantasy; the only question was with whom, or perhaps what, the romance would occur. For example, Canadian Martine Leavitt's moody *Keturah and Lord Death* (2006), which has something of the feel of a darkly sumptuous Pre-Raphaelite painting, introduces us to a serious young woman who finds herself courted by Death himself, who is portrayed as rather chivalric. Although vampires have dominated the teen horror market and particularly the supernatural romance for nearly a decade, other monsters, as Meyer's werewolves clearly demonstrated, also have the ability to speak to teens on a deep emotional level. Melissa Marr, in the series that begins with *Wicked Lovely* (2007), is one of a number of writers who domesticate fairies: she places them in a modern urban setting, involving them heavily with the currently popular fad of tattooing, and following the Young Adult supernatural romance model. She both enrols them in high school and has one of them become romantically involved with her female protagonist. Holly Black, perhaps the finest author working this particular trope, in the very dark *Tithe: A Modern Faerie Tale* (2002) features a young heroine who becomes entangled with warring faerie kingdoms against the backdrop of a grungy and believable blue-collar New Jersey. For the werewolf lovers, the best of the new fictions may be Stuart Hill's *The Cry of the Icemark* (2005), which was also part of a revived interest in prehistoric and early medieval fantasy settings; Martin Millar's ironic *Lonely Werewolf Girl* (2008); Maggie Stiefvater's highly readable *Shiver* (2009) and its sequels; and the ever-transgressive Catherine Jinks with her *The Abused Werewolf Rescue Group* (2011). Even angels get a shot at romance in such volumes as Becca Fitzpatrick's *Hush, Hush* (2009) and the Australian writer Rebecca Lim's *Mercy* (2010).

Stiefvater's *Shiver*, to consider just one popular example, largely follows the same formula as *Twilight* and other supernatural romances aimed at teens. Grace, who lives in a small town in northern Minnesota, has always been attracted to the wolves who spend the winter in the nearby woods, particularly one with yellow eyes, and this fascination continues even after she has been attacked and bitten in her own backyard. Eventually, however, she meets Sam, a boy with the same kind of eyes, and discovers that he's part of a local werewolf pack. It seems that what causes werewolves to change is not the time of the month but the cold. They become wolves when the temperature drops below freezing and every spring it becomes harder and harder to change back again. Grace must then face a decision. Should she try to save Sam and keep him human or should she allow herself to become a werewolf too? Up against both human hostility towards the wolves and various werewolf pack rivalries, Grace soon finds herself in danger, both sides of her double life spinning rapidly out of control. *Shiver* and its sequels tell a powerful tale of love, loyalty and, as is usually the case in such books, the desire for agency.

The plot of *Shiver*, and of other novels in the new paranormal romance, raises new issues. Supernatural romances tend to be solipsistic. Although the protagonist may occasionally have concerns for the larger community, as in Molly Cochran's *Legacy* (2011), the heavy emphasis is on the problems of the protagonist herself and perhaps those closest to her. Most important, of course, are her romantic difficulties with her supernatural love interest. Bella may occasionally worry about her parents or her surrogate family, the Cullens, particularly when one or more of them is in danger, but is otherwise largely fixated on Edward and Jacob, her two monstrous but enormously cute suitors. Even when the new paranormal teen fictions seek to give women agency, it is noticeable that they structure the adventures of their heroines around the succour of men. For those of us brought up in the 1960s and 1970s, that the woman got to rescue the Prince once felt radical, but in the 2000s it is beginning to feel slightly different, as if a woman's adventure must still be motivated by male need. In Cochran's *Legacy*, for example, Serenity Ainsworth, who insists on being called by her more prosaic middle name, Katy, has lived with her father for most of her life but now, at sixteen, finds herself enrolled at a snobby prep school in her long-dead mother's home town of Whitfield, Massachusetts. There she quickly discovers that her mother's people and indeed much of the town (including one very attractive and emotionally damaged young man) are descended from the very real witches who fled the witch trials in Salem during the late seventeenth century. Being a witch does not make you either better or worse, she finds, but it does give you powerful agency, the ability to do great evil or great good. In a classic example of wish fulfilment fantasy, Katy gradually realizes that a great (and sentient) evil has intruded upon and eventually plans to take over Whitfield (and eventually, of course, the world) and she is the only one with the power to repel or even delay it. Doing this, of course, will also save her new boyfriend, something that, as is often the case in such stories, seems to have almost equal weight in Katy's mind.

In Becca Fitzpatrick's *Hush, Hush* (2009), the first in a series, Nora Grey, a college sophomore, meets Patch Cipriano, a fabulously good-looking senior who, we eventually discover, just happens to be a fallen angel who, and this is not good, has an angel of death named Dabria for a girlfriend. Patch was originally considering killing Nora as part of an elaborate plan to transform himself into a completely human being, but has now fallen in love with her. Eventually he saves her life and becomes her guardian angel. Rebecca Lim's *Mercy* charges things up by making the titular female protagonist the fallen angel. Sent repeatedly back to Earth by an apparently capricious deity and injected into a series of human bodies, Mercy is searching for her lost love, an angel named Luc. Unlike the majority of protagonists mentioned in this chapter, she seriously worries about people other than her nearest and dearest. Mercy is forbidden from interfering in human problems but seems to operate out of a strong ethic of caring which, within a plot concerning jealousy between high school choir sopranos, eventually leads her to save the life of a kidnapped girl who also happens to have a cute brother named Ryan.

Many of these stories of transformation turn into metaphor the sometimes wrenching physical, emotional and intellectual changes that, as any parent or teacher will tell you, can make the young borderline crazy. Often in such tales the protagonist finds herself transformed after being infected by a monster. Sometimes this change is very much against the protagonist's will, but sometimes it is something that, after suitable hesitation, she realizes that she wants, a change comparable to and as right for her as the scary leap into adulthood or sexuality. On other occasions, however, the protagonist discovers something within her, a monster that has lurked in her genes, unknowingly inherited from one or both parents. The biggest difference between these two forms of transformation is that the infection model is likely to leave the protagonist isolated from her birth parents, often by her own choice, taking up a new life with a new family; the inheritance model, whether seen as the passing on of the parent's moral corruption, or more often as a terrifying but ultimately worthwhile inherited gift, may serve to draw the protagonist back to her family, resulting in the revelation of heretofore unknown family secrets. This latter trope is even more obvious in another form of fantasy that developed alongside the paranormal romance, the paranormal family narrative.

This plotline, like the paranormal romance, has a certain antiquity: the Addams family and the Munsters, popular monstrous families of 1960s US television (with the original Addams family cartoons by Charles Addams going back to 1938), satirized the desire we all have for our families to be both like and yet not like others, to have families with dark and wondrous secrets we can enter into and celebrate. In the teen paranormal this begins to emerge in the popularity of families gifted with witchcraft or other supernatural powers among those (writers and readers) who had grown up reading authors such as Diana Wynne Jones (particularly the *Chrestomanci* series) or J. K. Rowling. Alison Waller has noted that, like the paranormal romances, 'witchcraft narratives tend to focus on the affirmative qualities of the fantasy rather than any fearful properties of black magic (unless they are part-horror). Most protagonists in witchcraft novels are female and it seems that authors are eager to explore issues of matrilineal power and contemporary female identity through mythological and historical frames.'[7]

A strong example of this can be found in Cassandra Clare's two related series, *The Mortal Instruments*, beginning with *City of Bones*

(2007), which takes place in modern New York City, and the *Infernal Devices* series, beginning with *Clockwork Angel* (2010), which takes place in Victorian England. Both series feature talented, competent young women who discover the existence of an age-old society of Shadowhunters, angelic beings with a variety of superpowers and tattoos (not to mention rather Byronic romantic tendencies), who are destined to hunt and destroy demons, vampires, fairies and a range of other evil supernatural creatures. Clare's books, although a bit predictable, are well-written and very popular. Clare has a knack for action sequences, and her major characters are both attractive and powerfully drawn.

Australian Justine Larbalestier and Canadian Kelbian Noel have also produced interesting novels along these lines. Larbalestier's *Magic or Madness* trilogy, beginning with *Magic or Madness* (2005), tells the story of Reason Cansino and her mother, who have spent years in the Australian outback, on the run from Reason's grandmother, supposedly an evil witch. Reason eventually discovers what her mother has kept from her, that she herself is magical and faces a horrible choice: if she uses her abilities, she will die young, but if she doesn't she, like her mother, will go mad. In her *Roots: Witchbound Book One* (2013), Noel offers a multicultural, multi-ethnic take on this meme, with her heroine Baltimore, the child of a light-skinned, red-haired woman of Native American descent and an African-American man. She has apparently inherited witchcraft which she does not desire from both sides of the family. The novel begins when Baltimore skips out on a school trip to visit her runaway brother in California, only to discover that he has signed on with a local coven with a taste for sacrificial magic, and she is on the menu. Baltimore's trajectory, however, is inwards to reintegration with a grandparent, a cousin, the child of her mother's best friend. Love here will reconstruct her family rather than take her away from it.

Whether we examine the paranormal romances or the paranormal familial tales, these are all essentially consolatory fantasies, and fantasies of status acquisition. They all deploy a trajectory towards incorporation of the teen into the adult body politic, with an emphasis on family, whether heteronormative (the paranormal romance) or matriarchal (the witchcraft families). Margaret Finders, in *Just Girls: Hidden Literacies and Life in Junior High* (1997), posited two quite different groups of girl readers, and although we would argue for a greater overlap than Finders suggests, she does point to a different functionality for different types of fantasy. Finders argues that this consolatory, incorporative fantasy is read by those who seek to construct or confirm a group identity (seen today in the tendency for paranormal fantasy to attract extensive online engagement): literature enables them to confirm the structures of popularity and social status they enjoy within the group.[8] However, there is an alternative trajectory: Finders notes that there are other readers (or perhaps the same readers in a different mood) who use their literacy more individually to assert their outsider status and also their belief that this is not their time, that they will live through this period and emerge stronger.[9]

For Finders's second category, those who understand themselves as outsiders, far more important than integration to the group can be integration of the self. For many writers, the engagement of magic with the social side of young adulthood is rather fraught. If fantasy for children and teens prior to the 1980s assumed the protagonists would leave behind childish things, fantasy of the 1990s increasingly looked to integrate magic into adulthood, in much the same way as most people in their twenties in America and Europe no longer see why they should give up the interests of their youth, whether these be video games, music, books, attending science fiction conventions or cosplay. All of these things are now the stuff of adulthood; magic, it seems, *is* compatible with being a grown-up.

In Patrice Kindl's *Owl in Love* (1993) Owl is a teenager, struggling to get along at school, wanting to fit in, and with a crush on her science teacher. She is also a wereowl who in an attempt to pass at high school tucks the mouse tail from her lunch in between two slices of bread and suffers a stomach ache from the bread all day. She lives with parents who are so engaged with magic they cannot quite understand her difficulties. At night she hunts. She lurks in a tree outside her teacher's house and watches him sleep. But one night she meets a rather inept young male wereowl, and as she helps him adapt, her affections move from the teacher to the starving teenage boy. In showing the misplacement of teenage affections, Kindl does an excellent job of demonstrating that first love is not the only love, but where this very gentle book shines most is in its delicate exploration of what living as a magical creature might involve.

Less gentle, but also in its odd way rather sweet, is Melvin Burgess's *Lady: My Life as a Bitch* (2001). Burgess has acquired a reputation of producing very hard-hitting, controversial novels, but in reality they are rarely as radical as the critics fear. *Junk* (1996), for example, is a classic Victorian morality tale in which the use of drugs has only one possible ending. *Lady* is different in that the ending runs utterly counter to the moral lessons which fiction in general, and fiction for young people in particular, frequently feels obliged to perpetuate: that the trajectory of adolescence is rebellion, repentance, conformity and absorption. When

Sandra Francy is seen having sex in the park by a local tramp, he turns her into a dog. For much of the novel Sandra is trying to get herself turned back, and during her quest discovers the tragedy behind the tramp's power: everyone he has ever truly loved he has also transformed in a moment of anger. *Lady* is no tale of delightful superpowers or a special kid; underneath it is a story of what specialness can really mean. Nagging at the back of Sandra's mind is the fact that, if she can avoid the pound, life as a dog is not all that bad; in fact, when it comes to no one yelling at you for having sex, it's really pretty good. But it is still a shock when she decides she wants to stay a dog after all. This isn't the kind of growing up that is usually desirable in fantasy, where the release from transformation is almost always the desired conclusion.

Michelle Paver's prehistoric fantasy novels *Chronicles of Ancient Darkness* are almost entirely concerned with this. In *Wolf Brother* (2004) Torak's father is killed by a bear that is possessed by a demon and he finds himself on a quest in company with a man he later realizes helped create the bear, as well as a wolf whom he thinks he may have to sacrifice. In *Spirit Walker* (2005) Torak is threatened by his own uncle who wishes to eat his heart and become a spirit walker. In *Outcast* (2007), having by this time been marked by the *Soul Eaters*, Torak is cast out from his people, and in *Ghost Hunter* (2009), the last of the sequence, Torak finds himself under attack by almost every dark spirit in the land in an escalation that is an almost classic horror structure that reinforces Torak's specialness. So, again, growing up and magic are now frequently inseparable and, as often as not, essential: when a magical character does not grow up, modern fantasy sees it as sinister rather than endearing. In Sarah Singleton's *Century* (2005), for example, Mercy and her sister discover that they have been living the same day over for many years in a Gothic Groundhog Day since their father – trapped in his grief for their mother – took them all out of time. This sense of a childhood trapped or thwarted can also be seen in C. Butler's *Death of a Ghost* (2006) where Ossian realizes that his own coming adulthood may be thwarted by the death of an adolescent boy many centuries before. In Rhiannon Lassiter's *Ghost of a Chance* (2011) no one is growing up if Evangeline doesn't work out who killed her, before they can kill again.

## Adults can't be trusted

For many writers adolescence is precisely the period in which one realizes that the sheltering power of adults is cracking: Libba Bray's

*Gemma Doyle* trilogy, beginning with *A Great and Terrible Beauty* (2003), is a reflection of this. Set in the nineteenth century and in a boarding school, this is a dark vision of adolescence: Gemma's mother is dead (suicide) and her father is addicted to laudanum. Gemma's school seems to be in the grip of a magical power, while Gemma herself and her friends discover they can spirit-travel. Unravelling what has happened and is happening in the school leaves one friend dead and little consolation. In the sequel, *Rebel Angels* (2006), Gemma must deal with madness, issues of abuse and the slow corruption of magic. The final novel, *The Sweet Far Thing* (2007), however, sees a loss of both love *and* magic. This is not an either/or choice – the two have become so integrated that to lose one is to lose both and to embark on a different kind of adulthood.

Darker still are the three volumes of Holly Black's *Modern Faerie Tale* series. In the aforementioned *Tithe* (2002) sixteen-year-old Kaye Fierch lives what some teens might think was a dream life, touring with her mom's rock band, Stepping Razor, but they'd be wrong. Kaye's world is seedy and violent, the dirty reality behind the glamour of sex, drugs and rock and roll. After various entanglements with the faerie world, Kaye discovers that she is a pixie changeling and is in imminent danger of becoming a 'tithe', a pawn in the complex and bloody political machinations between the Seelie and Unseelie Courts; in contrast to the paranormal romances, belonging and absorption are threats to self-identity rather than supports. In *Valiant* (2005) and *Ironside* (2007) recurring themes include the danger of trusting adults, addiction, problematic gender identification and, as in most Young Adult fantasy, the importance of gaining agency and becoming an adult, all in a world where magic is never far away, even when, as *Ironside*'s faerie protagonist insists, your final goal in life is simply to open a coffee shop. Black plays games with a wide variety of fairy and folk tales as well as works of classic fantasy, referencing everything from 'Tam Lin' to 'The Three Billy Goats Gruff', from Emma Bull's contemporary fantasy novel *War for the Oaks* (1987) to the comic strip *Prince Valiant* (1937 to present), from the game *Vampire: The Masquerade* to various manga.

Nalo Hopkinson's *The Chaos* (2012) is also precisely about the integration of self into magic. Hopkinson had already pursued this theme in her adult novel, *New Moon's Arms* (2007), in which a middle-aged woman discovers with the onset of menopause that the magic she rejected to take refuge in a greyed-out, dutiful but angry adulthood, is flooding back. In *The Chaos* Scotch, seventeen years old, with a white Jamaican father and a black Canadian mother, is struggling to integrate her ethnic identity, her family identity (good girl), school identity (dancer and sassy wit) and sexual identity (straight, monogamous) with her friendships (gay friends, polyamorous friends), her experience of bullying and her betrayal of her brother to her parents. Plus, there are the invisible horse heads she can see at her shoulders and the creeping black leathery substance taking over her skin. In some ways Scotch is a wannabe Susan who is not quite comfortable with all that would entail. When her brother is dragged through a magical portal and into the phone system, Scotch follows and we quickly enter a wonderland every bit as chaotic as that of Alice, with a heavy dose of Russian fairy tale. Integration in this book is less about preserving a blended identity than it is about learning to understand how identities sit alongside each other. Hopkinson's work, however, is an outlier in its presentation of teens. Overall, the Young Adult fantasy field is relentless in its portrayal of sexual relationships as heteronormative. The exceptions, such as Malinda Lo's *Ash* (2009) and *Huntress* (2011), which feature a lesbian protagonist, or Elizabeth Hand's *Radiant Days* (2012), which features the gay, transgressive poet Rimbaud, remain rare and usually emphasize the trajectory outwards from the group.

### Understanding the role of Young Adult fantasy

The role of reading as a support for being an outsider is anything but new. One of the most vivid depictions of its role in constructing the fantasy reader can be found in Jo Walton's novel *Among Others* (2011), which tells the story of a lonely 1970s bookish teenager. This novel is revealing because it emphasizes the solipsism of the young reader and the belief (eroded by a reading club in the novel, and in modern life by the internet) that the reader is the *only one*. Alison Waller has argued, 'Fantasy provides private meanings for adolescence, acting as an intrinsic facet of identity rather than merely providing the epic scope for heroic actions.'[10]

   As we have already suggested, the emphasis on the *adult* in Young Adult is misleading. Young Adult books are in many ways Over-Aged Children's books, intended, in part, to support young people in the belief that their lives *really are important*. The difficulty for many teens is, and has always been, that their lives are not particularly important, at least to the world at large. It can even be argued that the Young Adult form, which replaced the Juveniles of the 1950s, is precisely not about growing up in that it is not about entering the adult world, but rather about occupying a class of people that, at any time prior to the 1960s, would have overwhelmingly been in the workplace.[11] For all the media argument that children are forced to grow up too soon (are sexualized or inducted into commodity culture), the children of the middle-class West have never been more protected, their adolescence often extending into their mid or late twenties, and they are frequently raised in rigid peer groups, rather than vertical groupings containing significant numbers of younger and older people.

In this context, fantasy literature has become a place where teens can play at the kind of adolescences their grandparents might have lived, engaged in work and socialized into the adult world. One way in which teen fantasy of the 1990s and 2000s refocused itself was to move away from the modern period where a teen involved in serious issues might feel implausible, and turn to historical fantasy, where a space existed to explore the lives of people their age genuinely occupied with adulthood. The location of many of the coming-of-age fantasies which became popular in the 2000s has been in the apprentice model which has all but fallen out of favour in the real world. This helps to explain the appropriation of Trudi Canavan's *Black Magician* trilogy (*The Magician's Guild*, 2001) which was written for adults but later repackaged for the Young Adult market. *The Magician's Guild* tells the story of Sonea, whose innate magic is strong enough to break the protective barrier the magicians use when clearing the slums, in a world where magic is usually restricted to the higher orders. The trajectory of the series is important to this discussion because it is part of a wider cultural narrative: Sonea is first identified as innately special, then brought into the institution, and finally rises high enough to preserve the institution by amelioration that reduces external resentment. Growing up, it seems, involves abandoning the desire to ferment revolution.

The same trajectory of a child picked out for specialness and then integrated with the institution runs through Pullman's and Rowling's work of course, but it has become endemic. We can see it in Mindy Klasky's *The Glasswrights* series (2000–4), and in Alison Goodman's *Eon* (Australia, *The Two Pearls of Wisdom*, 2008). *Eon* reads in some ways like a combination of Tamora Pierce's work (Eon is secretly female) and that of Anne McCaffrey, who has not been discussed here as her work is technically science fiction, but whose *Dragonsong* (1976) and *Dragonsinger* (1977) were marketed separately for teens and can be read as fantasy. Eon is not just talented but super talented, able to see all twelve dragons in her mindsight. Eon is not just chosen by a dragon, but is chosen by the Mirror Dragon who has been missing for 500 years, and when Eon finally masters her dragon by seeking its name, it is, once again, to preserve a system that had become corrupted.

In Malinda Lo's *Huntress* (2011), two young women are selected for a world-saving quest to confront the Fairy Queen. Both are selected for their education – Taisin, a sage trained in magic, and Kaede, completely unmagical but a well-trained daughter of the aristocracy with all the political awareness of that class – and we can read the novel as their journeyman test, at the end of which, interestingly, they choose different paths from the ones for which they were trained. However, Lo's work particularly stands out because the two young women are lesbians: although their sexuality is accepted within the world, the requirement of Kaede to make an advantageous match and Taisin to stay celibate overwhelms this, so that the trajectory of the book is away from compliance and Kaede at least finds a new way to live in the world, as a Huntress trained by fairy folk. The move in Lo's work away from compliance has been a theme in science fiction for children since the 1970s with the abandonment of the career novel and a conviction instead that the parents are wrong, deluded or lying. This belief seems to have taken rather longer to show itself in fantasy but eventually such stories began to imply both that the world offers less promise and magic less wonder and rather more threat than had previously been the case in fantasy written with teens in mind.

Whether Young Adult fantasy is integrative (the paranormal romances or the apprenticeship novels) or reinforces self-identity and being an outsider, all the novels discussed so far reward their protagonists and end, more or less, with the promise of satisfactory futures. The most significant underlying trend of the 1990s and 2000s may have been the one which moved away from this, towards disappointment, bitterness and desolation.

## The bitterness of Young Adult fantasy

This section begins with a book that was marketed for children, but in many ways did more to set the tone for what could be achieved in fantasy for younger teens, Philip Pullman's *Northern Lights* (1995; US, *The Golden Compass*). At the start of *Northern Lights*, Lyra Belacqua is still a child, perhaps a pre-teen on the edge of puberty, although a careful reader will realize that Pullman ages her awfully fast towards the end of the three books. Lyra lives in an alternative Oxford, as a ward of the Master of Jordan College. In its setting the novel clearly calls to mind the alternative Britain of Joan Aiken's *Wolves* chronicles (*The Wolves of Willoughby Chase*, *Black Hearts in Battersea*, etc.). The book begins when Lyra observes the Master attempting to poison Lord Asriel, and intervenes. Lyra's world is in the grip of a theological controversy about the particles of Dust that appear to adhere to adults rather than children, and to the heretical possibility of other worlds. Not by coincidence, children in the area have begun to disappear. In the meantime Lyra is sent to live with the mysterious and glamorous Mrs Coulter, carrying with her the alethiometer (essentially a Ouija board). When she discovers that Mrs Coulter is in charge of the Oblation Board, which steals children, Lyra flees, falls in with the Gyptians, and heads north to look for her missing friend Roger. At this point, the real adventure, spread over three books and complete with witches, talking bears, prophecies, a knife that can cut through worlds and a meeting with God, begins. Pullman's tale is a genuine epic, not only in its world-shattering consequences but in the stage on which it is set.

The trilogy *His Dark Materials* by Philip Pullman (1946–) is one of the most honoured works in the history of children's literature, with various volumes winning the Carnegie Medal, the Guardian Children's Book Award and the Whitbread Book of the Year Award, the last of which, it should be noted, had never before been given to a children's book. Pullman has also received the Astrid Lindgren Award for his career in children's literature and *Northern Lights* was voted the Carnegie of Carnegies as the greatest of all winners of the Medal in a public poll in 2007. The books, however, have not been received with unanimous praise and, in fact, are among the most widely attacked in children's literature, due largely to their author's willingness, both in the novels and in various articles and speeches, to criticize all manner of status quo institutions, including the Church of England (despite receiving support from former Archbishop of Canterbury, Rowan Williams), religion generally and the British educational system. It has been widely suggested that *His Dark Materials* is an attack on and rebuttal of C. S. Lewis's Narnia books, and Pullman, quoting William Blake, has described himself as 'of the Devil's party'.

Three elements lift *Northern Lights* and its sequels above the crowd. The first of these is Pullman's choice of rhetoric. *Northern Lights* is set in a full immersive world; it is Lyra's primary world, and as such, the reader enters it entirely through her unquestioning eyes. The result is that the veracity of the fantasy world is continually reinforced, which helps the reader to feel like an insider (in contrast to Rowling's work where we and Harry Potter are both explorers in a strange place). The second element is the role of the daemons, the *souls made visible* of every individual on the planet. The daemons appear as animals, usually but not always of the opposite sex to their human, and retain a range of forms until puberty, when they settle to one form. Of central importance are Lyra's relationship with her daemon, Pantalaimon, the airman Scoresby's relationship with Hester his hare, and the terrible distress of the children sundered from their daemons by the Oblation Board in an attempt to protect them from sin. The third factor is the sheer bitterness of the novels, both individually and as a sequence.

Bitterness, not darkness, is more often than not the hallmark of the Young Adult fantasy from the 1990s onwards and this separates it from the children's market. Take Pullman's work and compare it to Frances Hardinge's *Gullstruck Island* (2009), a book about genocide in which many, many people die. Yet not one of the people who die after the opening is someone whom *both* the protagonist and the reader are close to, and the novel ends with its protagonist Hathin stepping into the clapping game and – at least for a short time – shrugging off her cares the way only a child can. The darkness is not left unmitigated. In Pullman's *Northern Lights* sequence, however, Lyra loses her friend Roger. She discovers that Lord Asriel and Mrs Coulter are her parents, but by that time she despises and distrusts both of them. In *The Subtle Knife* (1997) Scoresby and his daemon Hester both die, while Lyra's friend Will Parry fails to rescue his mother from the beings who are draining her of health and sanity, and discovers his father just in time to see him killed by the witch who had loved him unreciprocally. The end of the series (*The Amber Spyglass*, 2000) is no lighter. Although Will and Lyra succeed in defeating both Lord Asriel and Mrs Coulter, they discover that the knife lets Dust leak into the universe and creates the dark spectres that prey on humans. Furthermore, as neither can live in the other's world for more than ten years without fading, they must be separated.

Lyra is left waiting at a bench each year, thinking of Will in his own world. In a set of novels that is in part about whether the Fall is a good or bad thing, which positions Lyra as a New Eve, this separation posits the Fall as a permanent presence embodied in loss, in memory and in mourning. For a novel (and it is really one novel) that began as a child's adventure and which in its vocabulary remains accessible to a fluent young reader, it is shockingly bitter, yet it is a bitterness that we consistently see in books for this older age group.

Take, for example, Gail Carson Levine's *Ella Enchanted* (1997). On the one hand this is a light tale of the truth behind the Cinderella story but, although told affectionately, it is also a relentlessly bitter story of a mother who declines the medicine that will save her life, leaving her only

214 Children's Fantasy Literature: An Introduction

child alone; of a man too blind to see his new wife for what she really is; and of a fairy too in love with her own powers to understand the consequences of what she has done. Lucinda has endowed Ella with the gift of obedience, not realizing that she has created a slave, and later compounds the problem by 'blessing' her father and stepmother with the desire to constantly be with each other, which wars with their mutual hatred. Ella is intelligent and lively but the gift is a curse which, rather than making her docile, turns her into a rebel. The result is that Ella spends her life in painful resistance to what is – once her stepsisters realize the situation – torture. When Ella falls in love with the Prince, she realizes that far from this being the happiest day of her life, she is facing potential tragedy; for if she can be forced to agree to do anything, she can be forced to kill the Prince or betray her country.

In another distractingly subtle version of Cinderella, *Chime* (2011) by Franny Billingsley, another confused and angry young woman, Briony, knows herself responsible for both her stepmother's death and her twin sister's brain damage. When the first railroad comes to town and the nearby swamps are about to be drained, the Old Ones who live there, and of whose existence only Briony is aware, fight back by spreading a deadly plague, forcing her both to forgive herself and to find a balance between waning magic and encroaching technology. As the story unravels we begin to realize that the adored stepmother may not have been quite as lovely as Briony remembers, while the sister to whom Briony is enslaved turns out to be a much more complex being. The bitterness of the novel is focused both on the betrayal of discovering oneself used, and on discovering that one has deceived oneself.

Bitterness is at the core of many of these novels. The light-hearted tone of Catherine Jinks's *The Reformed Vampire Support Group* (2009) is a foil to, rather than distraction from, the reality of being a fifteen-year-old vampire when this means being confined for years to your mother's basement and being grateful that the internet was invented. China Miéville's *Railsea* (2012), part of the steampunk wave which is a subgenre of both science fiction and fantasy, is based on Herman Melville's *Moby Dick* with not a little of *Peter Pan* on the side. On a planet where rails run from the city into the hinterlands in a complex web and monsters can churn through the earth, the protagonist finds himself on a ship where the captain is infected with the desire to capture the giant mouldywarpe (or giant mole), which once ate her arm. The novel, although at times exhilarating and heroic, ends in death and disaster; successfully walking away from the debacle itself becomes a victory.

In *The Voyage of the Dawn Treader* (1952), Prince Caspian rescues one of the Lords of Narnia from the Island Where Dreams Come True who warns them that there is a difference between the pleasantries of day dreams, and the reality of the uncontrolled, random dreaming that works its way into one's worst nightmares. Several of the new Young Adult fantasy writers seem to have taken teaching teens this lesson as their core mission. Rhiannon Lassiter, Elizabeth Knox and K. A. Applegate, for example, have all played with the power of dream worlds. In Lassiter's *Bad Blood* (2007) four children, having moved into an old house, find themselves playing an old game once played by three girls. There is a collection of children's books in which the names of characters have been crossed out. With each such erasure on the page, a hope or dream was sacrificed. Now two new children are fighting for a name and an identity and the game knows exactly how to appease them. When Catriona and Katherine both erase each other's names they are reduced to small, miserable Cats, embodiments of the nickname they each treasured. They can be lifted out of the dream only when their (step)brother John pulls their identity out of their old one so they become Iona and Erin, and when John too chooses to leave his name behind. The loss of identity is both terrifying and exhilarating, an intensification of the charged changes of puberty. In Knox's *Dreamhunter* (2005; UK, *The Rainbow Opera*) and *Dreamquake* (2007), dreams can be caught and captured and distributed as dramas, but by the second book it is clear that the dreams are being used to control convicts and that the dreams are more important and integral to the well-being of the people of Southland than has been realized.

Applegate's dream world is the portal fantasy of *Everworld*, which begins with *Search for Senna* (1999). In one sense it is a fairly simple set-up – four teenagers follow a classmate, Senna, into another world. But that is where things start going awry for this is not a full fantasy world in which a nice mage figure guides the protagonists through the rules, but rather a pocket universe in which the gods of various cultures (Roman, Norse, African, among others) have taken refuge with a stock of carefully chosen followers to reproduce their cultural environments. Over the course of the twelve books (really 'part works' which stand together, each one narrated from a different point of view) the teens find themselves in different worlds with different mores, often under attack. Towards the end the alien gods of another pocket universe begin to invade. Unlike in many portal fantasies, there is no easy time-slip to allow the children to return to their own world in time to make things right; the series ends without reconciliation. Reminiscent of Charlotte, in Penelope Farmer's *Charlotte Sometimes* (1969), while the teens have been in the pocket universe, shadows of their own selves have been operating their lives. Each night they dream of high school. Under the pressures of this dual life, of the conflicts between what they believe and what they must face, and the ways in which the Gods have homed in on their secrets, their fears and their weaknesses, the teens have begun to go insane. The tale ends inconclusively: there is no salvation either for the pocket universe or for the protagonists; no one has turned out to be the Great Hope of the portal world, and it is not even clear that they can or would choose to go back.

This absence of hope and of salvation is connected to the pain of giving up power which also runs as a thread through many of these books. When the quest writers of the 1970s adapted Tolkien's structures to their purposes, one of the most significant changes that we saw was the switch from the rejection of power, in the moment when Gollum bites Frodo's finger and with both finger and ring falls into the volcano at the top of Mount Doom, to a narrative in which power is sought and embraced, as in the conclusion to David Eddings's *Belgariad*. In the work of Knox, of Applegate and others we can see a return to Tolkien's initial premise, that power is ultimately destructive and corrupting, of both cultures and individuals. In Jonathan Stroud's *Heroes of the Valley* (2009), built from Norse myth and the tale of Beowulf, for example, Hailli Svenson learns as he grows older that most of the tales of the founding of his valley are worn thin to the bones, twisted to accommodate different actors for each family, and probably contain little more than a nugget of truth – although admittedly this turns out to be the most important nugget, the one that may help him stay alive through the night. In the process Hailli leads innocent men to their death and exposes his entire clan to vengeance. Although he learns lessons, it may well be too late, and the novel ends with Hailli and his friend Aud standing on a rock waiting to greet the monsters. L. J. Adlington's *Night Witches* (2013), a supernatural science fiction fantasy, pits two groups against each other (one with telekinesis, one without) and runs in a conventional Romeo and Juliet pattern with a certain amount of destinarianism; but whereas a previous generation would have granted Rain Aranoza love, destiny and the merging of her peoples, war does not work that way and by the end much of the world Rain knows is in ruins.

Perhaps the bitterest elegy on the misuse of power is found in Kathleen Duey's *Resurrection of Magic* trilogy. Duey, a US writer, brought out

*Skin Hunger* in 2007 at the stage when the Harry Potter novels, for all their cataclysmic ending, had created a trend in fantasy for magic to be relatively easy, a talent which protagonists delighted in. *Skin Hunger* is set in a world which fears magic, and has relentlessly weeded out its magic users. Into this world emerges a man who would revive magic, and knows only one way to do it, to make a child so desperate that he will use magic to save himself; to this end boys are gathered into a school and starved until they can feed themselves with magic. *Skin Hunger* is told from two perspectives, that of Sadima, a young woman from a family that still practises magic in a world without it, and Hahp, the expendable younger son of a wealthy merchant who is sent to the academy to learn magic. Eventually we figure out that they live in two different time periods. In Sadima's time, a young nobleman named Somiss obsesses over returning magic to the world and, with his friend and servant Franklin, and eventually Sadima's assistance, may succeed in doing so. In the second time period it seems Franklin has succeeded but the school of magic he has created is only open to the families of the wealthy and is shockingly harsh. Told across two time frames, before and after the revival of magic, the book is intensely political, engaged both with the nature of a society that deprives the poor of the relief of magic (a lightly veiled comment on the US health care debate, one suspects), and with how personal politics can shape an entire new movement, the misogyny and sadism of a leader becoming embedded in the tenets of that movement or, as Pratchett memorably put it in *Small Gods*:

> The merest accident of microgeography had meant that the first man to hear the voice of Om, and who gave Om his view of humans, was a shepherd and not a goatherd. They have quite different ways of looking at the world, and the whole of history might have been different. For sheep are stupid, and have to be driven. But goats are intelligent, and need to be led.[12]

The second book in Duey's trilogy, *Sacred Scars* (2009), continues the story, but the third has not yet been published and, if we can see Somiss's endeavours converging on Hahp's present, we cannot see where Hahp's narrative will conclude, and are thus left with a scenario in which, simply put, abuse is a route to power. Stories of the abused child acquiring power are of course not new – Stephen King's *Carrie* (1974) is a classic – but a greater willingness to discuss the nature of abuse has lent many of these stories an extra edge. In the Canadian author Arthur Slade's *Dust* (2001), children kidnapped so their souls may power a rain-making machine do not survive. There is no happy ending, no immediate welcome into their parents' arms, and no recovery from trauma. Nor can it all be blamed on stranger danger, for the parents, like those in *Skin Hunger*, have been complicit, unwilling to question the miracles they desire.

Nigerian American Nnedi Okorafor's *The Shadow Speaker* (2007) takes place in 2070 in West Africa, and is set in motion when the protagonist, fifteen-year-old Ejii, witnesses her father's beheading. As she journeys to find her father's killer she encounters talking camels, superpowers and powerful magicians. *Who Fears Death* (2010), marketed for adults, because of its violence perhaps, but with protagonists who are all teens, takes fear and abuse onto a wider stage with the story of Onyesonwu who grows up in a post-apocalyptic Sudan where the light-skinned Nuru oppress the dark-skinned Okeke. The protagonist is an Ewu, the product of war rape, and as she grows up she develops magical powers inherited from her sorcerer father. Onyesonwu experiences a range of abuse, from the day-to-day punishment that comes with being an outsider and the symbol of something people would prefer to forget, through the abuse intrinsic in her own culture as she is subjected to genital mutilation. Forgiveness has traditionally been the end point of earlier fantasy, but at the conclusion of *Who Fears Death*, Onyesonwu inflicts infertility on the mass of the enemy population. This is a vengeance narrative, and as such – engaged precisely in perpetuating the cycle with which it began – it is a story that doesn't end, but instead creates more stories.

Oisín McGann's Young Adult work engages with a similar cycle of bitterness and vengeance. McGann, an Irish writer, has written both science fiction and fantasy for the children's market and for early teens, but only one series for older teens, *The Wildenstern Saga*, made up of *Ancient Appetites* (2007), *The Wisdom of Dead Men* (2009) and *Merciless Reason* (2012). The series is unusual in a number of ways: it is set in an alternative nineteenth-century Ireland at a time of tenant revolts, and its initial protagonist is bisexual, having relationships with both his serving-man and his wife. By the second book he is also disabled and then dies, and a second protagonist is forced onto the stage. Nate Wildenstern belongs to an unusually long-lived family – so long-lived that they have Rules of Ascension which outline who may, and may not, be assassinated. All of this is thrown into chaos when a funeral reveals three bound bodies of Wildenstern ancestors, who promptly begin to revive. By the rules, these Norman ancestors are the heads of the Wildenstern house. In the second book the clan begins to realize that there may be reasons for their powers, connected perhaps to their ability to find living machines, *engimals*, which appear to buck the rules of evolution and which frequently (the living toaster for example) are impenetrable to the discoverer until some equivalent made thing appears in the wider world. There are more important issues to worry about, however, because local women are spontaneously combusting and in the meantime the head of the clan, Berto – Nate's brother and the only one left standing at the end of the previous book – is worried once more that he will be a target for assassination. By the third book we are into alternative physics as Gerald Wildenstern begins to experiment with intelligent particles to explain the mystery of the engimals. The books are complex, adult and dark; they end in death and destruction, but as in some other books here, destruction is liberating, allowing a new world to arise from the old.

The same can be said for Tom Pollock's *The Glass Republic* (2013), a sequel to *The City's Son* (2012), which seems to be aimed at older readers. This assumes that the reader himself or herself is ageing with the protagonist, an issue to which we will return. In this book Beth, the protagonist of *The City's Son*, has been taken over by the poisons of the Chemical Brothers and is turning into a manifestation of the city. Her skin is grey and looks like paving and her teeth are breaking out in spires and skyscrapers. But this is not Beth's story, it is Pen's. Pen ended the previous book embraced by living barbed wire. When *The Glass Republic* opens there have been no miracles: she is badly scarred, and her hijab is no longer only a religious covering but a disguise for hair loss and a ruined scalp. But Pen has created an alter ego in the mirror world to which she was introduced, and when bullying drives her away, she talks to Parva. When Parva disappears, she follows her into the looking-glass world of the mirrorstocracy, where the rich are allowed asymmetrical faces like human beings, but the working poor have faces that are perfectly symmetrical, indicating that they actually only have half a face which is repeated on both sides of their heads. In this world Pen's scarred face is the ultimate in beauty, every scar enhancing her highly desirable asymmetry. So, although the series is as yet unfinished, from the very beginning we understand that Pen's victory will be a loss.

This sense of loss runs through a range of different kinds of fantasy written for Young Adult readers. The metatext, which relies on the readers' awareness of previous fantasies, has become particularly popular in the past decade. China Miéville's *Railsea* riffed on *Moby Dick*; Tom Pollock's *The Glass Republic* is a darker view of the world beyond Alice's Looking Glass (and deliberately emphasizes the *looking into the glass* of that text). In Chris Wooding's *Poison* (2003), another changeling novel, the title character uses her knowledge of fairy tales to negotiate with the

Bone Witch and the Wraith-Catcher Bram, and sets out to retrieve a dagger from the castle of the spider-woman Asinastra and return it to the Lord Aelthar, in a trajectory very close to that of Dorothy in *The Wizard of Oz*, including the discovery that Lord Aelthar has no intention of helping her to return home. But beyond the metatext are those books which explore the power of the text as physical object. The most interesting of these are Roderick Townley's *Sylvie Cycle*, Martine Leavitt's *The Dollmage* and Markus Zusak's *The Book Thief*.

The first of Townley's *Sylvie Cycle* is *The Great Good Thing* (2001). Princess Sylvie sits by her lake and talks to the trout that occupies it, wishing to do a great good thing, when she becomes aware that for the first time in many years her book has a reader, and she rushes into place so that she and the other characters can begin the story. But as the tale develops it is her relationship with the reader that becomes the heart of the story, and when tragedy strikes and the book is destroyed, Sylvie finds a new home in the book as *re*-written and published by her reader. The book ends with a sense of loss and a sense of change: because readers change, even fiction cannot stay the same.

Martine Leavitt's *The Dollmage* (2001) is precisely about the devastation that resistance to change can bring. It is a book about the bitterness of terribly wrong decisions. The dollmages of the valley quite literally make the material world around them, in the form of stitchwork – quilts, wall hangings. Narrated by one character in the first and second person (she is talking directly to the village), the book begins at the end with the dollmage Hobblefoot explaining how her own prejudice against a woman in the valley led her to ignore the magic in the woman's baby, and perhaps worse, to ignore her own awareness that two dollmages had been born, and not one. This wrong choice leads to an unfolding in which one child is blessed and spoiled, and the other left vulnerable and abused until such time as a crisis point is reached and the abused child, Annakey, does the one thing that the village cannot tolerate: she breaks a promise, a terrible action even though the promise was to marry the boy who raped her. The novel is relentless; it begins at a stoning. At the end of the dollmage's story we have no idea whether the stoning will go ahead, or whether the dollmage, who has spent her entire life in the creation of new endings, will succeed in persuading the villagers not just to free Annakey, but to allow her to become their new dollmage. There is no consolation here.

There is a question as to whether we should even be including Marcus Zusak's *The Book Thief* (2005). This novel about a child who borrows books in Nazi Germany has very little of the fantastic about it, yet as it is narrated by Death it is clearly a posthumous fantasy (in which fantasies take place after the death of the protagonist). Its rhetoric uses the elegiac voice of the liminal fantasy, but this is a form grounded precisely in uncertainty about what is or isn't fantastic. Furthermore, it is aligned with fantasy in taking advantage of the rarely commented-upon affection in the fantasy field for *books about books*, which we have already seen in the work of Funke, Townley, Wooding and many others. While metatextual narrative is not fantasy per se, it has been adopted by the fantasy genre, as most commonly seen in the increasingly knowing ways that other texts are deployed by authors. Modern fantasy is as much an argument with itself as it is about an original mode of fantasy.

Folk tales and folk tale legacies run through these darker Young Adult books but they are rarely the straightforward retellings of the 1980s (or even the mapping we find in Jones's *Fire and Hemlock*, 1984). *Ella Enchanted* may well be the simplest. Instead in the new Young Adult novel we see folk tales being treated as *ur*-stories. Some have happy endings, but only after much suffering has occurred. Robin McKinley, whose *The Hero and the Crown* (1985) we have already discussed, produced some impressive fantasies which used fairy tales as their base but entwined them with other folklore as well as with original material to produce far more bitter stories. *Deerskin* (1993) retold Perrault's 'Donkeyskin', with Lissar, a princess, fleeing her widowed, grief-maddened father's castle only after he rapes and impregnates her. Lissar miscarries and almost dies, but her life is saved by a goddess who transforms her face and gives her magical powers. Later, she must confront and punish her rapist father before she is able to accept the man who genuinely loves her. *Spindle's End* (2000) reworked the story of Sleeping Beauty in surprising fashion, sending the princess into hiding with a humble adoptive family that teaches her the duties of a working-class country girl and veterinarian; oddly enough, it is hinted that the tale takes place in the same world as *The Hero and the Crown*. Published prior to the full emergence of the Young Adult market, these two works were rather too dark to be considered for children at that time, and were instead presented as adult fiction, but are now widely seen as suitable Young Adult fare.

In Franny Billingsley's *The Folk Keeper* (1999), clearly published as a Young Adult book, the appeasement of elven folk is elevated (or depressed) to new levels as fifteen-year-old Corinna Stonewall is employed to sit with the gremlins under the caves of Rhysbridge and appease their anger while pretending all the time to be a boy. Later, having taken on an even more dangerous folk-keeping assignment, Corinna discovers why she has always felt uncomfortable in what she thought was her own skin; she is actually a selkie, a seal woman, and must spend at least part of her life in the sea.

Helen Oyeyemi, a British writer of Nigerian origin, has deployed both African and Cuban mythology in her work. *The Icarus Girl* (2005) is a tale of haunting: eight-year-old Jess visits Nigeria for the first time and is haunted by a little ragged girl called TillyTilly. *White is for Witching* (2009) is a Gothic tale (with an implicit political agenda) of household haunting and sundered twins, drawing on both African and European traditions of twinning and doppelgangers. Miranda suffers from a rare and apparently hereditary eating disorder that causes her to eat chalk; she can also feel the ghosts that haunt the old family house in Dover and they are calling to her. The house itself appears as a spirited and not particularly nice character.

Marcus Sedgwick, who works across both fantasy and mimetic fiction, produced a particularly impressive novel, *Blood Red, Snow White* (2007), which intertwines a tale of Arthur Ransome's time as a journalist and British agent in Russia just prior to the 1917 revolution with an evocation of Ransome's narration of *Old Peter's Tales* (mentioned in Chapter 4), in which the Old Bear becomes the representative of Old Russia. In *Midwinterblood* (2011), there is a ritual slaying on the island of Blessed, where rumour has it that no children are born and no one ages, and an old story from a thousand years before begins to play out as two souls strive to be reunited under different moons.

Alan Garner, who had been silent for over a decade, returned to the field in 2003 with *Thursbitch*, a novel which mourns both for life and for lost belief. Returning to some of the ideas in *Red Shift* (1973), this novel is set in both the eighteenth century and the present day, and grounded in the bull worship of some of the Roman military units stationed in the north of England. In 2012 he published *Boneland*, a conclusion to and commentary on *The Weirdstone of Brisingamen* and *The Moon of Gomrath*. While these earlier works had been very much books for children and young teens, *Boneland* was clearly intended for older young adults and for Garner's readers who were now adults. Colin, one of the two protagonists of the earlier book, is now middle-aged, and a highly regarded astrophysicist working at Jodrell Bank Observatory, but he has both lost all memory of events before his thirteenth birthday and developed an eidetic memory for everything since. Half mad with not knowing his past, he goes to a psychotherapist for help, with startling results. Both of these books are steeped in Garner's long fascination with regional archaeology and linguistic development. The use of almost dead languages is as much a part of the elegy they construct as are the plots.

Perhaps the most impressive, complex and also bitterest of the new Young Adult writers is Margo Lanagan, whose work brings together many of the strands discussed so far. Lanagan's early work involved writing teen romance for major mainstream publishers, but no one would call her fantasy either sweet or cuddly. In the short story 'Singing My Sister Down' (2004), a young boy takes part in a macabre family picnic where his mother feeds his sister as she sinks down into a tar pit, punishment for killing her own husband. Lanagan already had a flourishing career as a Young Adult writer in Australia before she published her first Young Adult fantasy story collection, *Black Juice* (2004).

Her gruelling but beautiful *Tender Morsels* (2008) is about the total destruction of an innocent who finds happiness and healing in a supernaturally imbued retreat from the world. The novel concerns Liga, who lives in what Lanagan refers to as 'some kind of fairy tale Eastern Europe'.[13] Horribly brutalized by her own father, she is later gang-raped by the young men of her town. Pregnant, she is taken by unknown supernatural forces to her own personal Garden of Eden in order to escape further trauma and find the time to heal. Eventually, however, the border between her idyllic pocket universe and the world that she came from proves permeable and is transgressed by both a wicked dwarf in search of riches and a kind young man who has been transformed into a bear as part of an annual fertility ritual in the local village. Liga's restless daughter Urdda, grown to young adulthood, yearns to see that world and eventually she, Liga and Urdda's fraternal twin, the peaceful Branza, do so. All three soon discover they must now confront the evils that damaged their mother in the first place.

Lanagan is a stylist, her words conjuring beauty on the page. 'The birds were bright in the sun, and the busyness of them flaunted and flapped the sunlight so that Urdda felt radiant with them, as if they were a kind of fire flaming across the top of her. What a grand idea this was!'[14] What lifts her above the average is her ability to use style to intensify the horror of a story. Raped by her father, Liga miscarries, all without really understanding what is happening to her:

> She fell to her knees in the snow. Inside her skirt, so much of her boiling self fell away that she felt quite undone below the waist, quite shapeless. No, look: sturdy hips. Look: a leg on either side. A blue-grey foot there, the other there. Gingerly, Liga sat back in a crouch to lift her numbed

knees off the snow. The black trees towered in front of her, and the snow dazzled all around. She heaved and brought up nothing but spittle, but more of her was pushed out below by the heaving.[15]

The book has been enormously controversial, with many reviewers and readers questioning whether it can be a teen book at all, but for some teens, this beautifully written tale is as much a part of their experience as any teen romance, if not more so. *Sea Hearts* (Australia, 2011; *The Brides of Rollrock Island* in USA and UK), Lanagan's most recent novel, offers a different bitterness, the bitterness of mothers' tears. The story is told, in part, from the point of view of one of the boys from an island, and we gradually grow aware that the island's women, called 'mams', are not just naturally taciturn and uninvolved, they are *something else*, selkies conjured from the waves, desperate to return to the sea. The trajectory of the book is of a child's disillusionment with its parents but with greater intensity, as the boys of Rollrock Island have to decide whether they will make the same choices as their fathers did, and one girl has to consider how much vengeance is worth. As seen here and in Billingsley's *The Folk Keeper*, the selkie tale seems a particularly apt vehicle for the grim worlds we are discussing.

Many of the writers in this chapter are deeply moral – authors who wish to help readers understand their world, and to ask of it some very awkward questions, and it is this that has helped them deal with the criticism they have received for the often terrifying stories they tell. Critics have decried violence in children's books for as long as such books have existed (see, for example, the work of the late eighteenth-century critic Sarah Trimmer, as discussed in Chapter 1), just as they have worried over the existence of sex in such books, and in every generation, it seems, new writers have pushed the borders of acceptability a little further. It seems highly unlikely that books like *Tender Morsels* or *Lady: My Life as a Bitch* or *The Chaos* could have been published as for teens even twenty years ago. That these are all positively reviewed, award-winning titles says much about the changing scope of the field.

## Evolution of a form

Throughout this book we have traced changing ideas about who children are and how they grow to adulthood. We have considered beliefs about their intellectual and moral capacity as those beliefs have evolved over the last several centuries, and have also examined the ways in which this evolution has shaped the genre of children's literature. We have seen the perceived status of children's fantasy shift from that of something potentially dangerous to young readers, to something that presents an ideal for young people to aspire to, and then to something that can help children find their own lives and gain agency in the world they live in. We have traced the growing sophistication of material, of sources and of language. Overall, we have described a tradition that began as relatively rare and experimental, then developed recognized forms and an identifiable readership before, in the current century, experiencing a sort of generic speciation event, with so many texts and subgenres now available that not even the most determined reader of fantasy fiction can consume all of it. It has, in fact, become increasingly possible to read *just* paranormal romance, *just* folklore fantasy or *just* urban fantasy. One has only to look at the children's market over the past two decades, taking note of the popularity of such bestselling fantasy franchises as the Harry Potter books (beginning in 1997), Christopher Paolini's *Eragon* trilogy (beginning in 2002), Rick Riordan's *Percy Jackson* series (beginning in 2005), Stephenie Meyer's *Twilight* (2005) and its sequels, and such related dystopian science fiction series starters as Suzanne Collins's *The Hunger Games* (2008), James Dashner's *The Maze Runner* (2009) and Veronica Roth's *Divergent* (2011) to recognize the extent to which the fantastic now dominates children's literature, particularly that designed for teens.

Why is this? Realism obviously has its advantages and its attractions for child readers. There will always be children, both pre-teens and teenagers, who prefer Jeff Kinney's *Diary of a Wimpy Kid* (2007) and its sequels, or such John Green novels as *Looking for Alaska* (2005) and *The Fault in Our Stars* (2012). Indeed, some children heavily prefer realism, others fantasy, while still others are omnivorous. To some extent, it is true, the reading of fantasy is a form of escapism. There is considerable comfort to be had in a trip to Middle Earth or Narnia or Hogwarts or even Forks, Washington. We hope, however, that we have shown that the best children's fantasy is, over all, far from escapist. The exotic settings of Tolkien, Lewis, Rowling and even the much maligned Stephenie Meyer may actually make it easier for children to deal with serious issues by presenting them once removed from reality, as they may otherwise be too threatening to confront. Beyond its possible bibliotherapeutic value, however, the best fantasy literature is simply an enormous pleasure, one shared by children, teens and adults, witness the increasing sales of such books ostensibly for children to adults. It is our hope, finally, that this book has conveyed our own love for the genre and perhaps convinced new readers to give children's fantasy a try.

# Notes

## Introduction

1 Kathryn Hume, *Fantasy and Mimesis: Responses to Reality in Western Literature* (London: Methuen, 1984), 5–6.

2 Brian Attebery, *Strategies of Fantasy* (Bloomington: Indiana University Press, 1992); Helen Young, 'Fantasy as Genre-Culture: A New Model of Genre', International Conference for the Fantastic in the Arts, Orlando, FL, 22 March 2014; Farah Mendlesohn, 'Peake and the Fuzzy Set of Fantasy: Some Informal Thoughts', in G. Peter Winnington (ed.), *Miracle Enough: Papers on the Work of Mervyn Peake* (Newcastle-upon-Tyne: Cambridge Scholars, 2013), 61–74, at 71–3; Farah Mendlesohn and Edward James, *A Short History of Fantasy* (London: Middlesex University Press, 2009).

3 Farah Mendlesohn, *Rhetorics of Fantasy* (Middletown, CT: Wesleyan University Press, 2008), xiii.

4 Ann Swinfen, *In Defence of Fantasy: A Study of the Genre in English and American Literature since 1945* (London and Boston: Routledge & Kegan Paul, 1984); Sheila A. Egoff, *Worlds Within: Children's Fantasy from the Middle Ages to Today* (Chicago, IL: American Library Association, 1988); K. V. Johansen, *Quests and Kingdoms: A Grown-Up's Guide to Children's Fantasy Literature* (Sackville, NB: Sybertooth, 2005); Colin Manlove, *From Alice to Harry Potter: Children's Fantasy in England* (Christchurch, NZ: Cybereditions, 2003); Pamela S. Gates, Susan B. Steffel and Francis J. Molson, *Fantasy Literature for Children and Young Adults* (Lanham, MD, and Oxford: Scarecrow Press, 2003).

## How fantasy became children's literature

1 Seth Lerer, *Children's Literature: A Reader's History, from Aesop to Harry Potter* (University of Chicago Press, 2008).

2 Gillian Avery, 'The Beginnings of Children's Reading to c. 1700', in Peter Hunt (ed.), *Children's Literature: An Illustrated History* (Oxford University Press, 1995), 1–26.

3 William Caxton, 'The History of Reynard the Fox' [1481], in Henry Morley (ed.), *Early Prose Romances* (London: Routledge, 1889), 4.

4 Ibid., 7.

5 Renée Kennedy, 'Introduction', in Richard Johnson, *The History of the Seven Champions of Christendom* (Portland, OR: Richard Abel, 1967), n.p.

6 Johnson, *History of the Seven Champions*, 9.

7 John Bunyan, *A Few Sighs from Hell, or The Groans of the Damned Soul* [1658] (Glasgow: Robertson, 1770), 108.

8 Philippe Ariès, *Centuries of Childhood: A Social History of Family Life* (New York: Knopf, 1962), 96–7.

9 Lerer, *Children's Literature*, 210.

10 Jack Zipes, *When Dreams Came True: Classical Fairy Tales and their Tradition* (New York and London: Routledge, 1999), 12–16.

11 Jack Zipes, *Fairy Tales and the Art of Subversion: The Classical Genre for Children and the Process of Civilization*, 2nd rev. edn (New York: Routledge, 2006), 30.

12 Jack Zipes, *Fairy Tale as Myth, Myth as Fairy Tale*, The Thomas D. Clark Lectures (Lexington: University Press of Kentucky, 1994), 22.

13 Ariès, *Centuries of Childhood*, 95.

14 Madame J.-M. Leprince de Beaumont, 'Beauty and the Beast', *Le Magasin des Enfants: Or, The Young Misses Magazine. Containing Dialogues between a Governess and Several Young Ladies of Qualitiy, Her Scholars* (London: S. Fields, W. Ware and T. Johnson, 1765), 38.

15 Ibid., 39.

16 Ibid., 39.

17 Ibid., 52.

18 Ibid., 55.

19 Zipes, *Fairy Tale as Myth*, 17, 23.

20 Avery, 'Beginnings of Children's Reading', 3–5.

21 Sarah Fielding, *The Governess; or The Little Female Academy* (Dublin: Bradley and James, 1749), 68.

22 Ibid., 176.

23 Sarah Trimmer, *The Guardian of Education: A Periodical Work*, 5 vols. (Bristol: Thoemmes, 2002), II.185.

24 Ibid., II.185–6.

25 Ibid., II.448.

26 See Maria Nikolajeva, 'Fantasy', in Jack Zipes (ed.), *The Oxford Encyclopedia of Children's Literature*, 4 vols. (Oxford University Press, 2006), II.58–63.

27 Samuel Taylor Coleridge, Letter to Thomas Poole, *Letters of Samuel Taylor Coleridge*, 2 vols. (Boston and New York: Houghton, Mifflin, 1895), I.16.

28 'Introduction', in Anna Jackson, Karen Coats and Roderick McGillis (eds.), *The Gothic in Children's Literature: Haunting the Borders* (New York and London: Routledge, 2008), 2.

### Fairies, ghouls and goblins: the realms of Victorian and Edwardian fancy

1 Selma G. Lanes, *Down the Rabbit Hole: Adventures and Misadventures in the Realm of Children's Literature* (New York: Atheneum, 1976), 3.
2 Colin Manlove, *From Alice to Harry Potter: Children's Fantasy in England* (Christchurch, NZ: Cybereditions, 2003), 14; Caroline Sumpter, *The Victorian Press and the Fairy Tale* (Basingstoke: Palgrave Macmillan, 2008), 9.
3 Rob Banham, 'The Industrialization of the Book, 1800–1970', in Simon Eliot and Jonathan Rose (eds.), *A Companion to the History of the Book* (Malden, MA: Blackwell, 2007), 273–90.
4 John Feather, *The Provincial Book Trade in Eighteenth-Century England* (Cambridge University Press, 1985), 29.
5 Sumpter, *Victorian Press*, 16.
6 W. B. Yeats, 'Irish Fairies', *Leisure Hour*, October 1890; *The Collected Works of W. B. Yeats*, vol. IX: *Early Articles and Reviews*, ed. John P. Frayne and Madeleine Marchaterre (New York: Scribner, 2010), 117–23.
7 Sumpter, *Victorian Press*, 26.
8 Ibid., 88–131, 132–75.
9 Guinevere L. Griest argues, persuasively, that far from expanding the book market, the circulating libraries of the mid to late nineteenth century may have actually confined it: because their orders were sufficiently large to shape the print run, they could demand that novels be produced in multiple volumes (to facilitate circulation) which drove up costs. Rider Haggard and other adventure writers such as Stevenson and Kipling broke with the form in the early 1890s. In 1884, 193 three-deckers were published; in 1897, only four were released. Griest, *Mudie's Circulating Library and the Victorian Novel* (Newton Abbot: David and Charles, 1970).
10 Humphrey Carpenter, *Secret Gardens: A Study of the Golden Age of Children's Literature* (London: Allen & Unwin, 1985), 17–18.
11 See Gretchen R. Galbraith for the role of second-hand and scavenging in the children's reading market of the nineteenth century: *Reading Lives: Reconstructing Childhood, Books, and Schools in Britain, 1870–1920* (New York: St. Martin's Press, 1997).
12 Carpenter, *Secret Gardens*, 13.
13 Manlove, *From Alice to Harry Potter*, 26–7.
14 C. S. Lewis, 'On Stories', in Lewis (ed.), *Essays Presented to Charles Williams* (Oxford University Press, 1947), 100.
15 Carpenter, *Secret Gardens*, 106.
16 Ibid., 186.
17 Ibid.
18 Manlove, *From Alice to Harry Potter*, 14.
19 This contained construction of the marvellous, in which a larger wondrous world is contained within a mundane item of the mundane world, has come down to us in the twenty-first century, long after it stopped being a

dominant theme in written fantasy, in perhaps the most instantly recognizable icon of British science fiction, the Tardis, which has probably lost all but its fantastical role to most younger viewers.

20 *The Wind in the Willows* [1908] (Mineola, NY: Dover, 1999), chap. ix, 187.

21 Maria Nikolajeva, 'Imprints of the Mind: The Depiction of Consciousness in Children's Fiction', *Children's Literature Association Quarterly*, 26/4 (2002), 172–87.

22 Carpenter, *Secret Gardens*, 41–2.

23 Although *Bevis* is not a fantasy, Jefferies was responsible for some science fiction, including the marvellous novel *After London* (1885).

24 Carpenter, *Secret Gardens*, 111.

25 Manlove, *From Alice to Harry Potter*, 22–4.

## The American search for an American childhood

1 Richard Lovell Edgeworth, 'Preface' to Maria Edgeworth, *Moral Tales* [1805] (Philadelphia, PA: Henderson, 1853), v.

2 Samuel G. Goodrich, *Recollections of a Lifetime*, 2 vols. (New York and Auburn: Miller, Orton and Mulligan, 1856), 1.169.

3 Brian Attebery, *The Fantasy Tradition in American Literature: From Irving to Le Guin* (Bloomington: Indiana University Press, 1980), 23.

4 Ibid., vi.

5 Selma G. Lanes, *Down the Rabbit Hole: Adventures and Misadventures in the Realm of Children's Literature* (New York: Atheneum, 1976), 6, 95.

6 Ibid., 94.

7 Ibid., 98.

8 Nathaniel Hawthorne, *A Wonder-Book for Girls and Boys* (Boston: Ticknor, Reed and Fields, 1852), 10.

9 Ibid., 9.

10 Attebery, *Fantasy Tradition*, 63.

11 Hawthorne, *Wonder-Book*, 62.

12 Ibid., 75–6.

13 Ibid., 9.

14 Gillian Avery, *Behold the Child: American Children and their Books, 1621–1922* (Baltimore, MD: Johns Hopkins University Press, 1994), 73, 77.

15 *The Last of the Huggermuggers* [1855], in *Three Children's Novels by Christopher Pearse Cranch* (Athens: University of Georgia Press, 2010), 32.

16 Attebery, *Fantasy Tradition*, 79.

17 Leonard S. Marcus, *Minders of Make-Believe: Idealists, Entrepreneurs, and the Shaping of American Children's Literature* (Boston: Houghton Mifflin, 2008), 47.

18 Avery, *Behold the Child*, 141.

19 Howard Pyle, *The Garden Behind the Moon; a Real Story of the Moon Angel* (New York: C. Scribner's Sons, 1895), 2.

20 Katherine M. Rogers, *L. Frank Baum: Creator of Oz* (New York: St. Martin's Press, 2002), 77, 245.

21 Marilyn Irvin Holt, *The Orphan Trains: Placing Out in America* (Lincoln: University of Nebraska Press, 1992), 26–7.

22 Avery, *Behold the Child*, 144–5.

23 Rogers, *L. Frank Baum*, 241.

24 Attebery, *Fantasy Tradition*, 109.

25 Ray Bradbury, 'Preface' to Raylyn Moore, *Wonderful Wizard, Marvelous Land* (Bowling Green, OH: Bowling Green University Popular Press, 1974), xi.

26 E. B. White, *Stuart Little* (New York: Harper, 1945), 8.

27 Marcus, *Minders of Make-Believe*, 176.

28 E. B. White, *Charlotte's Web* (New York: Harper, 1952), 77–8, 140.

29 Ibid., 184.

30 Eudora Welty, 'Life in the Barn Was Very Good', *New York Times*, 19 October 1952.

31 Marcus, *Minders of Make-Believe*, 195–6.

32 Attebery, *Fantasy Tradition*, 144.

33 James Thurber, 'The Wizard of Chitenango', *The New Republic*, 12 December 1934, 141–2, at 141.

34 Ibid.

35 Brian Attebery, *Strategies of Fantasy* (Bloomington: Indiana University Press, 1992), 148.

36 Ibid.

37 James Thurber, *Many Moons* (New York: Harcourt, 1943), 2.

38 Edward Eager, *Seven-Day Magic* (New York: Harcourt, 1962), 3.

39 Deborah O'Keefe, *Readers in Wonderland: The Liberating Worlds of Fantasy Fiction: From Dorothy to Harry Potter* (New York: Continuum, 2003), 92–3.

40 Edward Eager, *Half-Magic* (New York: Harcourt, 1954), 3–4.

41 Janice Bogstad, 'Penny Dreadful', III.233–5, and 'The Dime Novel', I.414–16 both in Jack Zipes (ed.), *The Oxford Encyclopedia of Children's Literature*, 4 vols. (Oxford University Press, 2006).

42 Michael Levy, 'Introduction' to A. Merritt, *The Moon Paul*, ed. Levy (Middletown, CT: Wesleyan University Press, 2004), xv, 277.

## British and Empire fantasy between the wars

1 A. A. Milne, *Once on a Time*, 2nd edn (London: Hodder & Stoughton, 1925), 5.

2 See Michael Paris, *Over the Top: The Great War and Juvenile Literature in Britain* (Westport, CT, and London: Praeger, 2004).

3 Milne, *Once on a Time*, 7.

4 Brenda Niall, *Australia Through the Looking Glass, 1830–1980* (Melbourne University Press, 1984), 200.

5 Geoffrey Trease, *Tales Out of School: A Survey of Children's Literature* (London: William Heinemann, 1948).

6 The independence of the Twenty-Six Counties only came in 1922, so many collections of 'British' fairy tales included those of Irish origin.

7 Kevin Crossley-Holland, *Folk-Tales of the British Isles* (London: Folio Society, 1985), 3.

8 Donna White, *A Century of Welsh Myth in Children's Literature* (Westport, CT: Greenwood Press, 1998), 9.

9 Brian Doyle, *English and Englishness* (London: Routledge, 1989), 25–7.

10 Richard W. Barber, *The Arthurian Legends: An Illustrated Anthology* (Woodbridge: Boydell Press, 1979), 3.

11 J. R. R. Tolkien, 'On Fairy-Stories'. Originally published in 1947, and in an expanded version in Tolkien, *Tree and Leaf* (London: Allen & Unwin, 1964); also in *Tolkien On Fairy-Stories*, ed. Verlyn Flieger and Douglas A. Anderson (London: HarperCollins, 2008), 29–30.

12 Until the 1950s, 'Indian' is the common label, and it is used to flatten out the differences between tribes. Only in the 1970s will Canadian writers become alert to the nuances of what are now referred to as the First Nations.

13 Cyrus Macmillan, *Canadian Wonder Tales* (London: John Lane, 1918), vii.

14 J. R. R. Tolkien and Douglas A. Anderson, *The Annotated Hobbit*, 2nd edn (London: HarperCollins, 2002), 5–6.

15 This is a remarkably accurate description of Quaker refugee hostels in Spain during the Spanish Civil War and was clearly the progressive ideal of child rearing for the period. See Farah Mendlesohn, *Quaker Relief Work in the Spanish Civil War* (Lewiston, NY: Edwin Mellen Press, 2002).

16 Michelle Landsberg, *Reading for the Love of It: Best Books for Young Readers* (New York: Prentice Hall, 1987), 165.

17 David Rudd, 'Toffee Shocks: Lands of the Magic Faraway Tree and Blyton's Schematic Fantasy', in Nickianne Moody and Clare Horrocks (eds.), *Children's Fantasy Fiction: Debates for the Twenty-First Century* (Liverpool: John Moores University Press, 2005), 191–206, at 193.

18 Ibid., 203.

19 For the history and problematic nature of the Golliwog, see the Jim Crow Museum at www.ferris.edu/jimcrow/golliwog (accessed 11 August 2015). This Golliwog is drawn by Eileen A. Soper as a young black boy in a sailor's uniform, with no caricature, and with every emphasis in the text on his dignity, intelligence and bravery.

20 *The Times Literary Supplement*, 2 October 1937. On this and other early reviews of *The Hobbit*, see Tolkien and Anderson, *Annotated Hobbit*, 17–22.

21 Trease, *Tales Out of School*, 13.

### The changing landscape of post-war fantasy

1 E.g. J. A. Appleyard, *Becoming a Reader: The Experience of Fiction from Childhood to Adulthood* (Cambridge University Press, 1990).

2 See e.g. C. Butler, *Four British Fantasists: Place and Culture in the Children's Fantasies of Penelope Lively, Alan Garner, Diana Wynne Jones, and Susan Cooper* (Lanham, MD: Scarecrow Press, 2006), 8–13.

3 Sheila A. Egoff and Judith Saltman, *The New Republic of Childhood: A Critical Guide to Canadian Children's Literature in English* (Oxford University Press, 1990), 232–4; K. V. Johansen, *Beyond Window Dressing? Canadian Children's Fantasy at the Millennium* (Sackville, NB: Sybertooth, 2007), 16.

4 Marcus Crouch, *The Nesbit Tradition: The Children's Novel 1945–1970* (London: Benn, 1972), 121.

5 Paul Berton, *The Secret World of Og* (Toronto: McClelland & Stewart, 1961), 109.

6 Elizabeth Baer, 'A New Algorithm in Evil: Children's Literature in the Post-Holocaust World', *The Lion and the Unicorn*, 24/3 (2000), 378–401, at 392.

7 There are interesting resemblances between Narnia and Catherine Anthony Clark's work: winters and talking animals are important to both of them. The thaw Lewis describes is remarkably like a Canadian thaw – fast and intense – and there are plenty of beavers in Canada. Lewis had a Canadian aunt and it is possible that he had read some of the hybrid Canadian fairy tales.

8 See Baer, 'New Algorithm in Evil'.

9 Peter Hunt, *An Introduction to Children's Literature* (Oxford University Press, 1994), 20.

10 Jane Yolen, personal communication, 8 August 2012.

11 Donna White, *A Century of Welsh Myth in Children's Literature* (Westport, CT: Greenwood Press, 1998), 83.

12 Susan Cooper, *Silver on the Tree* (New York: McElderry, 1977), 267.

13 Ibid., 267.

14 Joy Chant, *Red Moon and Black Mountain: The End of the House of Kendreth* (London: Allen & Unwin, 1970), 209.

15 Victor Watson, *Reading Series Fiction from Arthur Ransome to Gene Kemp* (London and New York: Routledge, 2000), 155.

## Folklore, fantasy and indigenous fantasy

1 Peter Bramwell, *Pagan Themes in Modern Children's Fiction: Green Man, Shamanism, Earth Mysteries* (Basingstoke: Palgrave Macmillan, 2009).

2 Marcus Crouch, *The Nesbit Tradition: The Children's Novel 1945–1970* (London: Benn, 1972), 128.

3 John Stephens and Robyn C. McCallum, *Retelling Stories, Framing Culture: Traditional Story and Metanarratives in Children's Literature* (New York and London: Garland, 1998), 135.

4 K. V. Johansen, *Beyond Window Dressing? Canadian Children's Fantasy at the Millennium* (Sackville, NB: Sybertooth, 2007), 23.

5 Ibid., 39.

6 Margaret Mahy, *The Changeover* (New York: Scholastic, 1985), 184–5.

7 Roderick McGillis, 'And the Celt Knew the Indian: Knowingness, Postcolonialism, Children's Literature', in McGillis (ed.), *Voices of the Other: Children's Literature and the Postcolonial Context* (New York and London: Garland, 1999), 223–36, at 224.

8  Ibid., 231.
9  Ibid.
10 Clare Bradford, *Unsettling Narratives: Postcolonial Readings of Children's Literature* (Waterloo, Ont.: Wilfred Laurier University Press, 2007), 85–7.
11 Ibid., 78.
12 Ibid., 79.

## Middle Earth, medievalism and mythopoeic fantasy

1  Marek Oziewicz, *One Earth, One People: The Mythopoeic Fantasy Series of Ursula K. Le Guin, Lloyd Alexander, Madeleine L'Engle and Orson Scott Card* (Jefferson, NC: McFarland, 2008), 67.
2  Ibid., 70.
3  Garth Nix has said that 'mainstream Australia, while geographically remote, is deeply connected to Western Culture': Leonard S. Marcus, *The Wand in the Word: Conversations with Writers of Fantasy* (Cambridge MA: Candlewick Press, 2006), 125.
4  Farah Mendlesohn, 'Peake and the Fuzzy Set of Fantasy: Some Informal Thoughts', in G. Peter Winnington (ed.), *Miracle Enough: Papers on the Work of Mervyn Peake* (Newcastle-upon-Tyne: Cambridge Scholars, 2013), 61–74, at 63–5.
5  Oziewicz, *One Earth, One People*, 84.
6  Donna White, *A Century of Welsh Myth in Children's Literature* (Westport, CT: Greenwood Press, 1998), 123.
7  Ibid., 74.
8  In Marcus, *The Wand in the Word*, 97.
9  Sandra J. Lindow, *Dancing the Tao: Le Guin and Moral Development* (Newcastle-upon-Tyne: Cambridge Scholars, 2012), 249.
10 Kath Filmer, *Scepticism and Hope in Twentieth-Century Fantasy Literature* (Bowling Green, OH: Bowling Green State University Popular Press, 1992), 47.
11 Brian Attebery, *The Fantasy Tradition in American Literature: From Irving to Le Guin* (Bloomington: Indiana University Press, 1980), 165–6.
12 John Stephens and Robyn C. McCallum, *Retelling Stories, Framing Culture: Traditional Story and Metanarratives in Children's Literature* (New York and London: Garland, 1998), 143.
13 Ursula K. Le Guin, *Tehanu: The Last Book of Earthsea* (New York: Atheneum, 1990), 32.
14 Robin McKinley, 'Newbery Medal Acceptance Speech' (1985), www.robinmckinley.com/essays/speech_newbery.php (accessed 11 August 2015).
15 Diana Wynne Jones, *The Tough Guide to Fantasyland*, rev. edn (New York: Firebird, 2006), 80, 174.
16 Mike Cadden, 'Home is a Matter of Blood, Time and Genre: Essentialism in Burnett and McKinley', *ARIEL: A Review of International English Literature*, 28/1 (1997), 53–67, at 62.
17 Ibid., 56.

### Harry Potter and children's fantasy since the 1990s

1 Barbara Sleigh, *West of Widdershins: A Gallimaufry of Stories Brewed in Her Own Cauldron* (London: Collins, 1971), 9.

2 John Feather, *A History of British Publishing*, 2nd edn (London: Routledge, 2006), 221.

3 One of the authors once spent part of a pleasant afternoon with his eleven-year-old daughter in London in 2000 repeatedly bouncing off a wooden barrier in King's Cross Station looking for Platform 9¾ and the Hogwarts Express. A bobby watched us the entire time without either smiling or suggesting that we stop. When we apologized to him for our actions, his response was, 'That's all right, sir. It happens all the time.' There is now a special corner in the station for Harry Potter fans, with someone taking official photographs, complete with props.

4 Arthur C. Clarke, *Profiles of the Future* [1962] (London: Gollancz, 1999), 2.

5 Frances Hardinge, *Gullstruck Island* (London: Macmillan, 2009), 493.

6 Kayla Ancrum, 'How to Write Women of Colour and Men of Colour If You Are White', http://mediadiversified.org/2013/12/19/how-to-write-women-of-colour-and-men-of-colour-if-you-are-white (accessed 30 January 2014).

7 Kimberley Reynolds, in Kimberley Reynolds, Geraldine Brennan and Kevin McCarron, *Frightening Fiction* (London and New York: Continuum, 2001), 1.

8 Patrick Jones, *What's So Scary About R. L. Stine?* (Lanham, MD: Scarecrow Press, 1998), xi.

9 Ibid., 37.

10 R. L. Stine, *One Day at Horrorland* (New York: Scholastic, 1994), 1.

11 Ibid., 8.

12 Ibid., 17.

13 Ibid., 112.

14 Rick Yancey, *The Monstrumologist* (New York: Simon & Schuster, 2009), 151.

15 Ibid., 454.

16 David Almond, *Skellig* (London: Hodder, 1998), 8.

17 Geraldine Brennan, in Reynolds et al., *Frightening Fiction*, 93.

18 Almond, *Skellig*, 167.

19 Neil Gaiman, *The Graveyard Book* (London: Bloomsbury, 2008), 23.

20 Christine Robertson, '"I want to be like you": Riffs on Kipling in Neil Gaiman's *The Graveyard Book*', *Children's Literature Quarterly*, 36/2 (2001), 164–89, at 168.

### Romancing the teen

1 Philip Pullman, 'The Dark Side of Narnia', *The Guardian*, 1 October 1998.

2 Roberta Seelinger Trites, *Disturbing the Universe: Power and Repression in Adolescent Literature* (Iowa City: University of Iowa Press, 2000), 116.

3 Beth L. Bailey, *From Front Porch to Back Seat: Courtship in Twentieth-Century America* (Baltimore and London: Johns Hopkins University Press, 1988), 29.

4 Michael Cart, *From Romance to Realism: 50 Years of Growth and Change in Young Adult Literature* (New York: HarperCollins, 1996), 105.

5 Ibid., 61.

6 Holly Virginia Blackford, *Out of This World: Why Literature Matters to Girls* (New York and London: Teachers College Press, 2004), 84.

7 Alison Waller, *Constructing Adolescence in Fantastic Realism* (New York and London: Routledge, 2009), 23–4.

8 Margaret J. Finders, *Just Girls: Hidden Literacies and Life in Junior High* (New York and London: Teachers College Press, 1997), 48–55.

9 Ibid., 83–90.

10 Waller, *Constructing Adolescence*, 63.

11 Farah Mendlesohn, *The Inter-Galactic Playground: A Critical Study of Children's and Teens' Science Fiction* (Jefferson, NC: McFarland, 2009), 18–19.

12 Terry Pratchett, *Small Gods* (London: Gollancz, 1992), 127.

13 Jeff VanderMeer, 'Margo Lanagan and *Tender Morsels*', *Clarkesworld*, 25 October 2008 http://clarkesworldmagazine.com/prior/issue_25.

14 Margo Lanagan, *Tender Morsels* (New York: Knopf, 2008), 71.

15 Ibid., 7.

# Further Reading

## Introduction

Attebery, Brian. *The Fantasy Tradition in American Literature from Irving to Le Guin* (Bloomington: Indiana University Press, 1980). The best critical analysis of American fantasy literature from the beginning through Le Guin's original Earthsea trilogy.

— *Strategies of Fantasy* (Bloomington and Indianapolis: Indiana University Press, 1992). Excellent theoretical volume.

Egoff, Sheila A. *Worlds Within: Children's Fantasy from the Middle Ages to Today* (Chicago: American Library Association, 1988). A solid survey of children's fantasy up until the mid-1980s.

Hume, Kathryn. *Fantasy and Mimesis: Responses to Reality in Western Literature* (London: Methuen, 1984).

Johansen, K. V. *Quests and Kingdoms: A Grown-Up's Guide to Children's Fantasy Literature* (Sackville, NB: Sybertooth, 2005). Intelligent reference work with solid critical content by a well-known Canadian fantasy writer.

Manlove, Colin. *From Alice to Harry Potter: Children's Fantasy in England* (Christchurch, NZ: Cybereditions, 2003). A veteran critic of science fiction and fantasy offers a somewhat idiosyncratic and sometimes brilliant view of the development of the genre in England.

Mendlesohn, Farah. *Rhetorics of Fantasy* (Middletown, CT: Wesleyan University Press, 2008). Not devoted to children's fantasy per se, though many children's books are mentioned, this study categorizes the four major ways in which the fantastic enters the text.

Mendlesohn, Farah and Edward James. *A Short History of Fantasy* (London: Middlesex University Press, 2009).

Nikolajeva, Maria. *The Magic Code: The Use of Magical Patterns in Fantasy for Children* (Stockholm: Almqvist & Wiksell International, 1988). Theoretical study of children's fantasy, substantially based in the work of structuralists like Vladimir Propp and semioticians like Mikhail Bakhtin.

# Chapter 1

Ariès, Philippe. *Centuries of Childhood: A Social History of Family Life* (New York: Knopf, 1962). Foundational text.

Hunt, Peter. *An Introduction to Children's Literature* (Oxford University Press, 1994).

Jackson, Mary V. *Engines of Instruction, Mischief, and Magic: Children's Literature in England from its Beginnings to 1839* (Lincoln: University of Nebraska Press, 1989). Useful analysis of the gradual evolution of children's literature and its role in society.

Nikolajeva, Maria. *The Rhetoric of Character in Children's Literature* (Lanham, MD: Scarecrow Press, 2002). Strong theoretical work which is particularly good on the differences between the portrayal of characters in children's literature and how they are shown in adult literature.

Salway, Lance. *A Peculiar Gift: Nineteenth-Century Writings on Books for Children* (Harmondsworth: Penguin, 1976). Important early essays on children's literature by Ruskin, Dickens, Molesworth and others.

Shavit, Zohar. *Poetics of Children's Literature* (Athens: University of Georgia Press, 1986). She is particularly strong on the shifts that take place in a story as it is retailored for child and middle-class audiences.

Tatar, Maria. *The Hard Facts of the Grimms' Fairy Tales* (Princeton University Press, 1987). Tatar analyses the way the Grimms gradually rewrote their tales from edition to edition, moving further and further away from the true folk material, cutting sexual material that might offend their nineteenth-century middle-class audience, but also making the stories more violent.

Zipes, Jack. *Breaking the Magic Spell: Radical Theories of Folk and Fairy Tales* (London: Heinemann, 1979). This early work by Zipes, also available in a revised edition (2002), is foundational to his later important work on political interpretations of folklore.

   *Fairy Tale as Myth, Myth as Fairy Tale*, The Thomas D. Clark Lectures (Lexington: University Press of Kentucky, 1994).

   *Fairy Tales and the Art of Subversion: The Classical Genre for Children and the Process of Civilization*, 2nd rev. edn (New York: Routledge, 2006). Recent thoughts by one of the greatest interpreters of fairy tales.


# Chapter 2

Carpenter, Humphrey. *Secret Gardens: A Study of the Golden Age of Children's Literature* (London: Allen & Unwin, 1985).

Gray, William. *Fantasy, Myth and the Measure of Truth: Tales of Pullman, Lewis, Tolkien, MacDonald and Hoffmann* (Basingstoke: Palgrave Macmillan, 2009). Traces the thread of Romanticism through nineteenth- and twentieth-century fantasy, with an emphasis on Pullman's place within, rather than in opposition to, that tradition.

Nikolajeva, Maria. *The Rhetoric of Character in Children's Literature* (Lanham, MD: Scarecrow Press, 2002).

Reynolds, Kimberley. *Radical Children's Literature: Future Visions and Aesthetic Transformations in Juvenile Fiction* (New York: Palgrave Macmillan, 2007). See Chapter Three, 'And None of It was Nonsense', for an exploration of the rhetorical structures of nonsense poetry.

Streatfeild, Noel. *Magic and the Magician: E. Nesbit and her Children's Books* (London and New York: Abelard Schuman, 1958). Noted study of the great turn-of-the-century fantasist by a Carnegie Medal-winning children's author.

Sumpter, Caroline. *The Victorian Press and the Fairy Tale* (Basingstoke: Palgrave Macmillan, 2008). Examines how the popular press of the day presented and sometimes transformed fairy tales, making them more available to the lower and middle classes, but also using them for a variety of sometimes subtle political and social engineering purposes.

## Chapter 3

Attebery, Brian. *The Fantasy Tradition in American Literature from Irving to Le Guin* (Bloomington: Indiana University Press, 1980). This foundational book is far and away the most important study of American fantasy literature.

Baum, L. Frank. *The Annotated Wizard of Oz: The Wonderful Wizard of Oz*, pictures by W. W. Denslow, ed. with an introduction and notes by Michael Patrick Hearn (New York: W. W. Norton, 2000). Hearn's edition of Baum is a treasure trove of interpretation and fascinating miscellaneous data.

Kidd, Kenneth B. *Making American Boys: Boyology and the Feral Tale* (Minneapolis: University of Minnesota Press, 2005). Child Studies-oriented analysis of how boy culture, and the literature that supports it, have been constructed in America since the nineteenth century.

Levy, Michael. *Natalie Babbitt* (Boston: Twayne, 1991).

Marcus, Leonard S. *Minders of Make-Believe: Idealists, Entrepreneurs, and the Shaping of American Children's Literature* (Boston: Houghton Mifflin, 2008). Award-winning social history of the development of book culture in the United States.

Rogers, Katherine M. *L. Frank Baum: Creator of Oz: A Biography* (New York: St. Martin's Press, 2002). Fine biography of the first great American children's writer.

## Chapter 4

Hettinga, Donald R. and Gary D. Schmidt. *British Children's Writers, 1914–1960* (Detroit: Gale Research, 1996). Useful reference book covering such writers as Enid Blyton, C. S. Lewis, Hugh Lofting, John Masefield, Mary Norton, A. A. Milne, P. L. Travers, Alison Uttley and others.

Rudd, David. 'Toffee Shocks: Lands of the Magic Faraway Tree and Blyton's Schematic Fantasy', in Nickianne Moody and Clare Horrocks (eds.), *Children's Fantasy Fiction: Debates for the Twenty-First Century* (Liverpool: John Moores University Press, 2005), 191–206. One of the very few considerations of Blyton's fantasy.

Shippey, T. A. *J. R. R. Tolkien: Author of the Century* (Boston: Houghton Mifflin, 2000). Perhaps the best of the many studies of Tolkien and his work.

Stephens, John and Robyn C. McCallum. *Retelling Stories, Framing Culture: Traditional Story and Metanarratives in Children's Literature* (New York and London: Garland, 1998). A wide-ranging study of the political and social implications of retelling traditional stories for young readers, with relevance to several chapters in this book.

Tolkien, J. R. R. 'On Fairy-Stories', in *Essays Presented to Charles Williams* (London: Oxford University Press, 1947), 38–89; also collected in *Tolkien On Fairy-Stories*, ed. Verlyn Flieger and Douglas A. Anderson (London: HarperCollins, 2008).

## Chapter 5

Butler, C. *Four British Fantasists: Place and Culture in the Children's Fantasies of Penelope Lively, Alan Garner, Diana Wynne Jones, and Susan Cooper* (Lanham, MD: Scarecrow Press, 2006). Perhaps the most significant contribution to the study of this period.

Filmer, Kath. *Scepticism and Hope in Twentieth-Century Fantasy Literature* (Bowling Green, OH: Bowling Green State University Popular Press, 1992).

Manlove, Colin. *From Alice to Harry Potter: Children's Fantasy in England* (Christchurch, NZ: Cybereditions, 2003).

Mendlesohn, Farah. *Diana Wynne Jones: Children's Literature and the Fantastic Tradition* (New York: Routledge, 2005).

Philip, Neil. *A Fine Anger: a Critical Introduction to the Work of Alan Garner* (New York: Philomel Books, 1981).

Rees, David. *What Do Draculas Do? Essays on Contemporary Writers of Fiction for Children and Young Adults* (Metuchen, NJ: Scarecrow Press, 1990).

Saxby, Maurice. *The Proof of the Puddin': Australian Children's Literature 1790–1990* (Sydney: Ashton Scholastic, 1993).

Ward, Michael. *Planet Narnia: The Seven Heavens in the Imagination of C. S. Lewis* (New York: Oxford University Press, 2008). Award-winning study of Lewis's use of astronomy and classical myth.

## Chapter 6

Bramwell, Peter. *Pagan Themes in Modern Children's Fiction: Green Man, Shamanism, Earth Mysteries* (Basingstoke: Palgrave Macmillan, 2009). Looks at the use made of pagan themes by Susan Cooper and others.

Meek, Margaret. 'The Englishness of Children's Books', in Meek (ed.), *Children's Literature and National Identity* (Stoke-on-Trent: Trentham Books, 2001), 89–102.

Niall, Brenda. *Australia through the Looking Glass, 1830–1980* (Melbourne University Press, 1984).

West, Máire. 'Kings, Heroes and Warriors: Aspects of Children's Literature in Ireland in the Era of Emergent Nationalism', *Bulletin of the John Rylands Library*, 3 (1994), 165–84.

White, Donna. *A Century of Welsh Myth in Children's Literature* (Westport, CT: Greenwood Press, 1988). Explores the lure of Welsh myths and their importance in children's fantasy.

## Chapter 7

Bradford, Clare. *Unsettling Narratives: Postcolonial Readings of Children's Literature* (Waterloo, ON.: Wilfred Laurier University Press, 2007). Important theoretical study of how settler societies use children's books as tools for regularizing the postcolonial world view. This book is also applicable to most other chapters in our study.

Cadden, Mike. 'Home Is a Matter of Blood, Time, and Genre: Essentialism in Burnett and McKinley', *ARIEL: A Review of International English Literature*, 28/1 (1997), 53–67.

*Ursula K. Le Guin Beyond Genre: Fiction for Children and Adults* (New York and London: Routledge, 2005). There are many good books that analyse Le Guin's work, but this was the first to centre specifically on her children's fantasy.

Crouch, Marcus. *The Nesbit Tradition: The Children's Novel 1945–1970* (London: Benn, 1972).

Manlove, Colin. *The Fantasy Literature of England* (Basingstoke: Macmillan, 1999). Very well-regarded study of English fantasy.

*From Alice to Harry Potter: Children's Fantasy in England* (Christchurch, NZ: Cybereditions, 2003).

Mendlesohn, Farah and Edward James. *A Short History of Fantasy* (London: Middlesex University Press, 2009). Intended as an overview of the fantasy genre for general readers, this offers a thorough reading list of the adult fantasy in which much medievalist fiction is situated.

Oziewicz, Marek. *One Earth, One People: The Mythopoeic Fantasy Series of Ursula K. Le Guin, Lloyd Alexander, Madeleine L'Engle, and Orson Scott Card* (Jefferson, NC: McFarland, 2008). Award-winning study of mythopoeic fantasy.

Perry, Evelyn M. *Robin McKinley: Girl Reader, Woman Writer* (Lanham, MD: Scarecrow Press, 2011). A close study of each of the author's books up to 2010.

Waggoner, Diana. *The Hills of Faraway: A Guide to Fantasy* (New York: Atheneum, 1978). Well-regarded if now somewhat dated study.

## Chapter 8

Baker, Deirdre and Ken Setterington. *A Guide to Canadian Children's Books* (Toronto: McClelland & Stewart, 2003).

Bryfonski, Dedria. *Political Issues in J. K. Rowling's Harry Potter Series* (Detroit: Greenhaven Press/Gale Cengage Learning, 2009). One of the more interesting of the many monographs and essay collections on Rowling's work, this book places the series within the political context of the contemporary UK.

Byatt, A. S. 'Harry Potter and the Childish Adult', *The New York Times*, 7 July 2003, A13.

Jackson, Anna, Karen Coats and Roderick McGillis (eds.). *The Gothic in Children's Literature: Haunting the Borders* (New York and London: Routledge, 2008). Another valuable essay collection.

Jones, Diana Wynne. *The Tough Guide to Fantasyland*, rev. edn (New York: Firebird, 1996). Hilarious spoof and critique of the cliches of secondary-world fantasy.

Jones, Patrick. *What's So Scary About R. L. Stine?* (Lanham, MD: Scarecrow Press, 1998). Well executed study of the most popular fantasy writer of his day.

Levy, Michael. 'Children and Salvation in David Almond's *Skellig*', *Foundation: The International Journal of Science Fiction*, 88 (Summer 2003), 26–32.

McCarron, K. 'Point Horror and the Point of Horror', in Kimberley Reynolds, Geraldine Brennan and Kevin McCarron (eds.), *Frightening Fiction* (London: Continuum, 2001), 19–52. A study of the development of the Point Horror series, which for the first time introduced horror fiction specifically written for children and younger teens.

Nel, Philip. 'Is There a Text in This Advertising Campaign?: Literature, Marketing, and Harry Potter.' *The Lion and the Unicorn*, 29/2 (2005), 236–67.

Pennington, John. 'From Elfland to Hogwarts, or the Aesthetic Trouble with Harry Potter.' *The Lion and the Unicorn*, 26/1 (2002), 78–97.

Rosenberg, Teya et al. (eds.). *Diana Wynne Jones: An Exciting and Exacting Wisdom* (New York: Peter Lang, 2002). Strong collection of essays on Jones's work.

## Chapter 9

Barfield, Steven and Katharine Cox (eds.). *Critical Perspectives on Philip Pullman's His Dark Materials: Essays on the Novels, the Film and the Stage Productions* (Jefferson, NC: McFarland, 2011).

Blackford, Holly Virginia. *Out of This World: Why Literature Matters to Girls* (New York and London: Teachers College Press, 2004).

Bodart, Joni Richards. *They Suck, They Bite, They Eat, They Kill: The Psychological Meaning of Supernatural Monsters in Young Adult Fiction* (Lanham, MD: Scarecrow Press, 2012). Solid basic study of the various monsters used in Young Adult horror and supernatural romance.

Clarke, Amy M. and Marijane Osborn (eds.). *The Twilight Mystique: Critical Essays on the Novels and Films* (Jefferson, NC: McFarland, 2010). Excellent collection of critical essays on *Twilight* and the *Twilight* phenomenon.

Jackson, Anna, Karen Coats and Roderick McGillis (eds.). *The Gothic in Children's Literature: Haunting the Borders* (New York and London: Routledge, 2008).

Johansen, K. V. *Beyond Window Dressing? Canadian Children's Fantasy at the Turn of the Millennium* (Sackville, NB: Sybertooth, 2007).

Oliver, Chantal. 'Mocking God and Celebrating Satan: Parodies and Profanities in Philip Pullman's *His Dark Materials*.' *Children's Literature in Education*, 43/4 (2012), 293–302. One of a number of strong essays on Pullman published by this journal, this piece explores some of the more controversial moments in the series.

Reynolds, Kimberley. *Radical Children's Literature: Future Visions and Aesthetic Transformations in Juvenile Fiction* (Basingstoke: Palgrave Macmillan, 2007). Chapters 6 and 7 are particularly helpful.

Rutledge, Amelia A. 'Robin McKinley's *Deerskin*: Challenging Narcissisms.' *Marvels & Tales*, 15/2 (2001), 168–82. This essay perceptively discusses McKinley's take on Perrault's incest-related fairy tale 'Donkeyskin'.

Silver, Anna. 'Twilight is Not Good for Maidens: Gender, Sexuality, and the Family in Stephenie Meyer's *Twilight* Series.' *Studies in the Novel*, 42/1–2 (2010), 121–38. An examination of what the author sees as Meyer's very conservative construction of female and family identity.

Stott, Belinda. 'Survival into the Twenty First Century: Reading the Victim in Virginia Andrews's *Flowers in the Attic*', in N. Moody and C. Horrocks (eds.), *Children's Fantasy Fiction: Debates for the Twenty First Century* (Liverpool: John Moores University Press, 2005), 111–26.

Waller, Alison. *Constructing Adolescence in Fantastic Realism* (New York and London: Routledge, 2009).

# Index